In Faith
Best, Wishes & Happy Birthday!

Arthur C Clarke

11/17/07

The
Bountiful Flower Garden

The Bountiful Flower Garden

Growing and Sharing
Cut Flowers in the South

Neil G. Odenwald & William C. Welch

Taylor Publishing Company
Dallas, Texas

Also by William C. Welch
Perennial Garden Color
Antique Roses for the South
The Southern Heirloom Garden
(with Greg Grant)

Also by Neil G. Odenwald
Attracting Birds to Southern Gardens
(with Thomas Pope and Charles Fryling Jr.)

Designed by David Timmons

Published by Taylor Publishing Company
1550 West Mockingbird Lane
Dallas, Texas 75235
www.taylorpub.com

Photo credits:
page viii—William C. Welch
Pages ii, x, xii, xv—G. Michael Shoup, Antique Rose Emporium

Library of Congress Cataloging-in-Publication Data
Odenwald, Neil G.
The bountiful flower garden : growing and sharing cut flowers in the south / Neil G. Odenwald & William C. Welch
p. cm.
Includes bibliographical references (p.).
ISBN 0-87833-235-9
1. Flower gardening—Southern States.
2. Cut flowers—Southern States.
I. Welch, William C. (William Carlisle), 1939– II. Title.

SB405.5.S68 O33 2000

635.9'66'0975—dc21 99-055702
10 9 8 7 6 5 4 3 2 1

Printed in the United States of America

The Bountiful Flower Garden is dedicated to
Robert S. ("Doc") Reich, a teacher who has devoted
his life to being an inspiration to others. The authors
acknowledge with gratitude his influence on their lives
and careers through the years.

Contents

Thoughts About the Authors

Fate assured that I could not have known one without knowing the other. Their paths have been personally and professionally intertwined for more than thirty-five years. Although they live in different states, there is no boundary their ideas cannot cross, compare, and cultivate. To watch them in action is akin to watching the flow of a fast-moving river, full of energy, speed, and focus, but with slight need of control. Unrestricted, their ideas can chart new courses without major intent—a landscape created in process, although planned precisely on paper.

In knowing their mentor, Dr. Robert Reich, one sees the influence of the teacher, a man of quiet dignity but strong resolve. In many ways he took the horticulturist and turned him into a landscape architect and took the landscape architect and turned him into a horticulturist. In both men he instilled the love of sharing one's knowledge that has resulted in careers reaching literally thousands of gardeners throughout the country. As mentors in their own right, they have influenced the development of successful young professionals who are themselves becoming well-known and recognized in horticulture and landscape architecture fields.

The symmetry of their lives is interesting. Both have spent their professional years in education; both have been involved in consulting, writing, lecturing, and serving in leadership positions in related associations. Both have been recognized by national gardening organizations. Perhaps most importantly, both have callused hands that reflect their love for trying yet another plant and planning, installing, weeding, and watering yet another garden plot. To travel with them is to be relegated to the rear, surrounded by flats and shovels and politely ignored unless involved in Latin translations of the plant genus or discussion of the design influences of early English herbaceous borders and French *parterres*.

It was on such a venture that the idea for this book was initiated. It would be their first literary collaboration, a project of pleasure and purpose with appeal to those sharing their love of plants and flowers. In addition, it would be the gift of gratitude to the teacher held in such high esteem. And perhaps the outcome would be the creation of unbridled enthusiasm in yet one more individual for "taking up the trowel," planting the seed, and becoming transformed by the products of their labors.

One would think it peculiar that they should ask a perpetual gardening novice to make comment. The defense lies in the ability of a long-term observer who appreciates their talents and provides objective insight and structural response to their creative ideas. To the "husband" and the "best man" I convey my thanks for taking me along on the many garden explorations and adventures.

DIANE THAMES WELCH

Foreword

I am pleased to have been invited to comment on the work of my former students Neil G. Odenwald and William C. Welch. Among the joys of being associated with the School of Landscape Architecture for over fifty years has been my long-standing friendship with Neil and Bill.

Throughout his many years at Louisiana State University, Dr. Neil Odenwald conducted superior courses in plant materials and planting design. His teaching had three primary results: guiding students to identify a multitude of ornamental plants, developing their skills in the effective use of plants while building sound horticultural practices in planting design, and most importantly, developing among his students a strong empathy for plants.

As teacher and director of L.S.U.'s School of Landscape Architecture, he was a great inspiration to faculty, students, and the general public. He regularly conducted schools, short courses, and tours to educate the public on how best to use plants in landscape design.

Neil's first book, *Southern Plants for Landscape Design*, with sketches by another former student, James Turner, was published in 1980. It clearly illustrates his sensitivity for and thorough knowledge of plants. This reference is found in practically every landscape architect's office in the South and in many homes and libraries throughout the region. A second edition was published in 1987 and a third in 1996. To further assist people in the use of plants, he collaborated with Dr. Thomas E. Pope and Charles Fryling Jr. in the publication of *Plants for American Landscapes*. This book abounds in beautiful color prints of the most important plants covered in his first book. He co-authored another book, *Attracting Birds to Southern Gardens*, with Pope and Fryling, which received outstanding reviews among bird and plant enthusiasts.

Neil has been actively involved in both the L.S.U. Hilltop Arboretum in Baton Rouge and the John James Audubon Arboretum at Gloster, Mississippi.

His own home is a perfect example of the excellent landscape planting practices he constantly strives to teach others. He enthusiastically helps those who are interested in the effective use of plants, also a primary goal of this new book.

Dr. William C. Welch is another great plantsman. His enthusiasm for plants has led him to try many plants that are new or little used, including both the woody ornamentals and the herbaceous perennials that traditionally have not been in great use in Southern gardens. An example is his reintroduction of the pistachio trees that have become very popular, especially for their outstanding autumn color in the South.

He has spent many hours visiting early American gardens, abandoned housesites, and cemeteries to rediscover and study old roses and other plants on these historic sites. His enthusiasm for the cultivation of old roses and herbaceous perennials led to the publication of three great books: *Perennial Garden Color*, filled with beautifully colored plates, *The Southern Heirloom Garden*, and *Antique Roses for the South*. In addition, he has authored several publications on popular gardening topics.

Bill is extremely enthusiastic about flower arranging. I look forward to his visits to Baton Rouge because on the Sundays he is in town, Bill meets me at the University Methodist Church at 7:30 A.M. to help with the altar arrangement.

For many years Bill has been a major contributor to the nurseryman's association programs and to garden club activities throughout the nation. Numerous honors have been bestowed upon him by these groups. In his work through the years he has helped to educate the public about the joys of working with plants.

DR. ROBERT S. ("DOC") REICH

Acknowledgments

Numerous individuals had a role in making this book possible. As we worked on the manuscript, we were reminded just how many people could have their names included in the book. Many flashbacks occurred—recalling the individuals who first introduced particular plants to the authors, and in most cases leading to our remembering the private garden visits where the plants were first seen growing. A plant book could hardly be written in a vacuum or in isolation because of the great diversity of plants covered and the broad range of growing conditions that occur over the region. Consequently, we have benefited from the experiences of many people who have grown the plants that were ultimately chosen to be included. So to all those gardeners and friends over the years who have shared their plants and knowledge we say a hearty thanks and recognize your valuable contributions to this work.

Although there are hundreds of gardeners and friends whose names do not appear in print, we acknowledge several special people who provided information and encouragement. First, special thanks are extended to Diane Thames Welch, who conceived the book in the first place and believed that the long-standing friendship between the authors was worthy of some type of collaborative effort to celebrate our close ties and love of plants through the years.

In addition to those noted above, Neil is most appreciative for the support of several other people who were especially helpful. These include Dr. Thomas E. Pope, who has always been a readily accessible, highly qualified plant consultant, friend, and the source of many plant photographs used in the book. When you have a Pope as a friend, you benefit from many special revelations. Lucy S. Pope unscrambled a network of computer files in the final days of manuscript preparation. Leonard W. Martin of Editorial Excellence, Inc. in Baton Rouge provided valuable editorial assistance for several chapters. Special gardeners, horticulturists, landscape architects, and friends who provided valuable information and encouragement include: Lou W. Riddle, Dr. Robert S. Reich, Sadik Artunc, Bruce Sharky, Margie Jenkins, Marion Drummond, Wayne Womack, and Genevieve M. Trimble.

We are most appreciative to the people who shared slides and photographs from their private collections. These include Dr. Thomas E. Pope, Jo Kellum, Greg Grant, and Charles F. Fryling Jr.

In addition to all those Neil has mentioned, Bill would like to extend special thanks to Cynthia W. Mueller for valued research and editing assistance and to Greg Grant for his contributions to the plant sources list. Others who have graciously shared their time, talents, and gardens include Frances Parker, Pamela Puryear, Weej Broderson, Elizabeth Williams, Neil Sperry, Cleo Barnwell, Patti McGee, Mary Martha Blalock, Jason and Shelley Powell, Linda Askey, Dr. Brent Pemberton, Felder Rushing, Dan Gill, Dr. Jerry Parsons, Keith Hansen, Bill Adams, Tom Leroy, Robert Richter, Marge Hurt, Hazel McCoy, Nell Zeigler, John Thomas, Mike Shoup, Henry Flowers, Suzanne Turner, John Begnaud, Debbie Frost, Dottie Woodson, Dr. Steve George, Dr. Don Wilkerson, John Van Beck, Ruth Knopf, Peggy Cornett, Flora Ann Bynum, Tom Christopher, Florence Griffin, Jane Symmes, Nancy Haywood, and Shingo Manard.

The
Bountiful Flower Garden

One

Garden Enlightenment

The enthusiastic interest in growing flowers and other ornamental plants that has persisted in the Western world for several centuries has been influenced by many factors. Some powerful influences came from abroad, especially Europe and England, while other ideas responsible for the rapid growth of horticulture and gardening originated in this country. At the turn of now another century this fascination for growing flowers continues at an all-time high. What are some of the milestone events that have shaped our attitudes toward gardening and instilled in many of us an ever-increasing interest in growing flowers?

THE WESTERN TRADITION: EUROPE AND ENGLAND

Love of flowers and plants is part of our humanity, which seems always to have existed across all centuries and country boundaries. Humankind has always been interested in the beauty of flowers as separate from the need for food plants, whose products were first gathered by early man and then later cultivated. Archaeologists excavating a neolithic grave in Europe several years ago discovered the remains of plant offerings which evidently were laid over the deceased at the time of burial. It was still possible to identify the wildflowers involved, through study of the pollen grains at the site.

Not much in the way of written records still remains to us concerning details of flowers known and cultivated by the ancients, although almost everyone is familiar with the concept of the Garden of Eden, the hanging gardens of

Babylon, and elaborate gardens of the Persians and Moghul princes of India. The floating gardens of Xochimilco and the plant treasuries of the Aztecs were discovered by the Spanish as they travelled through Mexico, spreading their own Moorish traditions to the Western world—their ideas all combined to influence the garden concepts of the Americas.

However, our modern passion for ornamental gardening is deeply rooted in the traditions expressed in early European and English gardens.

Although people have expressed their love for flowers and other plants throughout the ages, it has only been in relatively recent times that others than the elite of any culture have been able to indulge in the simple luxury of growing flowers for pleasure, rather than plants with food, herbal or medicinal uses. In the history of the Western world, we find that when the French popes resided in Avignon, France, the papal palace in the mid- and late 1300s had a special garden inside the fortress and its ramparts for the pope, just under his windows, which received only the morning sun. Accentuated by a fountain with a cut-grass lawn (scythed, of

Hampton Court, an example of Victorian-style ribbon bedding. NGO

Sunken garden at Hampton Court, indicative of a time when geometric garden settings changed to more brightly colored annual plantings. NGO

course), the garden contained roses and beds of violets, vines, and all the sweet-smelling plants available at the time. Most of the recorded garden history of the Western world reflects works by and for the rich and famous. The middle class was historically very small until the time of the industrial revolution, and peasants were preoccupied with the struggle for survival. Also, the number of plants "native" to England and Europe was very small before explorations and the opening of trade routes brought in exotic and hitherto unknown species.

The cut-flower garden was familiar to Europeans of the sixteenth century, and was referred to by the French as *jardin bouquetiers,* an integral part of the pleasure garden, as contrasted to those areas of the garden laid aside strictly for growing foodstuffs and herbs. Usually not more than a quarter of the garden would be set aside for flowers. During the time of Louis XIV, flowers were grown in abundance in the *parterre*

fleuriste, which corresponded to our modern *picking garden,* for the flowers were used for indoor decoration. Louis XIV took great interest in the flowers grown for the royal table and frequently visited the *parterre fleuriste.*

In the grand gardens of Italy, France, and Spain of the seventeenth and eighteenth centuries, the emphasis was primarily upon powerful architectural form and pattern. Flowers played a relatively minor role, sometimes being used within the context of the strong patterns of the clipped evergreen hedges in early Renaissance gardens. The flowers and exotic plants that were used for interior decorations were normally grown out of sight behind walls in the service areas of the estate.

That restrained approach to the use of ornamental plants was abandoned in the Victorian Age, a period when flowers became a preoccupation of a more affluent society. When Queen Victoria ascended the throne of England in 1837, interest in floriculture

leaped to new heights. Her passion for flowers was legendary.

The nineteenth and early twentieth centuries brought a tremendous expansion in plant science and experimentation, with many new plants being created through application of newly discovered genetic theories. Elaborate plantings of flowers and exotic horticultural specimens— *bedding out* and *carpets of flowers,* or *carpet/ribbon bedding*—were commonplace in the landscapes of the wealthy. Flowers were even designed into floral clocks, or *floral timekeepers,* with designers going to the extreme of methodically placing plants in strategic locations to correspond to the clock hour when petals would open and close. Also popular was the *dial bed* in which mixed plants, ranging from water lilies to chicory and morning glories, could be seen opening and closing with the hours. Both Linnaeus and the well-known English garden writer, John Claudius Loudon, give lists of suitable plants for this project.

Herbaceous border, Canterbury, England. Where space is limited, taller plants can add another level of interest. NGO

Anne Hathaway's historical garden illustrates the simpler beginnings of the cottage garden. WCW

BEDS—BEDDING OUT— BORDERS—PARTERRES

In the 1830s English gardens began to display many more brightly colored annuals, often originating from South Africa or the West Coast of America. The hybrid offspring of these plants bloomed over a much longer period of time than the more delicate old-fashioned flowers, producing masses of bloom continuously in the same area for an arrangement that would last through much of the growing season. Flowers of the same color were worked into *sheets* or into geometric designs much like the carpets in vogue during Victorian times. When plants are massed together for a designed effect, they form a *planting bed* and when mostly low, compact foliage plants are grouped into carpet-like designs, the result is called *carpet bedding*. Outlines of these beds could be as simple as a circle or as fancy as flags, shields, or insignia. Originally these were created of

very low-growing foliage plant material, depending on leaf color and structure for contrast rather than flowers to form flat designs. These gradually changed into floral displays which might be raised at the centers or on the back side to aid in viewing, at first having only a few larger, more graceful plants. Later the larger, more flamboyant specimens became known as *dot plants*.

Parterre work consists of geometric placement of ornamentally shaped beds separated by a pattern of walks, turf area, or low hedging such as boxwood, preferably laid out to be seen to best advantage from above. The simplest of these might be four beds arranged symmetrically around a central ornamental feature such as a fountain, large ornate pot, or taller inside planting. The most complex might contain elaborate scroll designs resembling embroidery.

A *ribbon bed* is a long arrow-shaped strip with a special pattern conforming to its length. American gardeners in the 1870s followed

detailed descriptions of typical ribbon plantings, including even the heights, spacing, and exact color variations for each plant variety to produce stylish results. Such beds were intended to parallel paths or drives, with the pattern rhythmically repeating the same design. More gaudy plant materials composed these beds, and as this craze took effect the old-fashioned, more delicately-colored perennials previously occupying the garden tended to be discarded.

The *flower bed* means any shape of bed. There may be a great many varieties of flowers inside it, although not a part of a general pattern. No limitation of height, type of plant, or arrangement exists for this kind of bed. A gardener could mix perennials with annuals, or spring bulbs with low-growing annuals which will soon take over as the leaves of bulbs wither and disappear. In the beginning, plants will seem small and too far apart, but as they mature a space about 2 feet square will be needed for each larkspur, phlox or

The cottage garden at Sissinghurst. The formal evergreens, walk, and container of tulips contrast with the informal groupings of annuals and perennials in the rest of the garden. WCW

chrysanthemum, and even more room for rosebushes. Smaller annuals can get by each with a one-foot square space requirement.

Beds and borders may be of any length, but a 6 foot width will generally prove to be the easiest to maintain. Skillful gardeners who can maneuver through the plantings can tend to a bed as deep as 12 feet.

The *herbaceous border* reappeared as interest returned in plantings that were not so labor intensive, or so short in duration, and didn't require such large stocks of material to maintain through the winter or until of a size to plant out. Such a border was usually composed of mixtures of hardy perennials and small shrubs; *biennial* (those flowering in their second spring) and annual plants added filler to the permanent groupings.

The industrial revolution and the advent of plate glass and structural iron and steel brought another new dimension. This period provided the necessary materials, building expertise, relief from the expensive tax on glass, and wealth to build elaborate temperature-controlled glass houses where plant collections could be exhibited. Ever-expanding botanic gardens like Kew and Wisley in London and the Royal Botanic Garden in Edinburgh became influential centers of scientific research. Sir Joseph Paxton's grand glass houses at Chatsworth, Kew's imposing Crystal Palace, and similar structures throughout England and Europe provided controlled conditions for serious plant collections, as well as becoming status symbols of wealth and prominence in horticultural circles. Families of means had entire ranges of glass houses to devote to the needs of their ever-expanding collections of exotics—and to claim a renowned position in the community. Robert Leuchars' 1854 book, *Practical Treatise on the Construction,*

Heating, and Ventilation of Hot Houses, brought a special focus on the use of these structures. His work influenced the widespread expansion of greenhouses in England. However, Leuchars admonished gardeners rather sternly about the use of such houses:

> *Some are of (the) opinion that greenhouses are of no further service than merely to store away a miscellaneous assortment of rubbish during the months of winter, for the obvious purpose of preserving them until the next summer. . . . What is or ought to be, the chief ornament of the garden, (is) deprived of its character, for want of taste, and divested of its interest, for lack of skill. Visitors say, "Let us have a look at the greenhouse." "No," replies the gardener apologetically, "it's not worth your while going in, for there is nothing there to see." A humiliating acknowledgment, but full of truth.*

London's Horticultural Society formed in 1804 (later renamed the Royal Horticultural Society) provided another major impetus to horticultural expansion. This influential organization provided a forum for scientific discussions and investigations. Its membership included plant enthusiasts from around the world.

The results of plant-breeding research staged in the new conservatories and laboratories opened the floodgate of horticulture ever wider with people from virtually every part of the world coming under the influence of this constantly-expanding industry. The simple, elegant formal garden styles of early Europe became greatly embellished with the new exotic flowers that had been grown in the heated glass houses of the wealthy Victorian aristocracy. Colorful flower carpets could

be changed seasonally. Designers went to such extremes as copying elaborate designs from carpets and wallpaper to use in their huge garden beds.

Flowers became so important they adorned nearly everything—carpets, wallpaper, mirrors, all types of furniture, frames for paintings, lace and other fine handwork, silver, textiles, pottery, and even the handles of pistols. The Great Exhibition of 1851 featured floriculture in a high society. The floral arts and crafts movement became a way of life during the Victorian era. Flower arrangements—which had been introduced in the 1700s—embellished the already ornate interiors of the Victorian home. The *floral nosegay*, a tight clustering of flowers arranged in an upright container or wrapped for holding in the hand, extended the personal use of flowers into lavish parties and other social gatherings. Pressed flower and foliage specimens were treasured keepsakes of the times. Some were framed for decorative wall hangings, while others were enshrined in albums, accompanied by notes about the special meaning of the time and place where a particular specimen had been gathered—or perhaps received from an eager suitor. Botanizing and collecting plant specimens were favorite pastimes for the affluent during the nineteenth century. Ferns were among the most sought after plants for personal collections and exhibitions.

During the mid-nineteenth century, flowerbeds began to be set in the midst of a new type of green carpet—turf, cut by the new invention of the day, the lawn mower, which made its appearance around 1830. Owning one of these machines became yet another way of asserting status among the wealthy.

Expeditions to faraway lands brought another special dimension to an atmosphere already filled with a passion for flowers. Any

Suzanne Turner's Baton Rouge, Louisiana, garden provides bouquets of cut flowers and a pleasant view for the public, and includes a very well-planned color scheme. WCW

new and exotic plant that an intrepid explorer might bring back from his travels would receive rave reviews in the expanding horticultural press. Celebrations were staged for certain plants upon their arrival in England and Europe. These plants eventually made their way to the United States. Adventuresome plant explorers like Charles Sargent, E. H. Wilson, Robert Fortune, Henry Bates, Allan Cunningham, John Veitch, Joseph Hooker, and numerous others made extensive botanical excursions to collect exotics. The period between 1750 and 1850 is sometimes called the "golden age" of plant introductions. Wilson is reported to have shipped over 1,000 new species to the Arnold Arboretum in Boston from his explorations in China, while Sargent was equally zealous in his search for plants in Japan. Their finds were carefully stored, with many plant newcomers placed in Wardian cases (sealed

glass containers) where they were prominently displayed in the homes of the wealthy as objects of great curiosity and conversation.

There was great enthusiasm for any new introduction. Such was the case when England's Robert Fortune introduced the Golden Lily of Japan, *Lilium auratum*. It is reported that the enthusiasm for some plants was so great that gentlemen, expressing awe for a plant, would remove their hats in the presence of a fine specimen being introduced. On the other hand, some of the stories told by these early explorers greatly exaggerated their findings, and made certain plants out to be much more important than they would eventually prove to be in English and American gardens.

Not only explorers but also artists and writers have shown a passion for flowers and ornamental plants, and theirs has been the more constant affection. Their work has surely had an impact on

how we view flowers and the role of horticulture in our lives. The West was first captivated by the paintings of the old masters, who depicted flowers and fruit in formal still-life settings. Those works were particularly important to the royal aristocracies of England, Germany, Holland, and France. The great European impressionists Renoir, Monet, Cezanne, Van Gogh, and Pissarro later brought new insights to observing gardens, as they captured in their paintings the essence of garden character and the romantic qualities of the flowers they painted.

The work of the impressionists came during the period that has been called the "Golden Age of Horticulture." During that time the love of artists for flowers seemed to reach new heights. It is known that Renoir situated his studio so that he could paint his much-beloved olive orchard from indoors during his period of failing health. We are familiar with

The cottage garden at the Schultze House in San Antonio includes many heirloom plants from the area. WCW

the importance of Monet's two and a half acre garden, Giverny, to his grand body of work. It is reported that Monet constructed a special roof-covered boat, so that he could paint on the pond at his beloved Giverny in all types of weather. This garden, with its exuberance of colorful flowers, remains today among the most frequently visited and photographed showplace gardens of the world.

During the last half of the nineteenth century, an old garden type, but a new fashion trend, hit the English garden scene. The *cottage garden*, a diverse mix of floriferous plants, became the rage in England. That country offered a perfect setting and climate for small gardens filled with brightly colored flowers in this traditional, but newly elevated, garden style which, as a contemporary commentator explained, "lets the flowers tell their story to the heart" (*Victorian Flower Gardens*, Andrew Clayton-Payne, Weidenfeld). The true cottage gardens had been those surround-

ing the homes of the rural working class, or tenants of large landowners in earlier times. However, what started out to be a recognized garden character of the working class had become *the* garden theme for the affluent across England by the end of the nineteenth century.

The popularity of this kind of garden grew tremendously, in part due to the fairyland-like images that were created by several talented English painters. These artists' works often depicted quaint, colorful gardens surrounding small, rural, picturesque, thatch-roofed cottages. Several of the most influential painters of the late nineteenth-century period were Myles E. Foster, Helen Allingham, Charles E. Wilson, Arthur C. Strachan, Beatrice Parsons, Thomas Tyndale, and Henry J. Sylvester Stannard. For many of us today, however, our impressions of the cottage garden were formulated from the drawings by Beatrix Potter in her books for children.

The cottage garden concept continues to captivate gardeners

around the world, although garden writers warned would-be gardeners a century ago that these gardens are terribly labor intensive. Nevertheless, the interest persists, perhaps because to create and tend such a garden meets a deep inner need of many people who sincerely love to tend to flowers. Some of the most common plants to be found in such gardens are hollyhock, aster, carnation, pinks, sweet william, wallflower, stock, sweet pea, pansy, delphinium, phlox, and columbine.

THE CUT-FLOWER GARDEN CONCEPT IN VICTORIAN TIMES

William Robinson, the great English plantsman whose opinions have greatly influenced garden planning from late Victorian times to the present, wrote of the necessity of planning reserve and cut-flower gardens. Although he is well known for his dislike of the ribbon beds and stiffly formal borders which had currently been in vogue, instead favoring more random and free-form masses of plants, he was well aware that not all plants could survive in a mixed border for long. He wrote that hardy plants could be divided into two broad groups—those which will thrive in and near woody growth and those which cannot. Easily overwhelmed kinds, such as carnations and dianthus of all sorts, phloxes, anemones, ranunculus and other bulbs, delphiniums, irises, chrysanthemums, grasses and delicate plants intended to be dried for winter displays, need to be planted in rows and treated almost as a market gardener would, in a special plot in or near the kitchen garden, sheltered from wind and cold, but not shaded. To his mind, an eighth of an acre was a workable size for the cut-flower garden, although even the smallest garden should have a small plot of this kind. With these perennials (aided by the rose and other bush and tree flowers around the garden) can be grown the annuals needed to supply floral

decorations for the house or hospital, or to exchange with friends and neighbors, in the generous way of all true gardeners. This kind of garden plot also serves the gardener as his nursery for maintaining replacements or for starting out rare or delicate plants.

Many of Robinson's ideas seem surprisingly modern—for instance, his instructions to alternate narcissus with rows of delphiniums and hardy fuschias for color during two different seasons of the year, or to mix together plants of an entirely different nature in the same plot to discourage insects and disease. He suggests rotating beds or strips of plants so that deeply rooted types are followed by shallow-rooted ones "in order to keep up the freshness of the garden." Robinson encouraged readers to utilize the spaces between and under roses with bulbs or carefully thought-out choices of ground covers and shorter plants, to gain maximum color and interest.

CUT-FLOWER GARDENS IN THE UNITED STATES

Albert D. Taylor, a well-known landscape architect whose book, *The Complete Garden* (1916), was a mainstay in garden planning for many years, wrote that the first principle in successful development of any flower garden is to determine uses for which it will be put. Plantings developed to create an interesting garden picture, or sweeps of color, are different in character from the cut-flower garden from which blooms, as soon as they are mature, are usually cut for table decoration. Best success in garden development is obtained by drawing a clear-cut line between the cut-flower garden and the flower garden as a piece of landscape design, so that as plants develop their blooms and are at the height of effectiveness in terms of color and interest, they are not cut down for table decorations and the effect spoiled. For this reason a reserve or cut-flower area should be kept, containing

A kitchen garden at the Antique Rose Emporium in Independence, Texas, includes 'Archduke Charles' roses and other low-maintenance perennial heirloom plants. wcw

Cottage gardens often contain folk art such as this whirligig in Greg Grant's Arcadia, Texas, landscape. wcw

both annuals and those perennials with the lasting qualities to hold up well after cutting and whose flowers are of sufficient substance to be effective.

DIRECTIONS OF INTEREST IN HORTICULTURE

Any major movement or cause—artistic or otherwise—can generally be traced to influential individuals who have taken it to heart and made a dedicated commitment to it. Such is the case with the intense interest in horticulture. One example is the work of the Dutch with tulips in the seventeenth century. The craze for breeding and collecting choice varieties at that time resulted in what has ever after been referred to as *Tulipmania*, as demand for tulips became so extreme that bulb prices soared until the speculative financial bubble burst. Royalty in early days were especially influential in promoting particular plants. One such example is the universal passion for roses, which came to great heights during Empress Josephine Bonaparte's reign, and later, Queen Victoria's rule, and which has continued to this day.

Another such influential person was England's Gertrude Jekyll (1843–1932), who brought a new level of artistic expression to flower gardening. While she is probably best remembered for her understanding of the use of color in herbaceous border plantings, her contributions go far beyond this single aspect of garden design. To a period of English garden design that emphasized beds made up of flowers of every description while seeming indifferent to rather random placements of trees and shrubs, Miss Jekyll brought a level of artistic restraint seldom practiced then. Her plantings were designed with drifts of colors, rather than the solid blocks of color used by most garden designers of the period. Working closely with the influential English architect Edwin Lutyens, she pioneered the concept of compartmentalizing gardens to provide "rooms" where plants would be protected in micro-climates from harsh winds. Decades later Vita Sackville-West, following the same concept, referred to her Sissinghurst garden as a "garden with all its separate rooms and sub-sections." Few contemporary individuals have been more gifted or had a more profound effect on gardening than Jekyll. She made her mark by arranging plants in carefully-orchestrated color combinations. Her plantings were noted for grading the sequence of colors from warm to cool, or cool to warm, as one moved along the edge of the planting. Sometimes warm colors were in the center of a border planting, with cool colors on either end. Her garden designs and plant combinations continue to influence flower garden lovers. Her books include *Color Schemes for the Flower Garden, Wood and Garden, Home and Garden,* and *Roses for English Gardens.*

THE EASTERN TRADITION

The great gardens of Japan and China never had the impact on the American scene that gardens of Europe and England did. With our mostly European ancestry, it was only natural that, through remembered garden imagery, the new American gardens would take on Western styles and characters. Most Americans did not grasp the deep abstract or philosophical meaning associated with garden designs in Japan and China. Japan, moreover, was virtually a closed society from the mid-1600s, until the first plant collectors were allowed into carefully-selected areas of Japan in 1860. That period constituted a huge block of lost time during a critical period of formative garden design development in the United States. The Japanese concept of designing an entire garden on a small parcel of land was foreign to the expansive American mind; our early gardens normally covered multiple acres.

While Oriental garden design principles, or "styles," were seldom embraced, what would our American gardens be today without the hundreds of species of plants that found their way, primarily via England and Europe, to this country from Asia? The list of individual plants introduced into the United States by this means is far too extensive to give here in total, but consider just these few of our most widely used species from Japan or China: camellia, azalea, hydrangea, Bradford pear, Japanese maple, cycad, deutzia, Japanese persimmon, Japanese plum, many ferns, gardenia, junipers, aucuba, fatsia, bamboos, tea olive, flowering almond, cotoneaster, cryptomeria, barberry, buddleia, boxwood, ginkgo, hosta, Chinese hollies, Japanese iris, many ornamental grasses, crape myrtle, Oriental magnolias, ligustrums, liriope, mondo, and hibiscus. Clearly, much of our present plant diversity, in both woody shrubs and trees and even the herbaceous flowers, is owed to the horticulturally rich lands of China and Japan.

THE AMERICAN TRADITION

Although it has a short history when compared to other countries of the world, America has nevertheless played a significant role in the evolution of Western horticulture and garden design. Early American settlers and later pioneers had little time or inclination for ornamental gardening. Their primary concern was taming wild nature in order to survive on newly-acquired lands. They also usually lacked the resources to create and care for the types of flower gardens from back home. Their first cultivated plantings, as would be expected, were normally essential food plants like corn and other grains, beans, several types of squash, and sunflowers (primarily for the food value of their seeds, not for their flowers). Other essential plants were the herbs and special plants that provided for medicinal needs. Plants from which dyes were extracted were also important in early settlements. Not a necessity, but a highly-valuable commodity that was traded throughout the world, tobacco was also widely planted in the South.

As time and resources would permit, early settlers returned to their native countries of England, France, Italy, and Spain and brought back images of the grand pleasure gardens in their lands. They would translate these places into their own vernacular landscape expressions in their new land. Fortunately, we have rather comprehensive records and plans of gardens at several early American historic sites, like Washington's Mt. Vernon, Williamsburg, and Thomas Jefferson's Monticello in Virginia. Those gardens apparently closely resembled the gardens of the English nobility, but with an emphasis on practical reproduction that would have been reflected in the aristocratic English gardens of the eighteenth century.

The love of flowers and ornamental gardening tended to reassert itself rapidly after early settlement of an area was completed. After realizing a degree of independence and affluence, inhabitants soon began expressing their inherent love of plants by importing huge quantities of favorite plants from their homelands. During this same period many of our native plants were

A perennial garden at Dumbarton Oaks is enclosed by a hedge, rather than walls. WCW

being shipped to England, Holland, and Germany, where they underwent extensive hybridization, to be returned to this country later as highly prized garden flowers. Plant introductions reached a new high in the mid-nineteenth century as great celebrations took place when plants from Japan and China reached the Eastern shores of the United States.

Nineteenth century American gardens, while rich in horticulture, could hardly be compared to the powerful architectural imagery of gardens in England and Europe, products of much more mature cultures. American tastes by contrast have been more eclectic. In her book *The Plantation South,* author Katharine Jones quotes the recollections of *London Times* writer William H. Russell of his 1863 visit along the Mississippi River corridor. His thoughts about one grand house, Houmas House at Burnside, Louisiana:

> *I ascended the bank, and across the road, directly in front, appeared a carriage gateway and wickets of wood, painted white, in a line of park palings of the same material, which extended up and down the road as far as the eye could see, and guarded widespread fields of maize and sugar cane. An avenue lined with trees, with branches close set, drooping and overarching a walk paved with red brick, led to the house, the porch of which was visible at the extremity of the lawn, with clustering flowers, rose, jessamine, and creepers clinging to the pillars, supporting the veranda. The view from the belvedere on the roof was one of the most striking of its kind in the world.*

We have been borrowers from other cultures since becoming a

country. Russell Page probably best summarizes our history in garden design in his book, *The Education of A Gardener* (Random House): "Styles from all over the world chase each other through the American scene, to be tried, accepted, modified, and then discarded."

While American gardens never reached the zenith of grandness and attention to detail of the old gardens of England, Europe, and Asia, beginning in the mid-nineteenth century grand-scaled flower plantings were included in the elaborate country and city estates of the wealthy, particularly in the Northeast. As tycoon families amassed untold fortunes, they built enormous mansions with gardens that did indeed rival those of England and Europe. The designs of those gardens were strongly influenced by the great English and European gardens their owners or designers admired. However, many of those estates also contained English cottage gardens, which were referred to by their new name, "old-fashioned gardens."

The power and prestige of family fortunes continued to grow in the late nineteenth and early twentieth centuries, with every part of the country eventually feeling the impact of the good times. The fifty-year period between 1890 and 1940 has been referred to as the "Golden Age of American Gardens" by Mac Griswold and Eleanor Weller in their book by the same title (Harry N. Abrams, Inc., New York). Others called that period the "Gilded Age" of American gardening. The owners of the lavish estates of the era believed strongly in the "M and M" gardening principle: "Money is the best manure." Both money and manure were spread lavishly over gardens that ranged in size from a few to several hundred acres. Renowned landscape architects and garden designers like Frederick Law Olmsted, Ellen

Biddle Shipman, Marian Coffin, and Beatrix Farrand were only a few of the big-name designers who participated in those lavish developments.

Nurseries and plant sales also flourished during that period. Mail-order catalog marketing of plants and seeds was a thriving business, with catalogs offering numerous varieties of a particular ornamental or vegetable. Garden magazines like *The Horticulturist, Gardener's Monthly,* and *The Garden Magazine* and books on horticulture like *Theory and Practice of Landscape Gardening Adapted to North America* by Andrew Downing, *What England Can Teach Us About Gardening* by Wilhelm Miller, and Guy Lowell's *American Gardens* added fuel to the fire of America's new love affair with gardening. Every part of American horticulture was enhanced during those prosperous times.

Arboreta and botanic gardens throughout the world played a leading role in horticulture research and the dissemination of useful knowledge. The United States had its prestigious research centers like the Morton Arboretum in Chicago, the Arnold Arboretum in Boston, the National Arboretum in Washington, D.C., and the great botanic gardens—the New York Botanic Garden, the Missouri Botanic Garden, the Brooklyn Botanic Garden, and numerous others. Land grant universities, one situated in each state, conducted research on regional plants and other horticulture issues. In the United States, prestigious plant societies like the Pennsylvania Horticultural Society (1827) and the Massachusetts Horticultural Society (1829) were equally enthusiastic about their work. All of these centers, along with countless other plant societies long focused on specialty plant research and promotion, have increased our awareness and appreciation for plants over many decades of intensive on-site work and explorations to remote places of the world to collect new materials.

There have been pauses along the way when the pace has not been quite so intensive. The Great Depression and World War II were two major periods when our thoughts and energies were focused on other issues. Now, however, America's great passion for flowers and other ornamentals is back, stronger than ever. All across this land we ride a high tide of enthusiasm for gardening. One of the objectives of this book is to celebrate the great bounty of garden plants that we now enjoy, which offers us the immeasurable pleasure of growing plants, cutting them for our homes and businesses, and sharing them with others.

CUT FLOWERS IN TODAY'S LANDSCAPES

Although Americans are spending more money in their gardens than ever, there are some modern constraints that impact the use of cut flowers in their gardens. Property size is shrinking. Also, gardening is in competition with many other activities for our time. Most homeowners simply don't have the time or space to create extensive separate cut-flower gardens. Although routine lawn maintenance done by professionals has become fairly widespread, trained gardeners capable of maintaining floral plantings are out of reach for most homeowners.

There are some practical ways to include flowers for indoor use when planning a modest size garden. Perhaps a small area can be devoted exclusively to cut-flower production by allocating several rows to zinnias, marigolds, poppies, and other seasonal annuals along with vegetables. Even modest size borders can usually accommodate drifts of various annuals and perennials useful for cutting, and flowering shrubs and trees can tolerate a reasonable amount of selective cutting. For rooftop or balcony gardens, cut flowers can be produced in large containers. Still another possibility for today's homeowner is to update the cottage gardening style so common in Texas and the South 50 to 150 years ago. A garden of this sort is particularly appropriate for town houses and other small properties where most modern landscaping efforts consist of a few uninteresting evergreen shrubs and ground covers unimaginatively placed against foundations of country homes.

There are a few rules to keep in mind when planning cottage gardens. Usually, they are modest in size and enclosed by low picket fencing, walls, or hedges, and contain a wide variety of plant materials selected by the owner for their beauty, emotional attachment, family favorites, or real usefulness. Cottage gardens reflect one of the best aspects of America's combined North European heritage— individualism. Since they should reflect the tastes of their owners, no two cottage gardens should ever be alike. Gardeners should study the countryside and older gardens in the area. Native plants, old garden roses, and other plants that have been successfully grown in local gardens for many years are often the best choices. One writer felt it was impossible for the true cottage garden to be in poor taste, relying as it does on the natural form of the plants. Andrew Jackson Downing (1815–1852), the great American architect and probably our first professional landscape architect, thought that the cottage garden was "perfect of its kind," and that the charm and attractiveness of these gardens made them "little gems of rural and picturesque beauty." Since the arrangement of plants in a cottage garden tends to be informal, taking cut flowers from it is less likely to diminish the overall effect. The key to success with any garden is planning. With some initial effort cut flowers and garden color can be provided for every season of the year. The fragrance, color, and beauty of flowers, foliage, and fruit can easily be produced in one's own garden and reflect the specific preferences of the owners.

WCW and NGO

Two

Sharing Flowers

A Southern Tradition

As long as there have been gardens, gardeners have loved sharing what they grow. Nowhere has this been more true than in the southern United States. The reasons for this region's tradition of floral generosity are not difficult to identify. The climate of the South itself sets the tone, providing gardeners throughout the region with long summers, brightly sunlit days, and mild winters. In addition, much of the region is extremely humid, providing in many places almost greenhouse growing conditions.

Until the explosion of urbanization that occurred throughout the South in the first three decades of the twentieth century, the region was almost exclusively rural in character. Rich or poor, people who live country lives necessarily live close to the land, and are often isolated from each other for long periods of time. What better conditions could there be to encourage the cultivation and giving of flowers as gifts, and to mark the important moments of life that necessarily bring people together?

But today, after a century of urbanization, the question must be asked, "Have we in the South begun to forget our tradition of growing and sharing flowers and other ornamental plants?" Our home gardens (or yards, as Southerners often call them, harkening back to a time when a family's homeplace was invariably surrounded by productive as well

as decorative and leisure activities) are still blessed by the bounteous local climate. They still offer plants that grow and flower quickly and an overall plant palette that is richer than that of any other United States region. It would be a shame if we wasted these advantages! Luckily, the respect that people in this region have for our traditional culture militates against that happening.

This book seeks to add its weight to the forces that favor the survival of the great Southern tradition of growing and sharing flowers and ornamental plants. In addition to identifying a broad spectrum of plants that flower, fruit, and offer interesting foliage in Southern gardens, it provides basic information on growing plants suitable for arrangements, and on cutting and preparing them for use in decorating our homes and marking the significant events in our lives.

ITS MANIFESTATIONS

Religious observances have long been the essential Southern communal experience. It is therefore not surprising that floral offerings have always occupied a central position in our places of worship. For many years most arrangements placed on or near altars were bouquets of fresh flowers, berries, and foliage from private gardens, or even wildflowers gathered from the fields and roadsides of the surrounding countryside. In the rural Mississippi of this author's youth virtually all flowers seen in church came directly from nature. This predominance continues in many Southern churches today.

Made from the best a garden has to offer on a particular Sunday, arrangements harvested from local gardens reflect the multitude of seasonal changes through which our gardens pass in the course of a year of Sabbaths. Not surprisingly, "dignified" flowers predominate in this usage. They include irises, lilies, and snapdragons. In early spring, for example, the long, arching branches of a group of favorite Southern shrubs, the spireas, proudly lift upward their long columns of delicate white flowers. Easter is often marked by the great "abstract" flower, the calla lily, beloved by generations of artists, and, in the

Floral offering of garden flowers at the Mangham United Methodist Church, Mangham, Louisiana. WCW

A table setting of garden flowers at Linden Plantation, Vicksburg. JOY BRABSTON

A buffet table arrangement of wildflowers, Southern Garden Symposium reception, St. Francisville, Louisiana. NGO

Victorian language of flowers given the supreme signification of *magnificent beauty*.

Another Southern church tradition, one that today has sadly almost faded away, was the wearing of a white or red rose to church on Mother's Day. A red rose signified that your mother was living, while a white one denoted she was deceased. Congregates of all ages wore a garden rose on this special day. For those without home-grown roses to wear, those more fortunate would always bring a supply to church from their own gardens.

During illness, it is a universal American custom for well-wishers to give the suffering friend or loved one plants or bouquets of flowers to express the desire for a full and speedy recovery. Although hospital stays can today be quite short and the rooms very small, bouquets of home-grown flowers still carry messages of concern and encouragement to those who are ill. We fortunate Southerners have some particularly stunning flowers and plants to present at such a time: in spring, the showy flowers of the "Indian" azalea; in summer the magnificent flower and foliage of the Southern magnolia or a bouquet of zinnias; in winter the unparalleled formal beauty of camellia flowers, perhaps set off with the more raffish flowers of the winter honeysuckle; around Christmas time perhaps a cheery little ardisia shrub from a shaded corner of our garden—the bright red berries against dark green foliage make it perfect for the season; and, in the darkness of late winter/earliest spring branches of the Taiwan flowering cherry or the Oriental magnolia.

Flowers play a leading role at times of sadness and bereavement. People have honored the dead with flowers from prehistoric times. While today most flowers given as expressions of sympathy have been commercially grown, this has not always been the case. Even today some occasionally gather garden flowers and give them in sympathy to the bereaved. Such home-grown offerings seem to carry an especially personal message of sympathy.

In south Louisiana, as in other places where the Catholic faith is strong, special respect is

Above: Flowers on a South Louisiana grave on All Saints' Day. NGO
Below: A bouquet of wildflowers on a grave in South Louisiana on All Saints' Day. NGO

paid to the deceased on All Saints' Day by decorating their graves. This practice has strong roots in the Spanish and Latin American cultures. Family members clean grave sites and sometimes give gravestones and vaults fresh coats of whitewash. On this day cemeteries seem to become flower gardens, as fresh bouquets, often of chrysanthemums, spread across the landscape. Many visit these quiet, park-like sites to commemorate the passing of loved ones, to see the glorious show of often homegrown flowers and to participate in special memorial services held in the cemeteries.

On Memorial Day, referred to as Decoration Day in some parts of the United States, the deceased are also remembered with floral offerings. Geraniums are often placed on the graves of the honored dead. Family members and others also take flowers to the cemetery to commemorate other special occasions such as Mother's Day (often marked by bouquets containing that fragrant star of Southern gardens, the gardenia), Father's Day, and birthdays and anniversaries of the deceased.

Home-grown zinnias at a farmers' street market. NGO

MODERN OPPORTUNITIES FOR ENHANCEMENT

Not all Southerners have gardens. The South is much more urbanized than it once was, so many now live in apartments and condominiums. Luckily, modern development in commerce makes it possible for those of us so situated to participate in the joy of sharing flowers. Anyone who travels abroad quickly learns how much more people of other cultures use flowers in their daily lives than do most Americans. Small, quickly-made bouquets are readily accessible in flower marquees and at other small flower and produce markets on the streets of major cities abroad. Seldom can one travel more than a block or so before one of these outlets appears. Flowers are very economically priced, and busy passers-by lose little time in making quick purchases of their favorite prearranged bouquets, or of a handful of loose flowers to arrange at home.

Flower shows across the nation have become a huge draw, with much to be learned from them. As the United States and the South move away from their rural and frontier roots, it is important to remember that flowers and ornamental plants can still enhance our lives, both in old and new ways.

NGO

Three

Annual Flowers for Cutting and Garden Display

Annuals are plants that complete their growing cycle in a year or less. They include many of the tried and true plants that have been traditional favorites for cut flower use. Some annuals are referred to as *reseeding*, which means if they are allowed to grow to maturity and their seed falls to the ground, they may return. There is something special about these plants being so fond of your garden that they return each year for another visit.

Since seed was a valuable commodity and money sometimes scarce, early Southern gardeners often saved seeds of favorite annuals from year to year, rather than gamble on the generosity of Mother Nature. Trading seed has always been a popular custom among friends, and families often handed down particular annuals, vegetables, and herbs from one generation to another. Seed can be saved just as successfully today, to be sown in pots or trays indoors, in the greenhouse, or directly into the garden.

Whether seed is collected and stored or allowed to fall and naturally germinate in the garden, it is important to remember that seeds gathered from modern hybrid varieties often do not produce plants identical to the original. Since they are not open-pollinated by commercial growers, seed saved from many of these modern types may produce flowers that bear little resemblance to the parent. Large and double flowers may return as smaller single types, and

once bright colors may be more muted, reflecting older forms of the plant. This may or may not be considered desirable, but can surprise the gardener new to seed saving.

If annuals are to self-propagate, the plants must mature their seed. Obviously, this cannot occur if the seed is picked before it ripens or, worse yet, if the plants are destroyed before they have had a chance to complete their growing and fruiting cycles. Sometimes this will mean tolerating plants for several weeks after they have passed their peak and are slipping into an unattractive senility.

Most seed keeps well in storage, if allowed to dry for a few days packed in airtight jars or self-sealing plastic bags and placed in the lower part of the refrigerator (where the temperature should range from about 40–45° F). Be sure to label the seed, since it may not be recognizable several months later when the time comes to plant it. If seed is not to be

stored, but rather allowed to germinate naturally in the garden, it is helpful to shake the seed pods or the entire plant upon picking to make sure the seed is properly scattered and not thrown into the compost along with the dead plant.

Annuals are sometimes classified into warm or cool season types. Because of our long warm season in the South, many of the warm season types may be replanted after completion of their spring and early summer flowering for an additional late summer/fall bloom. To help determine proper planting times, check the zone section in the heading of each plant, which classifies each as either cool or warm season.

Cool Season Annuals

Depending upon location, cool season annuals may be planted in the fall, winter, or early spring. In U.S. hardiness zones 8 and south, fall plantings are usually worth the risk of occasional cold damage.

Warm Season Annuals

These plants are sensitive to cold in varying degrees. Most should be planted after danger of frost is past in late winter or early spring. Some can be rejuvenated by pruning, watering, and fertilizing in late summer and produce beautifully again in the fall. Another option is to replant with new stock.

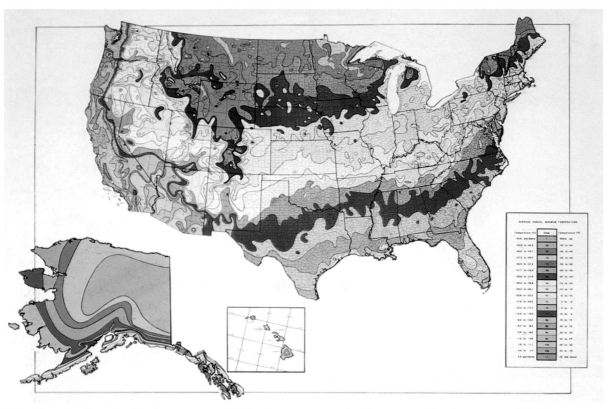

United States Hardiness Map. Hardiness zones provided in the text correspond to the zones on this reference map, which gives a range of average annual minimum temperatures for each zone. USDA

Ammi majus
(Am-ME MA-jus)

BISHOP'S WEED, FALSE QUEEN ANNE'S LACE

Family: Umbelliferae
Zone: all. Size: 2–3 feet, spring, cool season annual

Bishop's weed is very similar to Queen Anne's lace, but considered to be somewhat less invasive in the garden. It is excellent as cut material with lacy, snowflake flower heads 6 inches across. It grows best in full sun and is useful in borders. Foliage is divided into linear or threadlike segments. It is a wonderful filler in arrangements and blends with all color combinations. For best results sow the seeds in fall and thin to 8–10 inches apart. Bishop's weed will grow in most any soil, but prefers good drainage.

Anemone coronaria
(ah-NEM-o-nee cor-a-NAR-ee-ah)

ANEMONE

Family: Ranunculaceae
Zone: all. Size: 1 foot, spring, cool season annual

Anemones are excellent cut flowers that come in extremely vivid colors of red, purple, white, blue, and mixtures of these colors. They grow from oddly shaped tuberous roots planted in the fall or very early spring. Flowers are 1½–2 inches across and appear singly on long stems. There are single, semi-double, and double forms. The foliage is finely divided, somewhat like Italian parsley. Anemones like a sunny location with well-prepared and drained soil.

Bishop's weed is a more manageable plant than Queen Anne's lace for filler.

Above: Anemones provide vivid color from late winter until mid-spring. NGO

Below: Tall white snapdragons in the Hayward-Washington Garden, Charleston, South Carolina. WCW

Mulching newly emerging plants in November with pinestraw or hay can provide winter protection for areas north of zone 8.

Antirrhinum majus
(an-tir-I-num MA-jus)
SNAPDRAGON
Family: Scrophulariaceae
Zone: all. Size: 6 inches–2 feet, spring, summer, primarily cool season annual

Snapdragons are among the best cut flowers grown in Southern gardens. Mature height of the standard form is 18–24 inches; dwarfs are readily available but since the stems and plants are less than 8 inches tall, they are less valuable for cutting. In zones 8 and 9 plants set out in September or October have a reasonable chance they will make it through the winter unharmed.

Unfortunately, there are few nurseries currently handling snapdragons in the fall, and it may be necessary to grow your own from seed. Snapdragons are among the most impressive spike flowers we can grow and they thrive in a wide variety of soils as long as good drainage, sufficient moisture, and at least a half day of sunlight are available. Staking may be necessary to prevent blowing over. The terminal growth buds may be pinched to induce more but smaller flowers. Cutting the first spike usually results in forcing several smaller side shoots to bloom. A wide range of colors is available, including white, yellow, pink, red, rust, purple, and bi-colors.

Celosia cristata
(ce-LOW-see-ah CRIS-ta-ta)
COCKSCOMB
Family: Amaranthaceae
Zone: all. Size: 1–4 feet, summer, cool season annual

Various forms of cockscomb have been grown in American gardens since the eighteenth century. They thrive in hot Southern summers

Unusual forms and colors of celosias are exciting both in the garden and for bouquets. wcw

and are easily passed along from one gardener to another from seed or transplants, which tend to reseed freely in the garden. Cockscomb require a sunny location and well-drained soil to thrive. Although quite drought tolerant, they respond favorably to occasional watering. There are basically two types of celosias: crested and plumed. Both descended from *Celosia argentea*, a native of India and possibly China. All forms are useful as long-lasting, fresh-cut flowers or dried in winter bouquets. They are easily dried by hanging upside down in a dark, ventilated area for several weeks. The only annoyance I have associated with them is the shedding of small black seeds about the size of fleas. The dominant color in the crested forms is a bright purplish red. Yellow, pink, salmon, orange, and white forms are sometimes available. Cockscomb do not thrive, and should not be planted, until night time and soil temperatures are quite warm in late spring. They can be replanted in mid- or late summer for a fall display.

Top: Celosia comes in spike and crested forms, seen here in the Bynum Garden in Old Salem, North Carolina. wcw

Above: Plumed celosias are used fresh or dried. ALL-AMERICA SELECTIONS

Centaurea or corn flower, often referred to as bachelor's button, reseeds readily and provides some of the strongest blue shades available. WCW

Centaurea cyanus
(cen-TAU-ree-ah CY-an-us)
CORNFLOWER
Family: Compositae
Zone: all. Size: 1–2 feet, spring, summer, cool season annual

Cornflowers are known as "bachelor's buttons" in some parts of the country, but most of us in the South reserve that name for *Gomphrena globosa*, another good reseeding annual. Cornflowers are available in white, pink, lavender, and purple-flowering forms, and have naturalized along roadsides in North Texas and other areas of the South. They are excellent for cutting and return reliably each year in well-prepared soils. Full sun is the best location.

Chrysanthemum parthenium
(chry-SAN-the-mum par-THEN-ee-um)
FEVERFEW
Family: Compositae
Zone: all. Size: 18–24 inches, spring, summer, primarily cool season annual

Feverfew is a personal favorite for cutting as well as garden display. It has been popular for centuries. A literal translation of its Latin name, *febrifuge*, is "to drive away

illness." Victorians recommended it to keep the home fresh and sweet-smelling. Although often listed and sold as a perennial, I find it lasts only one season, or sometimes an entire year. It does, however, reseed in my garden and I often look for small seedlings to transplant or share with friends.

Probably the best time to start plants from seed is in the fall. For zones north of 8, early spring planting is recommended. I have had little success with the double-flowering types. The single one provides large sprays of dainty

Chrysanthemum parthenium, or feverfew, with its masses of daisylike single flowers, is excellent for cutting. WCW

Pink cleome in a Martha's Vineyard garden. NGO

white daisies with yellow centers. They are perfect to combine with old garden roses and other dramatic flowers. Pinching the plants when 6–8 inches tall results in bushier plants and more flowers. I have seen the cultivar 'Aureum', which has bright chartreuse foliage, in several gardens here and abroad, and find it attractive. Feverfew prefers well-drained and prepared soil and some afternoon shade, if possible. I believe it should be grown more extensively for commercial and home cut-flower use.

Cleome spinosa
(CLEE-oh-mee SPI-no-sa)
CLEOME, SPIDER FLOWER
Family: Capparaceae
Zone: all. Size: 3–4 feet, summer, cool season annual

Cleome is a heat-tolerant and easily grown plant. It thrives in the heat of summer and can become a shrubby mass of fluffy flower clusters with long, protruding stamens. Colors range from pure white to pink and lavender. Leaves and stems are clammy to touch and have a strong, although not totally unpleasant, odor. Both flowers and dry seed capsules are useful in arrangements. Plant cleome in sunny, well-drained areas of the garden. They will sprout and grow rapidly in warm or hot weather. Stems are spiny with divided leaves. A fall flowering season can be encouraged if plants are cut back in late summer.

Consolida ambigua
(Con-SOL-e-da am-BIG-u-ah)
LARKSPUR
Family: Ranunculaceae
Zone: all. Size: 2–4 feet, spring, summer, cool season annual

Larkspur is a wonderful, old-fashioned annual producing beautiful

Consolida, or annual larkspur, is an easily-grown cool-season annual. wcw

Cosmos are dependable self-seeding annuals. WCW

ORNAMENTAL KALE AND CABBAGE

Family: Cruciferae
Zone: all. Size: 1 foot, winter, spring, cool season annual

Ornamental forms of kale and cabbage have become very popular annuals in recent years. The heads may also be cut and used ornamentally indoors. Highly colored rosettes of pink, white, purple, and lavender are available in smooth leaf and fringed forms. The fringed types are usually referred to as kale. All are considered edible. For zones 8 and south cabbages and kales are usually winter-hardy and may be planted in late fall along with pansies. I am partial to traditional red and blue-green garden cabbage for ornamental use. Its bold texture contrasts nicely with other plants in containers, borders, and beds. Combine in the garden with spring-flowering bulbs such as daffodils, leucojum, and tulips. A sunny location and well-drained, fertile soil yield the best displays of kale and cabbage.

spike flowers of pink, purple, white, and mauve. They do not like being transplanted, but with extra watering this can be done in late fall or winter. Double-flowering forms often revert to singles in a year or two. They reseed so prolifically that thinning is usually necessary. If thinned to about 1 foot apart, larkspurs produce a full and impressive mass of color. Seed should be sown in September or October, in full or partially sunny areas that have been well-worked and fertilized. Larkspurs are relatives to the large-flowering delphiniums of the North, which are not well adapted to Southern gardens. Rather than perennials, they perform as short-term annuals and diminish quickly in early spring warm spells. There is an interesting but less showy perennial delphinium native to Texas, but it is rarely available in the nursery trade.

Cosmos bipinnatus
(COS-mos BI-pin-a-tus)
COSMOS
Family: Compositae
Zone: all. Size: 2–6 feet, summer, cool season annual

Cosmos occur in lovely pinks, lavenders, whites, purples, crimsons, and stripes and are popular for massing in the garden as well as cut-flower use. They are natives of Mexico and tropical America. The daisylike flowers occur on thin stems. Foliage is finely divided. They grow easily in sunny,

well-drained locations and bloom from late spring into summer, until the heat becomes too intense. Cosmos are also planted for fall bloom. When selecting cosmos flowers for cutting, choose newly opened flowers and immerse them immediately in cool or tepid water. The 'Sensation' series includes most of the colors listed, all of which combine beautifully. The 'Seashell' strain is interesting with its rolled florets. *C. sulphureus* comes in yellow and gold colors and tends to be more vigorous than *C. bipinnatus*. It is also available in a dwarf form that is less likely to take over the summer garden.

Ornamental kale at the Mercer Arboretum, Texas. WCW

Cucurbits, or gourds, come in many shapes and may be dried and fashioned into a wide range of decorative material. WCW

Cucurbita pepo ovifera, Luffa aegyptiaca, Lagenaria siceraria
(CU-cur-bit-ah)
GOURDS
Family: Cucurbitaceae
Zone: all. Size: rampant vines 10–15 feet, cool season annual

Gourds are easily grown and interesting annuals with a long tradition of usefulness and beauty in gardens. They require hot weather and produce best when the rangy vines are given the support of a fence, trellis, or other structure. Gourds will produce when allowed to sprawl on the ground, but the quality is better when the vines are given support. The dish-rag gourd, *Luffa aegyptiaca*, is among the most ornamental with its large yellow flowers and handsome foliage. It is a good choice for almost instant shade on arbors or pergolas. The 1–2 foot long cylindrical fruit is useful because of its fibrous interior, revealed after the gourds have dried and the outside skin removed. *Lagenaria siceraria* is better known as the "birdhouse gourd." It prolifically yields bottle- or dumbell-shaped fruit 1–2 feet long. Basket gourds range from 6 inches to 1 foot in diameter and are shaped somewhat like a large tomato. They do not produce as many gourds as other types I have grown, but are among the most desirable. *Cucurbita pepo ovifera* produces small ornamental gourds in various sizes, shapes, and colors. When harvesting wait until the vines are dry, then cut a piece of stem with each gourd. Hang them from their stems in a dark, warm, well-ventilated place where they can dry slowly. Once thoroughly dry, gourds may be preserved with a coat of paste wax, lacquer, or varnish. Gourds prefer fertile, well-drained soils and sunny locations and respond well to occasional deep watering.

Daucus carota
(DAW-cus car-AH-ta)
QUEEN ANNE'S LACE, WILD CARROT
Family: Umbelliferae
Zone: all. Size: 2–3 feet, spring, cool season annual

Queen Anne's lace may be found growing naturally along roadsides in most of Texas and the South. It is sometimes called "Wild Carrot" because cultivated carrots are a

Queen Anne's lace is an excellent reseeding annual for filler and gives a casual, cottage-style look to gardens and arrangements. NGO

Hyacinth bean is an easy, fast-growing vine for temporary arbors, pergolas, and trellises. T. E. POPE

variety of this plant. Although usually listed as a biennial, Queen Anne's lace is often grown as a cool season annual for its handsome umbrellalike 2- to 6-inch heads of tiny white flowers which are useful as cut flowers. Foliage is alternately arranged on the stems and similar in appearance to cultivated carrots. The flower heads dry nicely for use in winter bouquets. Plants tend to seed themselves in the garden after the first planting. Open, sunny areas and most any soil will produce satisfactory results. Fertile, well-drained soils produce larger flower heads. Plant seeds in early to mid-fall where they can be thinned to 8–10 inches apart and mature in place. Transplanting seedlings is possible, but direct seeding is easier and less troublesome. Queen Anne's lace is sometimes confused with Bishop's weed, *Ammi majus*, which is also useful as a cut flower but differs in having one colored floret in the middle of each *umbel* (umbrella-shaped flower clusters).

Dolichos lablab
(DO-li-cos LAB-lab)
HYACINTH BEAN
Family: Leguminosae
Zone: all. Size: rampant vines 10–15 feet, cool season annual

Hyacinth bean is a beautiful late summer and fall flowering vine that mounts an impressive display of sweet pealike flowers. It is probably of Old World origin,

though Thomas Jefferson grew it on interesting overhead structures made of tree limbs at Monticello, his Virginia home. Leaves are light green and divided, fanlike, into three leaflets. The stunning purple or rarely white flowers are followed by velvety, 2–3 inch pods of dark purple, popular for cutting and indoor use. In mild areas the

vines are perennial, but are usually treated as annuals and utilized primarily for fast summer shade on trellises, pergolas, and arbors. Seed may be easily saved and planted the next spring, although seedlings often return in the vicinity of last year's plants. Hyacinth beans prefer sunny locations and good garden soil, but are quite drought tolerant and thrive under a variety of conditions.

Eustoma grandiflorum
(you STO-muh gran-di-Fl OR-um)
TEXAS BLUEBELL, PRAIRIE GENTIAN
Family: Gentianaceae
Zone: all. Size: 1–2 feet, summer, cool season annual

Bluebells defy classification and are challenging to grow, but are well worth the effort. Anyone who has seen a field of their deep violet-purple flowers on a hot

Texas bluebells, or eustoma, are among the longest lasting and most beautiful of summer's flowers. WCW

Japanese hybridizers developed various color and flower forms from the native Texas bluebells. WCW

The common name "bachelor's buttons" can cause confusion when ordering seed from catalogs in the North where the name is often reserved for *Centaurea cyanus*, a plant usually called "cornflower" in the South. Under any name it is a true winner for Southern gardeners because it thrives in our summer heat and is very useful as dried material. A native of tropical Asia, bachelor's buttons have been fixtures in Southern gardens from at least as early as 1767, when Thomas Jefferson recorded them in his garden book at Monticello. Pioneer gardeners liked the way bachelor's buttons survived the summer heat with little or no irrigation. They would gather bouquets in late summer and fall, hang them upside down in a warm, dry, well-ventilated area and after several weeks arrange them indoors for winter bouquets. Flowers in the bouquets were crushed the next spring, yielding seeds for the next year's crop. This is another plant that does not want to be planted while the nights and soil are still cold. Wait

summer day cannot resist the temptation to have them in the garden. Bluebells are among the longest-lasting and most beautiful cut flowers that can be grown in our area, often lasting a week or more after harvest. They elude classification because in nature they are usually biennials, but in the garden may be annuals, or even perennials.

In the mid-1970s I was visited by several Japanese plant breeders interested in locating natural stands of these plants. Within a few years these hybridizers had developed white, pink, blue, and even double-flowering forms for the nursery and cut-flower industry. These are usually marketed under the name *Lisianthus*, which is one of the older genus names for bluebells. I have observed pink, white, and lavender variations as well as the more common deep purple in the natural environment. The native types have a black and gold eye that is absent in the hybridized forms. Foliage is blue-green and oval or lancelike. Nursery-grown plants set out in fall or early spring probably offer the best chance for success. The seeds are tiny, almost like dust, and challenging for the novice to handle.

If plants are allowed to mature their seed in the garden, seedlings usually come up the following fall. The natural stands and growing conditions provide some clues for success with bluebells. They are most often found in open fields of fairly heavy, alkaline soil where moisture is abundant in fall and winter but dry in summer. By cutting off the old bloom stems, I have usually gotten a second year of flowering from my plants. The hybridized forms of *Eustoma* are more commonly available than the native ones, which, in my opinion, are more graceful and natural in appearance. Although handsome in borders and mass plantings, bluebells may be best grown in rows as cut flowers where their somewhat inconsistent performance is more easily dealt with. Space plants about 12 inches apart and provide at least four to six hours of direct sunlight each day for best performance.

Gomphrena, or bachelor's button (globe amaranth), is among the most heat-tolerant of annuals. WCW

Sunflowers are among the most popular home-grown cut and garden flowers. CHARLES F. FRYLING JR.

to powdery mildew and other fungal diseases in the garden, and need full sun and good air circulation. For best results seed them directly where they will be grown in mid-spring. Large-flowering kinds are often referred to as "giant" or "mammoth Russians" and need irrigation to produce. Roasted sunflower seeds are popular people food, but birds relish them raw.

Iberis amara
(I-BER-is a-MAR-a)
CANDYTUFT
Family: Cruciferae
Zone: all. Size: 1–2 feet, spring, cool season annual

Candytuft is an old-fashioned favorite with its long stems of fragrant white, hyacinthlike flowers. For zones 8–10 it is best planted as a cool season annual along with pansies, snapdragons and other favorites. North of zone 8 candytuft is usually planted in early spring. The narrow, somewhat fuzzy foliage supports stems up to 15 inches long of round pure-white flower clusters. Candytuft is rarely available as transplants, but can be fairly easily grown from seed. It must have excellent drainage and at least half a day of direct sunlight since the plants are susceptible to damping off and other diseases resulting in sudden

until May or even June for best results. Four colors and dwarf forms are available but the old standard ones are most productive and satisfactory. Lavender-pink, white, and purple are the most common colors, although an orangish one ('Strawberry Fields') is also available. Dwarf forms are often sold under the name 'Buddy' and make compact mounds about 10 inches tall, but do not produce the long stems desirable for dried and fresh floral arrangements.

Helianthus annuus
(HE-lee-an-thus an-U-us)
SUNFLOWER
Family: Compositae
Zone: all. Size: 2–10 feet, summer, cool season annual

Sunflowers are coarse, hairy plants with spectacular flowers, some as much as 8–10 inches in diameter. Colors include yellow, orange, mahogany, and blends. The large-flowered types require rich soil and plenty of moisture.

Sunflowers consume considerable amounts of water after cutting. It is best to plunge them into water immediately after cutting and to re-cut the stems under water an inch or so above the original cut. They are susceptible

Candytuft, or iberis, is available in colors as well as in the traditional white. WCW

Ipomopsis rubra, or standing cypress, is useful for cutting and is among our most spectacular wildflowers. WCW

wilt and death. The flower spikes are excellent for cut-flower use and deserve more widespread availability.

Ipomopsis rubra
(ip-o-MOP-sis RU-bra)
STANDING CYPRESS
Family: Polemoniaceae
Zone: all. Size: 3–6 feet, summer, cool season annual

Standing cypress is among our most spectacular wildflowers. Its spikes of tubular red flowers can reach 6 feet in height, but are very narrow and most effective in masses. Native to the sandy, alkaline soils of Central Texas, standing cypress is sometimes biennial in habit. Dainty rosettes of finely textured foliage appear in late summer and fall, but give little clue concerning what is to come. Sometimes the plants bloom by late spring, but occasionally they will wait until the second year to flower.

A vivid coral-red color coupled with immense height makes standing cypress one of the most spectacular plants in the landscape. Hummingbirds are attracted in droves to their bright, tubular flowers. Starting new plants from

seed is not difficult, and once established they often reseed freely. A requirement for continued success is sandy, well-drained soil and a sunny location. Standing cypress requires little, if any, supplemental irrigation. Some of the most impressive native stands I have seen are along railroad rights-of-way, where they sometimes grow in the gravel near the tracks. Yellowish and whitish forms are occasionally found in the wild. Standing cypress is a spectacular cut flower and an impressive addition to the garden.

Lathyrus odoratus
(LATH-er-us O-dor-ah-tus)
SWEET PEA
Family: Leguminosae
Zone: all. Size: 4–6 feet vine, spring, cool season annual

Sweet peas are all-time favorite cut flowers. They are richly fragrant and brightly colorful in shades of purple, pink, white, and lavender, as well as bi-colors. The young seedlings can tolerate some frost and for zones 8 and south they should be planted in October or November. If you are north of zone 8, plant in late winter. Select a sunny area that has some protec-

Sweet peas are all-time favorites as cut flowers. WCW

Old-fashioned bi-colored sweet peas. wcw

Limonium sinuatum
(Li-MON-ee-um SIN-u-ah-tum)
STATICE
Family: Plumbaginaceae
Zone: all. Size: 1–2 feet, spring, summer, cool season annual

Statice is one of the best dried floral materials available. It may be grown as a cool season annual planted in the fall in zones 8–10, or set out in early spring for early summer flowers in cooler zones. Basal leaves are about 6 inches long and deeply lobed. The flower stems are distinctly winged. The showy *calyxes* (leafy, usually green part of the flower) are blue, lavender, or rose with white *corollas* (petals). Statice may be used fresh or dried. Drying may be successfully done by tying bunches of several or more stems together with string or raffia and hanging upside down in a dark, well-ventilated area such as an attic or garage space. Although the literature lists perennial forms, all I have grown in the South have been annuals. Plants may be easily started from seed, since nursery transplants are rarely available.

tion from winter winds, and where a fence, trellis, or similar support is in place. Sweet peas need loose, fertile, well-drained soil and plenty of moisture to thrive. Work the soil to a depth of about a foot, adding composted manure, peat, pine bark, or similar organic material. To plant the seeds, dig a V-shaped trench about 6 inches deep and set the seeds about 6 inches apart. Soak the seeds in water for several hours to hasten germination. Place about an inch of soil over the seeds, leaving most of the trench still there.

As the vines grow, gradually fill loose soil around their bases. The trench helps provide some protection from cold spells. Flowers should begin to appear in mid-spring and usually last until hot weather. Pick them every few days to encourage more flowers. Fertilize with water-soluble fertilizer every couple of weeks during the growing season. Pick your sweet peas often to encourage more flowers and a longer bloom season. Early flowering types are usually best for Southern gardens.

Statice, or limonium, is ideal for drying, but may also be used for fresh arranging. wcw

Fields of Texas bluebonnets at Wildseed Farm near Fredericksburg, Texas. WCW

Lupinus subcarnosus
(Lu-PIE-nus sub-CAR-no-sus)
BLUEBONNET
Family: Leguminosae
Zone: all. Size: 12–18 inches, spring, cool
season annual

In recent years bluebonnets have become available as fall bedding plants, along with pansies and snapdragons. This is an ideal way to use them, or plants from seed. To ensure even germination, commercial bedding-plant growers treat the hard-coated seed with sulfuric acid for periods of thirty minutes to one hour. This can be a dangerous process, since the acid is highly toxic. Another way to get through the seed coat of bluebonnets and other hard-seeded plants is to file it down or rub the seed over sandpaper.

Plant in September or October for best results. Bluebonnets normally reach about 1–1½ feet tall and wide. Many gardeners plant untreated seed on land that has been tilled or disced. Seed should be covered with ¼ inch to ½-inch of soil, then watered. Bluebonnets must have good drainage and prefer alkaline, infertile soils. They are quite tolerant

Bluebonnets combined with oxeye daisies and old-fashioned petunias in a Texas cottage garden. WCW

of dryness and rarely need watering. Actually, there are five species of bluebonnets native to Texas. *L. subcarnosus* is the most common native form and the one usually available as seed or transplants. Research horticulturists at Texas A&M University have recently focused on *L. havardii*, a species found in the Big Bend area of Texas. It has huge, deep blue spikes of flowers especially useful for cutting. *L. havardii* is not as easily grown as the common Texas bluebonnet, but the potential of 18–inch flower spikes for cut flower use has created considerable interest.

—32—

Malva sylvestris zebrina, or French hollyhock, is an easily grown heirloom grown by such notables as Thomas Jefferson. WCW

Like many of the other cool season annuals, *M. sylvestris zebrina* is worth the risk for fall plantings, but is occasionally damaged or killed from zone 8 north. Although best adapted to the cool season, they sometimes make it through the hot summer and bloom again in fall. *Alcea rosea* is the common hollyhock found in cottage gardens and borders all over the world. Spider mites, rust, and root diseases are challenges to its success in the South, although impressive plantings are sometimes found.

Matthiola incana
(Mat-te-O-la in-CAN-ah)
STOCK
Family: Cruciferae
Zone: all. Size: 1–2 feet, spring, summer, cool season annual

Stock is among the best and most fragrant of our cool season annuals. Flowers may be single or double and about 1 inch in diameter on 4–8 inch spikes. The color range includes white, pink, purple, lavender, red, and cream. Raised beds having fertile soil and sunny

Malva sylvestris zebrina
FRENCH HOLLYHOCK
Family: Malvaceae
Zone: all. Size: 2–4 feet, spring, summer, primarily cool season annual

M. sylvestris zebrina seems to be better adapted to the South than the common hollyhock. It is somewhat smaller, and has striped flowers of two shades of purple or purple and white. Occasionally a solid purple form is available. For best results French hollyhocks should be started in the fall or very early spring. They are often found in old gardens and were a favorite of Thomas Jefferson in his garden at Monticello. French hollyhocks reseed and return each year prolifically in my garden. My original stock came from Mattie Rosprim, a long-time College Station gardener who obtained them from her mother in the 1920s.

Stock comes in single and double forms. WCW

Bells of Ireland are a mainstay in all-green bouquets. wcw

impressively large spikes, provide frequent applications of water and fertilizer.

Nicotiana alata
(ni-kosh-EE-ana a-LAH-ta)
FLOWERING TOBACCO
Family: Solanaceae
Zone: all. Size: 2–5 feet, spring, summer, cool season annual

There is some debate whether this plant should be considered an annual or a perennial. In zones 9 and 10 it is usually perennial, although individual plants usually live no more than two years. Foliage is large and coarse, and best located in the center or rear of the border or in rows of the cut-flower garden. Although this species has pure white flowers, there are hybrids available in pink, purple, yellow, lavender, etc. The species forms are highly fragrant, especially in the evening.

Nicotiana prefers rich, well-drained soils, but is not difficult to grow. It usually reseeds abundantly in the garden.

Loose spikes of flowers may be cut with fairly long stems and are useful in arrangements for their flowers and fragrance. *N. sylvestris* is a similar species often reaching 5 feet tall when in flower. It also has extremely fragrant white flowers that grow in tiers. Many compact forms are available in a variety of colors, but the fragrance and grace of form are unique to the two species types.

exposure are best. In zone 8 and south it is worth risking frost damage to plant them in the fall along with pansies, snapdragons, and larkspur. Stock was once a very popular annual, but is no longer common as a landscape plant, possibly because of its susceptibility to root rot organisms. They are grown commercially for cut flowers and are popular for their fragrance and keeping qualities.

Moluccella laevis
(Mo-lu-CELL-ah LAH-vis)
BELLS OF IRELAND
Family: Labiatae
Zone: all. Size: 18 inches–2 feet, spring, cool season annual

Bells of Ireland are unusual and attractive as cut material. They may be single-stemmed or branched with flowers being carried almost from the base of the stems to their tips. The showy part of the flower is the bell- or shell-shaped calyx, a bright apple-green in color. The spikes are long-lasting as fresh-cut material and also attractive when dried. A sunny location with well-drained soil is best. Plant seeds or transplants in the fall for zone 8 and south, early spring elsewhere. For

Nicotiana, or flowering tobacco, adds evening fragrances to the garden and to bouquets. wcw

Top: A field of poppies at Wildseed Farm, Fredericksburg, Texas. WCW
Above: Old-fashioned poppies. WCW

Seed or transplants set out in fall will bloom early the next spring in zones 9 and 10. Early spring planting is probably best in cooler zones, unless protection can be provided for cold periods.

Papaver somniferum
(pa-PAV-er SOM-nif-er-um)
POPPY
Family: Papaveraceae
Zone: all. Size: 2–4 feet, spring, cool season annual

Poppies were grown in most nineteenth century gardens of our region. Single-flowered purples, pinks, and corals were most common, although double-flowering types have also been around for a long time. Poppies definitely resent any disturbance after they germinate in the fall. They like rich soils and full sun. Seed may be scattered on top of prepared soils and lightly raked in. The seed was used in cooking by our ancestors, and is still popular in German and Czech communities in Texas. North of zone 8, poppies should be planted in late winter or early spring. Thin the seedlings to about 1 foot apart.

Iceland poppy, *Papaver nudicaule*, is sometimes grown as an annual in the South. In mild areas they bloom in late winter and early spring with 3–4 inch silky flowers of orange, yellow, salmon, pink, cream, rose, or white that all blend together beautifully. 'Champagne Bubbles' is a good strain that is often available from seed sources. Iceland poppies are spectacular when they do well, but sudden cold spells often damage or kill the plants. Southern springs are usually too short for success with spring planting. Poppies are excellent cut flowers, but to keep

Double-flowered poppies. NGO

Ranunculus are superb cut flowers, but have a fairly short flowering season, due to their lack of heat tolerance. They require very well-drained and prepared soil, as well as a sunny location. The tubers can easily rot if watered too much before they sprout, but should be watered at planting so they will swell and germinate quickly. Although they are a bit tricky to grow, ranunculus are rewarding for their brightly colored and long-lasting flowers.

Rudbeckia hirta
(RUD-beck-e-ah HIR-ta)
GLORIOSA DAISY
Family: Compositae
Zone: all. Size: 3–4 feet, summer, fall, warm season annual

Gloriosa daisies are also known as black-eyed Susans, and are spectacular as cut flowers or in the garden. Wild forms commonly occur in the South as single with 2–4 inch orange-yellow daisylike flowers with dark centers. Garden types have larger flowers 5–7 inches wide in yellow, mahogany, and orange, often with bands of contrasting colors. Double and dwarf

them from wilting it is best to briefly sear the cut stems over flame before arranging and placing in water. Poppies, like poinsettias and some other plants, tend to bleed sap when cut, but the searing process coagulates the oozing material and extends the life of the flower.

Ranunculus asiaticus
(ra-NUN-cu-lus AZ-ee-ah-ti-cus)
RANUNCULUS
Family: Ranunculaceae
Zone: all. Size: 1–2 feet, spring, cool season annual

Ranunculus flowers are semi-double or double and are almost as formal in appearance as camellias. They grow from fall-planted tubers with numerous prongs that should point down and be set about 1½ inches deep.

Ranunculus provides early-spring color, but behaves as an annual in the South. NGO

Marigolds (Tagetes tenuifolia) come in a variety of colors and sizes, and endure hot summers well. NGO

types are also available. Stems and leaves are coarse and hairy. Gloriosa daisies prefer sunny locations and well-drained soil. They are often available as bedding plants or may be grown from seed. Although often listed as bi-annuals or perennials, gloriosa daisies are best grown as warm season annuals in the South.

Tagetes erecta, T. patula, T. tenuifolia
(ta-GEE-tees e-REK-tah, PAT-u-lah, TEN-you-i-fol-ee-ah)
MARIGOLD
Family: Compositae
Zone: all. Size: 10 inches–3 feet, cool season annual

Marigolds are well-known for their round flowers in bright yellow, orange, mahogany, and blends. They are fairly heat-tolerant traditional flowers for Southern borders. Dwarf forms are sometimes useful as edging material, but the larger types are more popular for cutting. The downside to their use as cut flowers is the pungent odor of the flowers and foliage. Some odorless varieties are now available. Marigolds thrive in the summer heat until it gets very hot. In July and August they sometimes wilt and die. Recent years have seen their popularity grow for planting in the late summer and fall, when spider mites are not as prevalent.

Tithonia rotundifolia
(ti-THO-nee-ah ro-TUND-i-fol-ee-ah)
MEXICAN SUNFLOWER
Family: Compositae
Zone: all. Size: 4–6 feet, summer

Tithonia is a bit coarse and gaudy, but quite useful as a background plant in borders and as cut flowers. Flower heads are 3–4 inches across with brilliant orange-scarlet rays and yellow centers. Take care with the hollow stems when using as cut flowers, since they are easily damaged. The leaves are velvety and green. Tithonia do best in sunny locations with good drainage and moderately low fertility. They are drought and heat resistant. Sow seed directly in the garden in spring and thin to 12–14 inches apart.

Tithonia, or Mexican sunflower, provides quick color for gardens and for bouquets. WCW

Old-fashioned trailing nasturtiums at the Claude Monet garden, Giverny, France. DOUGLAS F. WELSH

Tropaeolum majus
(TRO-pe-o-lum MA-jus)
NASTURTIUM
Family: Tropaeolaceae
Zone: all. Size: I foot or trailing vine to 6 feet, spring, cool season annual

Nasturtiums come in climbing and dwarf forms. Both are useful garden plants and have unique and fragrant flowers with round leaves perched on long stems. They add a peppery taste to salads, as do the flowers. The long-spurred flowers have a refreshing scent and may be yellow, maroon, red, orange, or creamy-white. Nasturtiums are easily started from seed and thrive in sunny or partially shaded areas in most any well-drained soil. Their season is relatively short since they are quite frost- and heat-sensitive. This limits their season in most of the South to late winter and spring. The seeds germinate easily and should be planted at about or just before the average date of last frost.

Nasturtiums are an easily grown old-fashioned spring annual. WCW

Nasturtiums do best when grown under low fertility situations so it is best to not add high nitrogen fertilizer to the soil before planting. The vining types may be used as a short-season ground cover or planted in a greenhouse during winter. Dwarf types are good as borders, masses, or in containers.

Violas are often combined with spring-flowering bulbs for a long season of color. WCW

Viola x Wittrockiana
(Vi-O-luh witt-ROCK-ee-ana)
PANSY
Family: Violaceae
Zone: all. Size: 6–10 inches, winter, spring, cool season annual

Pansies and their smaller cousins, violas, have become the most popular cool season annuals in the South. They appear in many colors and color combinations and are useful as cut flowers and for garden display. *Viola tricolor*, better known as johnny-jump-ups, are among the most delightful of the reseeding annuals. The common purple and yellow form has flowers about ½-inch across and is one of the parents of the larger-flowering pansy. Most pansies and violas are fragrant. The large-flowering types do not normally reseed. Plant in late fall in zones 8 and 9 where they are known for blooming all winter before succumbing to late spring heat. In cooler climates pansies are usually planted in early spring. They require well-prepared beds that are raised and fertile. Pick the flowers often to encourage continuous blooming.

Zinnia elegans
(ZIN-ee-ah el-ah-GANS)
ZINNIA
Family: Compositae
Zone: all. Size: 8 inches–3 feet, summer, cool season annual

Zinnias may be the all-time favorite summer cut flower. They are definitely warm weather plants and rarely produce until May or June. With adequate water and fertilizer they will continue to bloom all summer and into fall. Their round flowers vary in size from 1 to 5 inches. They also range from singles to semi-double and double forms. For cut flowers the larger types are best. 'Liliputs'

Zinnias, or old maids, are the all-time favorite for summer cut flowers. WCW

—39—

Bouquets of zinnias at market. NGO

are semi-dwarf plants about 1 foot tall that produce 1½–2-inch flowers, useful where smaller-scale flowers are needed. Large flowering types such as the State Fair series, dahlia-flowered and giant cactus flowered zinnias come in a wide variety of colors, including red, white, pink, lavender, orange, purple and variegated.

Plants are best started from seed in the garden. Thin seedlings to about 1–1½ feet apart when they are a few weeks old. Young seedlings may be transplanted if watering is carefully monitored. Zinnias must have at least a half day of direct sun to be productive and healthy. Powdery mildew is a problem that may be avoided if plants are in a sunny, well-ventilated area. Watering should be done without wetting the foliage, if possible. A second crop of zinnias is possible by planting seed in July or August. They don't really mind the heat if adequate water and fertilizer are available. Mulching with dried grass clippings, hay, or similar material can help to keep the root area cooler and prevent rapid drying of the soil. Although popular in garden borders and mass plantings, zinnias were most often grown by our ancestors in rows in the vegetable garden. Vernacular names like "old maids" and "cut and come again" refer to the prolific production when the blooms are picked often. Avoid bending the flower stems since zinnias have hollow stems that are easily damaged.

WCW

Four

Perennial Garden Color

erennials are versatile plants offering a variety of creative possibilities for the garden and home. By definition *perennials* are plants that return to your garden year after year from the same root part. Most die down sometime during the year, but many return from bulbs, rhizomes, or fleshy roots. From tiny terrace gardens of inner-city apartments to extensive country estates, perennials can add color, form, and texture for many years with minimal maintenance.

Growing requirements for perennials are similar to annuals, except for the concept of division. Many perennials become crowded after a year or more and benefit from being dug up, divided into single offshoots or plants and replanted in newly prepared soil. Division not only stimulates perennials, it propagates them as well. Although many types can be reproduced from seed or cuttings, division offers a quick way to "get a start" of a desired plant. There is no set period of time to wait before dividing your perennials. If they are not blooming well or look crowded it is probably time to divide. An easy and effective rule for when to divide is to divide perennials in the season opposite when they bloom. Divide spring-blooming plants in the fall, and fall-bloomers in the spring. Summer-flowering perennials are best divided in late winter or early spring.

Perennials as cut flowers offer numerous choices, with opportunities for almost every month of the year. A more comprehensive treatment of perennials for the South is included in my book *Perennial Garden Color* (Taylor Publishing Co., Dallas, 1989).

Achillea millcfolium
(ah-KILL-ee-ah mill-eh-FOL-ee-um)
YARROW
Family: Compositae
Zone: 3. Size: 1–2 feet, spring, early summer, fall

Yarrows are referred to as "sun ferns" because of their finely textured foliage. Although native to Europe, yarrow has naturalized in the Southeast to the extent that it is sometimes thought a wildflower. Although somewhat delicate looking, yarrows are actually quite hardy and tolerant of heat and drought. They prefer good soil

'Coronation Gold' yarrow is excellent fresh or cut. NGO

The easily grown, pest-free yarrows are available in a variety of colors. WCW

and little interference from trees and other competitive plants but can live in less hospitable surroundings. The large, flat heads of small flowers bloom over a long time, beginning in early spring. They are excellent cut flowers when used fresh or dried.

Their most common color is white, but it is usually not a pure white and is less welcome in my garden than some of the purple forms. 'Fire King' is probably the most popular and available of the pink-flowered selections of the naturalized species. The color is deep pink in spring, then fades to a paler color as the summer heat intensifies. The yellow- or gold-flowered yarrows are another species, *A. filipendulina*. 'Coronation Gold' is a commonly sold cultivar that grows well in our area, except for a strip of a hundred or so miles from the Gulf of Mexico, where it struggles with the heat and humidity. Yarrows have few, if any, insect or disease problems and may be propagated from division or seeds. They prefer partial shade but will also thrive in sunnier locations.

Agapanthus africanus
(Ag-ah-PAN-thus af-ri-CAN-us)
BLUE LILY OF THE NILE
Family: Amaryllidaceae
Zone: 8. Size: 2–3 feet, May–June

Agapanthus can be spectacular in the garden or as a cut flower, but rarely naturalizes in the South. Its blue or white flowers appear in funnel-shaped, round terminal clusters during May and June. A white form, 'Albus', bears its showy flowers on tall stems. 'Peter Pan' is a dwarf, rarely exceeding 18 inches in height. In areas where they are not winter-hardy, agapanthus is an excellent container plant. Agapanthus is a fleshy-rooted perennial that should be divided every three to four years. They bloom better when their root systems are slightly restricted, which explains their popularity as container plants. The foliage is evergreen most winters in zone 9. A well-drained soil is required since the rhizomes will rot in wet locations. A 3–4-inch mulch on pinestraw, coast Bermuda grass, hay, or similar material is good insurance against winter damage and summer moisture stress. For mass effect, space plants about 18–20 inches apart.

Lilies of the Nile (agapanthus) are often grown in containers since they are not very cold-hardy. NGO

Giant alliums make outstanding displays that can be dried for ornamental use. They are best in the upper South. NGO

Allium
(AL-ee-um))
ORNAMENTAL ONIONS
Family: Liliaceae
Zone: all. Size: 1–3 feet, April–fall

There are numerous ornamental onions and garlic that can be used as cut material. Most of their stems and flowers are also used as dried floral material. The spectacular and large-flowering *A. giganteum,* does not normally perform as a perennial in southern parts of zone 8 and south. *A. tuberosum,* known as "garlic chives," grows well in all zones. It not only is easily grown, but reseeds and may become invasive. Its white flower heads appear in late spring or summer, exuding a pleasant scent. Leaves are flat and about 1 foot tall. *A. neapolitanum* is a native of Southern Italy and cold-hardy only to zone 8. It produces white, fragrant flowers in late spring that are excellent for cut use. *A. schoenoprasum,* onion chives, has small spheres of lilac-pink flowers in spring. It is easily grown in containers or in the garden and useful for garnishes.

Tulbaghia violacea, society garlic, is a favorite landscape plant in the South. It blooms almost continuously from spring through fall, bearing umbrellalike flower clusters of bright, lilac-violet colored flowers. Leaves are flat, garliclike, and about 1 foot long. 'Silver Lace' is striking with its white-margined foliage. I have found it to be much more challenging to grow than the green-foliaged cultivar. Society garlic is native to South Africa and is very well-adapted to the Gulf South. Bulbs may be divided and reset from late fall through early spring in good, well-drained garden soil. Full or partially sunny exposures are best. Landscape uses include masses or borders in herbaceous or shrub plantings. It is also a good container plant. All the ornamental onions and garlics have pleasant-scented flowers useful for fresh or dried use. The strong onion and garlic scents are released when the foliage and stems are cut or bruised.

Alstroemeria pulchella
(Al-STRO-mar-ee-uh pul-CHEL-ah)
PERUVIAN LILY
Family: Liliaceae
Zone: 5. Size: 2–3 feet, late spring

Alstroemerias are among the best cut flowers and are often available at supermarkets as well as florists. The azalealike flowers occur in terminal clusters and are among the longest-lasting cut flowers. The alstroemerias sold as cut flowers are *A. aurea,* or *A. aurantiaca.* Although occasionally successful as garden plants in the South, they are not nearly so easily grown as *A. pulchella,* commonly known as Peruvian lily, which, although native to South America, has naturalized in many Southern

Society garlic is easily grown and reblooms throughout the warm season. WCW

Alstroemeria is useful as a long-lasting cut flower. WCW

are dense and useful as summer shade on trellises and arbors, especially when used with other vines such as roses. One of the prettiest pictures in my fall garden is coral vine combined with an old 'Trier Rambler' rose. The rich coral blooms combine beautifully with the pale pink, almost white flowers of the rose. A white form of *A. leptopus*, 'Album', is sometimes available.

Propagation is from division or seeds. When starting with seeds, plant in early spring to give them time to develop tubers before frost. The foliage and stems die to the ground with the first hard frost. The tubers look much like sweet potatoes and are reportedly edible. Large stems of the flowers are wonderful as cut flowers. Their natural gracefulness suggests large weeping bouquets. In areas north of zone 8, coral vine is often grown in large containers where it can be protected during the winter.

gardens. It is so easily grown it might be classified as aggressive. Its flowers are reddish-orange with green edging to the tubular florets. Although an interesting color combination, it is not very striking in the garden and needs a strong green background. Peruvian lilies prefer partial shade and well-drained soils, although they will grow in less hospitable surroundings. Propagation is usually by division of existing clumps.

Antigonon leptopus
(AN-tig-uh-non LEP-to-pus)
CORAL VINE, ROSE OF MONTANA
Family: Polygonaceae
Zone: 8. Size: 10–15 feet, vine, fall

Coral vine is a native of Mexico widely cultivated in South Texas and the Gulf South for its large clusters of small, striking pink flowers. It is a vigorous plant that

needs support and can climb 12–15 feet in a single growing season. Although there is sometimes a showing of flowers in late spring or early summer, the big display is during late summer and fall, when it can frame the garden like fine lace. Heart-shaped leaves

Aquilegia spp.
(Ah-kwa-LEE-juh)
COLUMBINE
Family: Ranunculaceae
Zone: 5. Size: 18–24 inches, spring

Hybrid columbines, grown over much of the nation, tend to be cool season annuals in Texas and the South. Two species native to Texas, *A. chrysantha* and *A.*

Coral vine provides a wealth of cut material in late summer and early fall. T. E. POPE

Native yellow columbines from Texas bloom in shade or sun. D. GREG GRANT

den, but are also useful for garden display and cutting. *A. tuberosa* is the hardy butterfly weed most commonly available in the nursery trade with its 2–5-inch diameter flat-topped bright orange umbrella-shaped flower clusters. They are among the showiest of our native perennials. Butterfly weed blooms in mid- to late summer in a natural environment, but sometimes earlier in the garden. The flowers are long lasting when cut. Two factors, however, somewhat limit the use of *A. tuberosa* in landscape settings. It must have very good drainage and is adapted best to dry, rather sandy soils. The major problem, however, lies in transplanting. The long tuberlike roots

canadensis, are excellent garden plants useful as cut flowers. Columbines bloom and thrive in partially shaded areas. Their fernlike foliage emerges in the fall and grows all winter. By early spring the mounds of leaves may reach a foot or more tall and wide. *A. chrysantha* 'Hinckley' has striking long-spurred yellow flowers arranged handsomely in large clusters. *A. canadensis* blooms in a soft blend of red and yellow. Propagation is usually by seed, although division is also a possibility. Columbines cross-pollinate readily, making it difficult to keep a pure seed source if more than one species is included in the garden. Young seedlings are usually found near mature plants. Columbines prefer organically enriched soil that drains well. Fall is the best time to plant seeds, set out seedlings, or make divisions. They are native to stream banks in Central and West Texas.

Asclepias tuberosa, A. curassavica
(As-KLEEP-ee-as tu-BER-os-ah, CUR-ah-sa-vica)
BUTTERFLY WEED
Family: Asclepiadaceae
Zone: 6. Size: 2–3 feet, summer, fall

Asclepias are best known for attracting butterflies to the gar-

Above: Mexican butterfly weed is easy to grow and reseeds prolifically. WCW
Below: Butterfly weed, or asclepias, can be grown for cutting as well as for attracting butterflies. WCW

Autumn aster is an easily grown source of material for fall bouquets. WCW

must not be broken when being moved. Even young plants are sensitive to this problem and are best grown or obtained in containers and, after planting, left undisturbed in the garden. Once established, they tend to be long-lived and increase in floral display each year. Bright, sunny locations are best.

A. curassavica, sometimes called "Mexican oleander," is native to Northern Mexico and becoming quite popular outside of South Texas, where it has been an heirloom plant for many years. It is much easier to grow, but is somewhat limited by cold tolerance to zone 8 and south. This Mexican form reseeds prolifically in the garden and roots easily from cuttings. Clumps bloom continuously during the warm seasons with flowers similar to *A. tuberosa*. Yellow flowering forms such as 'Silky Gold' are also available. *A. curassavica* is one of the most productive and easiest-grown

cut flowers for the South. In addition to attracting monarch and other butterflies, their foliage and stems are a magnet for aphids. They seem to coexist without doing serious damage to the plants, but when aphid populations become excessive, loss of vigor and flowering may occur.

Aster oblongifolius
(AS-ter ob-LONG-ih-fol-ee-us)
AUTUMN ASTER
Family: Compositae
Zone: 6. Size: 2–3 feet tall and wide, mid- to late fall

This aster is a really easy and rewarding plant for the garden and the vase. Each fall the 2–3-foot mounds of small leaves are covered with 1½-inch lavender flowers with yellow centers. They appear in October and sometimes last until frost. It is the only aster I have found to be reliable in dry as well as humid areas of the Gulf Coast and Upper South. Any

sunny, well-drained site and reasonable garden soil usually produces good results. Propagation is by division or cuttings. Since the bloom season is in the fall, it is best to divide or start new plants in the spring. Highly fertile soils and extensive watering may result in tall, spindly plants. To avoid this, simply ignore asters during summer, except for an occasional watering, and pinch them back until about September 1, if they seem to be too tall. Staking is not usually necessary in sunny locations. Excellent perennials to plant for fall display and cut flower use that combine well with this aster are Mexican marigold mint (*Tagetes lucida*) and Mexican bush sage (*Salvia leucantha*). All three plants like similar growing conditions, and the colors and flower forms are wonderful for fall gardens and for cutting.

Canna foliage is often useful for cut use or garden accent. WCW

Bletilla striata
(Bleh-TILL-ah STREE-ah-tah)
CHINESE GROUND ORCHID
Family: Orchidaceae
Zone: 8. Size: 18 inches–2 feet, spring

The Chinese ground orchid is an excellent perennial for partially shaded areas of the garden. Stems of purple or white 1½-inch flowers appear on short spikes around Easter, and are lovely both in the garden and as cut flowers. It is one of the few terrestrial orchids suitable for garden cultivation in the South. *B. striata* has large and handsome foliage that somewhat resembles a smaller version of aspidistra. Combine them with columbine, leucojum and narcissus for variety in the garden and floral arrangements. They prefer well-prepared soil and partial shade, but I have seen them growing in sunnier locations and fairly heavy soil. Propagation is by division of established clumps in late fall. Unfortunately, Chinese ground orchid spreads and increases rather slowly.

Canna x generalis
(CAN-ah GEN-er-alis)
CANNA
Family: Cannaceae
Zone: 7. Size: 2–5 feet, summer, fall

Cannas are enjoying a renewal of interest in Southern gardens. Natives of the tropics and sub-tropics, they thrive in the South where their rhizomes may be left in the ground year-round. In colder climates they are dug after the first frost and stored until spring. Cannas are among the easiest of perennials to grow and are available in a wide variety of flower colors and plant sizes. The bananalike foliage varies from green to reddish-purple, bronze, pink, and variegated. Flowers occur from May through November in some areas. Rhizomes planted in spring will bloom prolifically the first summer if planted in reasonably good soil and in a sunny location. Few plants can withstand more abuse. Removal of spent flowers and seed pods encourages more blooms and provides a neater appearance. Pfitzer dwarfs range in size from 2½ to 4 feet tall and produce large heads of brightly colored flowers in yellow, pink, orange, salmon, and red.

Canna foliage is as useful as the flowers for cutting. 'Pretoria' and 'Striped Beauty' have handsome yellow-and-green variegated foliage, and 'Pink Sunburst', a fairly new cultivar, has a blend of green, cream, pink, and purple that varies with the season. Flowers are a beautiful clear pink and mature height is only about 2 to 2½ feet tall. Combine cannas with ornamental sweet potatoes, or coleus for contrast and to provide cut foliage for indoors. The only major pest of cannas is a leaf caterpillar whose depredations cause leaves to abort and become

Chinese ground orchid provides small spikes of lavender-purple or white flowers. WCW

Canna 'Bengal Tiger' has bright, striking foliage and flowers. WCW

Colors range from reds, purples, whites, yellows, pinks, and lavenders to bronzes—almost every color but blue. Chrysanthemums are sensitive to day length and produce flowers as the days become shorter in the fall. Spring's short days may also trigger bloom, but both quality and quantity of the flowers will be much better in fall's cool weather than at the onset of summer's heat. Since spring flowering also tends to weaken plants, any buds that do appear then should be removed. Thrifty gardeners often try to recycle potted mums from the florist's shop into their gardens after they have enjoyed the flowers in their homes. While the plants may survive, they really aren't worth the effort or space in the garden. Varieties that have been bred for greenhouse forcing and florists' sales are not nearly so well adapted to outdoor use as the garden varieties developed for landscape display.

Garden mums need full sun and well-drained, well-prepared soil. To remain vigorous in the South, the plants should be divided or restarted from cuttings each spring, as soon as they begin growing rapidly. To prevent dis-

unsightly. Applications of insecticide to the foliage or to the root zone with systemic materials will usually control the problem. Propagation is by division of rhizomes in the fall or early spring.

Dendranthema x morifolium
(den-DRAN-the-ma MOR-ah-fol-ee-um)
CHRYSANTHEMUM
Family: Compositae
Zone: 6. Size: 1–3 feet, fall

Garden mums are probably the showiest of all fall-blooming perennials and among the best for cut flower use. They are also remarkably easy to grow, though hobbyists and specialists often devote much time and effort to cultivating them to perfection.

Chrysanthemum 'Country Girl' is one of the best garden mums for the South. WCW

Shasta daisies are favorites for bouquets and gardens. NGO

ease problems, it is recommended that new side shoots be separated from the clump and reset. Take 4–6-inch tip cuttings in March or April, root them in a mixture of peat moss and sand or a commercially prepared potting mix, then plant them directly into the garden on 16–18-inch spacings. Mums are among the easiest of all plants to root and are usually ready to set into a permanent location three to four weeks after sticking. It is best to settle them into the bed or border before the arrival of really hot weather. Pinching is an important part of the cultivation of all kinds of garden mums, except the so-called "cushion mums." Most varieties should have the soft growing tips "pinched out" whenever they reach 4–6 inches long. For large plantings this can be a big job, but it can be done speedily and almost as well by using hedging shears. In our climate, pinching may be necessary every two or three weeks during May, June,

and early July. By mid-July or early August in northern parts of our area and September 1 along the Gulf Coast, pinching should cease so that the plants can put on a final burst of growth as the buds are beginning to set. Application of a balanced fertilizer according to label instructions every four to six weeks from early spring until mid-August is helpful since mums tend to be heavy feeders. They also need regular and generous watering during dry spells.

Garden mums are not always readily available from garden centers in the spring. Plants ordered from mail order sources tend to look pretty pitiful when they arrive, but these rooted cuttings will grow quickly and can produce spectacular effects by fall if well cared for. Some of the most useful mums I have grown have been given to me by fellow gardeners who have handed them down as heirloom plants among friends and family. Growing mums in the field for sale as cut flowers on All

Saints' Day is still practiced in some Gulf Coast communities, although not nearly so commonly as it once was. Among the best varieties I grow is one that goes by several names. In the Atlanta area it is often called 'Ryan's Pink'; in South Carolina I have seen it grown as 'Korean Mum', and in Texas it is often known as 'Country Girl'. It is a simple pink daisy mum that is particularly nice for cutting. Since chrysanthemums are so easily propagated from cuttings or divisions they are frequently shared and enjoyed among family and friends.

Chrysanthemum x *superbum*,
C. leucanthemum
(Chry-SAN-the-mum Su-PER-bum,
lu-CAN-the-mum)
SHASTA DAISY, OXEYE DAISY
Family: Compositae
Zone: 5. Size: 1–3 feet, spring

Shastas are perennials easily grown in the South. Their sparkling

The oxeye daisy is similar to, but blooms earlier than, the shasta daisy. NGO

white ray flowers appear in May and June in most of the South. *C. leucanthemum*, oxeye daisy, is a native that has performed better than shastas in my gardens. Oxeye daisies are somewhat smaller, and their foliage tends to hug the ground and be more compact. The biggest advantage of oxeye daisies over shastas is that they bloom a month to six weeks earlier, usually by mid-April in Central Texas. By blooming earlier they avoid the heat and dryness that usually accompanies late spring and early summer. Both these daisies like a deep, rich soil and fairly moist conditions. They prefer a sunny location, but seem to appreciate a little afternoon shade. Even with supplemental irrigation, I sometimes lose plants during the heat and humidity of August and September. The first rains of fall seem to give them new life and no amount of cold seems to cause them to suffer in the South. It is best to divide every fall, between the first of September and mid-December. Single divisions placed 1 foot apart at this time make a solid mass by spring. If planted later in the season, the divisions will take root and grow, but they will not produce the same quantity of flowers.

As soon as blossoms begin to fade, flower stems should be cut as close to the foliage mounds as possible. Shastas and oxeye daisies are among the best perennial cut flowers. They produce so many flowers that cutting some for the house detracts little from the garden display. Shastas are available in many forms, some of them double-flowering. I have found the double and giant forms to be poor performers. These daisies combine with many other annuals and perennials in the garden and are especially attractive with spike flowers such as larkspur, bells of Ireland, and snapdragons. The pure white flowers reflect light well into the evening and brighten the space they occupy.

Clematis spp.
(CLEM-a-tis)
CLEMATIS
Family: Ranunculaceae
Zone: 6. Size: climbing vines 6–20 feet, spring, fall

Although only marginally adapted to the Gulf South, the large-flowering clematis are spectacular *deciduous* (lose their leaves in winter) flowering vines. They require well-prepared and well-drained soils and heat protection for their root zones in order to perform satisfactorily. *C. armandii* is an evergreen clematis with handsome, leathery 3–5-inch leaves and 2-inch white flowers that occur in long, branched clusters. It grows well in the Southeast, where its foliage and flowers are sometimes used as cut material. Chances for success with *C. armandii* and large-flowering clematis such as *C. × jackmanii* (purple) and 'Henryi' (white) are enhanced by keeping the root zone cool with mulches or stones and planting in partially shaded locations. Some of the Texas native and introduced small-flowering clematis are better adapted to the heat and dryness present in Texas. The easiest of these to grow is commonly known as sweet autumn clematis. In the past it was listed as *C. paniculata*, but this has been changed to *C. maximowicziana*. By any name, it is a valuable and vigorous vine (to 25 or 30 feet) that produces great quantities of white, star-shaped flowers for several weeks in the early fall.

Although sometimes considered invasive in East Texas and the South, the vanillalike scent of its flowers and timeliness of the late summer bloom make this New

—50—

Kashmir-bouquet, or clerodendrum, performs well in partially shaded areas. NGO

to just above the lowest healthy set of leaf buds in late January or February. Although all clematis need at least a half day of sun to flower well, they all seem to like to keep their "feet" in shade where their roots receive some protection from summer heat.

Clerodendrum bungei
(kler-o-DEN-drum BUN-gee-i)
CLERODENDRUM, KASHMIR-BOUQUET, GLORY-BOWER
Family: Verbenaceae
Zone: 8. Size: 6–7 feet. summer

These tropical plants usually return from their roots reliably each year in most of zones 8 and 9. They have large, glossy leaves and flower over a long season. Flowering is usually more prolific following a mild winter.

Clerodendrum spread by suckers that can form thickets over time. When stems freeze back in winter, they should be cut to the ground in early spring. The fragrant flowers are rosy pink and come in clusters as large as 8 inches in diameter. They thrive in partially shaded areas. Propagation is usually from root sprouts that can become a pest in good soils. C. thomsoniae is known as "bleeding-heart" and is an evergreen vine in zone 10 that produces branched clusters of heart-shaped crimson flowers with white lower petals. It is best grown in greenhouses, solariums, and other protected locations. When used as a container plant, a heavier bloom may be induced since the plant's supply of water and fertilizer are more easily controlled. C. speciossimum is a large and striking plant in the garden and for cutting. It produces spectacular, pyramidal panicles of red flowers on 10–12-foot plants, followed by green and blue-black berries in showy clusters. It also prefers partial shade and blooms much better when it is not severely frozen back, making it more useful in zones 9 and 10 than further north.

Zealand native welcome in most gardens. *C. drummondii* is native to Texas and sometimes known as "old man's beard" or "virgin's bower." The dried seed pods of this vine are popular for use as decorations. *C. pitcheri* is another Texas native that is quite beautiful, although not very showy in the garden. The blooms are pendant and shaped like small urns in various shades of purple. Vines typically reach 6–8 feet. *C. virginiana* is also known as virgin's bower and is native to Louisiana and other Southern states. Its 1-inch flowers are replaced by silky-tasseled seeds also useful as dried material. One of the most interesting of the native clematis is *C. texensis,* sometimes known as "scarlet clematis." It has pitcher-shaped blooms similar to *C. pitcheri*, but in a handsome crimson color. This species created a great deal of attention in England, where it has been considered the only source of crimson flowers among the clematis and was used in breeding to create varieties such as 'Duchess of Albany'.

Pruning clematis is often puzzling to gardeners who try to grow them. The stems are so tiny and lifeless in appearance that they are easily damaged or removed in error. Large-flowering types should be pruned at planting to just above the lowest pair of vigorous-appearing leaf buds. Once established, all except the evergreen *C. armandii* may be pruned

Coreopsis 'Baby Sun' keeps its compact shape and provides bloom over a long period. WCW

Coreopsis lanceolata
(ko-ree-OP-sis LAN-see-oh-la-tuh)
COREOPSIS
Family: Compositae
Zone: 6. Size: 1–3 feet, late spring, summer

Coreopsis is among the more popular native perennials of our region. They are tolerant of both heat and drought and require little care to produce lavish amounts of color in the garden. Daisylike flowers of 1½–2 inches appear on long, slender stems from mid-spring until really hot weather in July or August. Coreopsis are excellent cut flowers but their stems are weak and not suitable for use in florist's foam. They arrange well when placed directly into containers that provide some support for their thin, wiry stems. The native perennial form of coreopsis (*C. lanceolata*) tends to be rather tall and flops over after wind or rain. Preferable for garden use are the dwarf types like 'Baby Sun', 'Early Sunrise', and 'Sunray', which are more compact and less sprawling but still have stems long enough to cut. *C. tinc-*

toria is the annual form of coreopsis, coming in a variety of colors such as yellow, orange, maroon, bronze, and reddish, sometimes with bands of contrasting colors. Threadleaf coreopsis (*C. verticillata*) grows best in zone 8 and north. Their shorter stems make them less appropriate for cutting, although they are quite attractive in the garden. Cultivars such as 'Zagreb' (golden yellow flowers) and 'Moonbeam' (pale yellow) are commonly available perennials.

All coreopsis seem to prefer sunny locations and well-drained soil. Even the types listed as perennials tend to be short-lived, lasting about two years. Dividing every year or two helps, but many seedlings usually appear around established plants. These often do not breed true, so to maintain the dwarf character of special cultivars, it is necessary to propagate them through division of existing clumps, or purchase fresh seed or plants. Mature clumps sometimes form plantlets called "proliferations" on the tips of floral stems that may be removed and set in moist potting soil, where they quickly root. These proliferations will develop the same form and size as the parent plant.

Crinum bulbispermum
(CRY-num bul-bis-PER-mum)
CRINUM, MILK AND WINE LILY
Family: Amaryllidaceae
Zone: 7. Size: 2–3 feet, spring, summer, fall

Crinums are among the most common heirloom plants in Southern gardens. They often naturalize in bar ditches, around old home sites, and in cemeteries. Although there are many species and cultivars, *C. bulbispermum* is the most common and easily recognizable. Fountains of blue-gray clumps of foliage with large lilylike

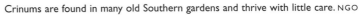

Crinums are found in many old Southern gardens and thrive with little care. NGO

Pink hybrid Crinum x 'Carnival' is a fragrant and beautiful hybrid. WCW

aware that the bulbs are large and at least part of the bulb plate must be retained for them to live. The bulb plate is the round structure on the bottom of the bulb from which the roots emerge. Since bulbs are often a foot or more into the ground, this can be a challenging job on a hot summer day. They may be successfully transplanted or divided at any time, but late summer and early fall are ideal. It seems that the most attractive crinums are slower to multiply than the more common ones.

The better crinums are becoming more available through mail order and nursery sources, but tend to be expensive due to their slowness to propagate. Some of the best include 'Mrs. James Hendry', a Henry Nehrling cross from the early 1900s. It is solid pink, very fragrant with attractive foliage, and reblooms prolifically throughout the warm seasons. 'Ellen Bosanquet' was bred about 1930 by Louis Percival Bosanquet, a Floridian of English descent. The flower is a favorite among Southern gardeners. 'Peach Blow', a choice T. L. Mead hybrid from the early 1900s, and 'White Queen', a frilled white

flowers, usually white with pink or reddish stripes, are most common, but the white form 'Alba' and wine-red 'Rubra' are also sometimes found. Many of the crinums found on old sites are hybrids of *C. bulbispermum* and *C. scabrum*. These are collectively known as *C. herbertii* and often have white flowers striped with pink or burgundy. Other forms may be crosses with *C. scabrum*, *C. zeylanicum*, or *C. erubescens*. The foliage of most crinums is floppy and coarse, but their flowers are fragrant and beautiful. Some forms have reasonably good foliage as well. All crinums are useful as cut flowers with their tall amaryllislike scapes of fragrant flowers that keep opening from buds several days after cutting. Crinums are extremely easy to grow, living in almost any soil and water conditions. They thrive in good soils and bloom best where

they receive at least a half-day of direct sun. When digging or dividing old clumps of crinums, be

Crinum 'Mrs. James Hendry' is a beautiful and fragrant reblooming perennial for the South. WCW

Montbretia 'Lucifer', or crocosmia, provides graceful stems of bright red flowers. NGO

trumpet from Luther Burbank, are excellent choices. *C.* × *powellii* 'Alba' is a vibrant and beautiful pure white. *C. rattrayi* blooms in late spring but is only cold-tolerant outdoors in zones 9 and 10. It has beautiful foliage and gorgeous pure white flowers in spring that closely resemble Dutch hybrid amaryllises. Among the more modern hybrids, 'Carnival' is an outstanding red of unusual hardiness; 'Wm. Herbert' has a vivid red stripe; 'Parfait' has an outstanding blush; and 'Sangria' is an unusual and large-growing cultivar with handsome red foliage and pink blooms bred by Scott Odgen. *Crinodonna corsii* 'Fred Howard' is known as an Amarcrinum and is well adapted to zones 9 and 10. Beautiful solid-pink flowers arise from mature foliage clumps during August and September.

Crocosmia crocosmiiflora
(kro-KOZ-mee-uh kro-KOZ-mee-uh-floor-uh)
CROCOSMIA, MONTBRETIA
Family: Iridaceae
Zone: 8. Size: 2–3 feet, late spring, summer

Crocosmias are native to the tropics and South Africa, but have naturalized from old plantings in the South. The corms are smaller than those of gladioli, but similar otherwise. The foliage is swordlike and the red-orange 1½-inch flowers occur on tall, branched stems in late spring or early summer. They are excellent as cut flowers and very easily grown. For best results plant them in a sunny area having well-drained soil. Divide the clumps every other year and fertilize early in the growing season with a balanced fertilizer. Although other colors are sometimes listed in catalogs, I have

only been successful with the brilliant orange-red form so common across the South. In good soils crocosmias may become invasive, but they are easily removed from unwanted areas. The stems are thin, but have enough body to be easily arranged in floral foam. The flowers often last a week and continue to open their buds for several days after cutting.

Cuphea micropetala
(ku-FEE-uh my-kro-PET-ah-luh)
CIGAR PLANT
Family: Lythraceae
Zone: 8. Size: 2–4 feet, fall

The cigar plant has attractive shiny, dark green foliage and a mounding form that make it welcome in the garden even when not in flower. It is valuable for its easy care and for its spikes of tubular-shaped red and yellow-green flowers in the fall. They are

Cigar plant, or cuphea, attracts hummingbirds to the fall garden. WCW

Mexican heather is less cold-hardy than cigar plant and its small flowers are less useful for cutting. Both forms are natives of Mexico and are distinctive garden plants.

Delphinium elatum
(del-FEN-ee-um e-LAH-tum)
DELPHINIUM
Family: Ranunculaceae
Zone: 8 as annuals, 7 and above as perennials, 2–6 feet, spring

Delphiniums are spectacular garden and cut flowers, but are finicky and short-lived in the South. In zone 8 and higher they may be grown as cool season annuals with some success. Spectacular spikes of blue, purple, dark blue, white, lavender, and pink are favorites where they can be grown. Delphiniums like a sunny location with rich, well-drained soil and plenty of moisture. In the South they last longer if grown in areas where they receive some afternoon shade. Taller strains need to be staked. In late winter or early spring, as new shoots develop, it is best to

very attractive to hummingbirds, often blooming from September until hard frost. The flowers last well when cut and are sufficiently prolific to gather a large bouquet from a single clump. For best results, plant in spring in a sunny area with well-drained soil. Cigar plants thrive in acid or moderately alkaline soils and are quite drought-tolerant. Propagation is usually from cuttings or division of mature clumps. *C. hyssopifolia* is commonly known as false heather or Mexican heather. It has tiny flowers of pink, purple, or white, which occur in abundance during the summer and fall.

Delphiniums are magnificent flowers usually grown as cold-season annuals in the South. WCW

'Magenta Pink' dianthus, a mat-forming type. WCW

remove all but two or three of the strongest. After flowering, cut back the spent flower spikes and fertilize to encourage a second set of blooms. Pacific hybrids may reach 5–6 feet tall but others such as 'Blue Springs' and 'Magic Fountains' are in the 2–3 foot range. For best results start to seed in late summer or early fall and transplant in October or November. Larkspur (*Consolida ambigua*) was once classified as a delphinium but now has been assigned its own genus. It is much better adapted to the South and Gulf South than delphiniums and often reseeds in the garden. For more complete information, refer to its description in the annuals section of this text.

Dianthus spp.
(Die-AN-thus)
GARDEN PINKS AND CARNATIONS
Family: Caryophyllaceae
Zone: 6. Size: 6–18 inches, spring, summer

Depending upon the cultivar and growing conditions, dianthus may be annual, biennial, or occasionally, perennial. Their foliage and highly fragrant flowers have been popular in cottage gardens of England and the United States for hundreds of years. The carnations are classified as *D. carophyllus*. Most florist carnations are poorly adapted to Southern gardens, but a double red, ever-blooming type is sometimes found in cottage gardens of rural Texas. It has dark green foliage and may reach a height of 18 inches when in flower. The small, double red, fragrant flowers are borne in abundance in spring and fall and intermittently through the rest of the year. This useful antique can sometimes be found in garden centers specializing in perennials. The propagation of this cultivar is similar to that of the other dianthus, with cuttings taken in the fall being the most successful home method. *D. barbatus*, sweet William, is one type often seen in Southern gardens, though it often performs as an annual. Its solid or multi-colored combinations of hues are striking and useful as cut flowers.

All dianthus are best planted in the fall. They prefer some shade from hot afternoon sun and must have well-drained soils. Frequent sprinkler irrigation can be deadly since root and stem rots are common. Some of the mat-forming pinks do fairly well in the South.

A bi-color fragrant clove pink dianthus with long stems. WCW

Dianthus hybrid 'First Love', a popular new multicolored type which succeeds well in Southern gardens. WCW

Although their stems are quite short for cutting, *D.* × 'Bath Pink' is a good ground cover for small areas and covers its fine-textured blue-gray foliage with single, lavender-pink flowers in spring. A dark green-foliaged mat-forming dianthus with striking semi-double, fuschia-purple flowers on 4–6-inch stems in spring is sometimes available in nurseries and frequently handed down among Southern gardeners. A fairly new and popular introduction is *D.* × 'First Love'. It changes from dark to light pink and stands about 1 foot tall when in flower. Stems are long enough for use as cut flowers and they are quite fragrant. 'First Love' is being sold as a perennial, but the recent winters have not been sufficiently challenging to determine its hardiness. It is quite handsome in masses, borders, or as cut flowers. Dianthus were popular in medieval times for their delightful fragrance, which was welcome in homes of the era because of the lack of plumbing and personal hygiene. Some of the new hybrids have lost their fragrance, but older forms nearly all are scented. Most dianthus are relatively long-lasting and handsome material for cutting.

Echinacea purpurea
(ek-ih-NAY-see-uh PUR-pur-ee-uh)
PURPLE CONEFLOWER
Family: Compositae
Zone: 4. Size: 2–3 feet, spring, summer, fall

Purple coneflowers are among our loveliest wildflowers and are easily grown perennials in the garden. The 3–4-inch daisylike flowers occur in abundance in spring, repeating well in early summer and fall. *E. purpurea* is closely related to *E. angustifolia*, which is native from Texas northward to Canada. Flowers of the native form are usually less intense in color with more "clasping" petals, and the plants are less compact in growth habit. Purple coneflowers tolerate drought and thrive in alkaline or acid soils. They perform best where they have at least a half day of direct sunlight. Fall planting or division is recommended, although planting at almost any time is usually successful. For best results divide every two to three years in the fall.

Seedlings often volunteer in the vicinity of mature plants and are easily transplanted. The flowers last a long time both on the plant and when cut. Keep plants tidy by cutting old bloom stems back to foliage level after each bloom cycle, unless you want to mature a crop of seed. Trying to pull off the bristly cones without benefit of a knife or shears usually results in uprooting the entire plant. Echinacea was a highly regarded medicinal plant for Native Americans, and today's

Purple coneflowers are long-lasting for cut use. WCW

'White Lustre' variety contrasts nicely with the common purple forms of coneflowers. WCW

Endymion hispanicus
(in-DIM-ee-un hiss-PAN-ah-cuss)
SPANISH BLUEBELL
Family: Liliaceae
Zone: 4. Size: 12–18 inches, spring

This perennial bulb deserves wider use. Spanish bluebells are relatives of hyacinths and are similar in appearance to the loosely flowered sprays, rather than tightly formed heads of Dutch hyacinths. The most common color is a medium blue, but pink and white forms are sometimes available. I first obtained Spanish bluebell bulbs from Minnie Colquitt in Shreveport, Louisiana, about ten years ago. They are lovely naturalized on the edge of wooded areas in our College Station garden. A native of Western Europe and Northern Africa, endymion naturalizes well over all but the most southern parts of Texas and Florida. Bulbs should be planted in the fall, but seldom require dividing. The flowers are good for cutting and have a pleasant fragrance.

medical community is showing a renewed interest in it. A white form, 'White Lustre', is sometimes available, although I find it on the grayish side of white. Various cultivars of the purple forms are available. Sometimes reports occur about this plant being difficult, and I believe that may be because forms of the plant from other climates are being sold. If you find growing it to be difficult, try obtaining seed or plants from a local source.

Spanish bluebells naturalize well in most of the South. WCW

Joe-Pye weed is an impressive fall blooming perennial native. NGO

Eupatorium coelestinum
(yew-pa-TOR-ee-um ca-les-TIN-um)
HARDY AGERATUM, BLUE BONESET
Family: Compositae
Zone: 6. Size: 2–3 feet, fall

Hardy ageratum is valuable not only for its hardiness and adaptability, but also for its misty display of fluffy autumn flowers. It has a fairly long bloom season in fall and grows well even in poorly drained soils. Hardy ageratum combines well in the garden with *Tagetes lucida*, Mexican marigold-mint, autumn asters (*Aster oblongifolius*), and Mexican bush sage (*Salvia leucantha*). It is one of those plants that is so vigorous it is sometimes considered invasive, but its rhizomatous roots can be easily thinned or removed. It will grow in practically any soil and exposure. Since it blooms in the fall, existing clumps should be divided in spring. *E. maculatum*, Joe-Pye weed, is another useful native perennial, even taller and more robust with flowers occurring in dome-shaped clusters in fall. The flowers are purplish-pink and the plant is well suited to boggy soils that occur naturally along the edge of ponds or streams. Plants sometimes reach 6–7 feet tall with 10–12-inch flower heads useful as cut flowers. Some gardeners plant eupatoriums just to attract butterflies. They are among the best for that purpose.

Gaillardia x grandiflora
(ga-LAR-dee-uh gran-dih-FLO-ruh)
BLANKET FLOWER, INDIAN BLANKET
Family: Compositae
Zone: 3. Size: 1–3 feet, spring, summer

The blanket flowers available are hybrids of two native species, *G. aristata* and *G. pulchella*. They are easily grown plants and perform best in relatively poor soils and dry conditions. Although tolerant of a wide range of soil acidity, they are not tolerant of poorly drained soils and grow best in sandy soils with only occasional watering. Gaillardias are also popular for their tolerance to salty conditions, often growing naturally very near the Gulf of Mexico. The natural blooming season is from mid-spring into summer. Stems are thin but strong, and need to be cut with sharp shears. Trying to pull them off by hand usually results in uprooting the entire plant. If old blooms are cut off, the plants reward the gardener with a late summer and fall crop of flowers.

Although usually considered a perennial, gaillardias tend to be rather short-lived, especially where drainage is less than ideal. Flowers are usually single, but semi-doubles do exist. Colors range from yellow to red, with petals sometimes distinctively marked with yellow on their edges. Although thin-stemmed, gaillardias are useful for cutting when given the support of narrow-necked containers. 'Goblin' is probably the most popular variety, with large dark red flowers edged in bright yellow. 'Monarch' is a taller-growing variety with attractive combinations of red and yellow in the flowers. To maintain specific cultivars, existing plants must be divided. Seedlings in your garden usually display considerable variation in size and color. Blanket flowers occur in great masses along Texas highways in spring and early summer, with their display beginning about the time that bluebonnets decline. Most of the wild forms are annuals.

Gaura is useful for filler material in bouquets and in gardens. WCW

Gaura lindheimeri
(GAR-uh lind-HI-mer-eye)
GAURA, WHIRLING BUTTERFLIES
Family: Onagraceae
Zone 6. Size: 3–5 feet, spring, summer, fall

Gaura was first described botanically in the 1840s by the great Texas botanist Ferdinand Lindheimer from New Braunfels. It is native to Texas and Louisiana and becoming a popular perennial in the Southeast due to its ability to provide filler in the garden and its adaptability to various soil and growing conditions. Appearance is similar to baby's breath, but the flowers are larger and bloom over a much longer period. The 1-inch white or pink flowers open a few at a time, arising from many fine stems at the base. The branched stems are useful in flower arrangements for their airy quality. Propagation is by seed or division of mature clumps.

Gaura prefers a sunny location and well-drained soil. Although not a spectacular plant, it adds delicate mass to the garden and blooms over a long period. The rather deep, carrotlike roots should be kept intact when transplanted. Seedlings often volunteer in the vicinity of mature plants and usually bloom within a year of germination. Buds are pinkish and flowers open white, except for new cultivars such as 'Siskyou Pink' and other selections with darker buds and pink flowers.

Gerbera jamesonii
(GER-bur-uh jay-mis-SOHN-eye)
GERBERA DAISY, TRANSVAAL DAISY
Family: Compositae
Zone 8. Size: 18–24 inches, spring, summer, fall

Gerberas are large-flowering daisies that come in beautiful pastels of pink, coral, orange, red, yellow, and cream. Flowers may reach 5 inches across, usually single but sometimes semi-double, and occur over a very long season. The foliage is composed of clumps of large, dandelionlike leaves that provide a coarse-textured effect. Old foliage and bloom heads should be cut off to maintain a neat appearance. Gerberas are excellent and long-lasting cut flowers, but a bit difficult to grow. One reason is that most of the plants available for sale are highly bred for cut-flower production and are a bit finicky in the garden. For that reason it is best to seek garden forms. When just the right exposure is found, they can be very rewarding.

Gerberas are not competitive plants and do not flourish among ground covers. They should be planted in well-prepared, well-drained soil that is neutral to acid, where afternoon shade protects plants from hot summer sun. Mulching with pinestraw, bark, or similar material can help keep the soil cool in summer and warm in winter. Gerberas are not very cold-tolerant and occasionally are

Gerbera daisies are available in a range of strong colors. WCW

Gladiolus have impressive spikes. WCW

come in many solid colors as well as some bi-color combinations. They must be planted very early in the spring or even late winter so that they will flower before the arrival of summer's intense heat, accompanied by its onslaught of thrips (tiny insects that damage buds and flowers). Dwarf forms are available and generally better for landscape use since their compact growth habit reduces the need for staking. All glads prefer a sunny location and well-drained and prepared garden soil. Protection from the hot afternoon sun prolongs the life of the flowers.

All gladiolus produce excellent cut flowers, and rows of their swordlike foliage are a common sight in the cutting garden. For longer life cut the spikes just as the lowest buds begin to open. In Texas and the Gulf South, modern gladiolus corms must be dug and stored after they begin to die back each summer. At that time, their tops should be cut off just above the corm. Burn or discard the foliage since it can harbor botrytis infection and thrips. Dry the corms for several weeks in a shaded, ventilated area, then pull off and discard the withered roots

killed by cold even in zone 8. They are usually offered in mixed colors with the various hues blending beautifully. If you wish to have single-colored masses in your garden, divide existing clumps and reset the plants yourself or purchase plants in bloom.

Gladiolus x hortulanus
(gla-dee-OH-lus hort-ul-LAN-us)
GLADIOLUS
Family: Iridaceae
Zone: all. Size: 2–4 feet

Gladiolus are among the best cut flowers we can grow in the South. Some forms are excellent perennials as well. The common glads are available as corms and usually grown as annuals. Tall, swordlike spikes of funnel-shaped flowers

Byzantine or hardy gladiolus thrive in Southern gardens and are useful for cutting. WCW

Parrot gladiolus (*Gladiolus natalensis*) is a spectacular species that does well in the South. WCW

vigorous white form, cv. 'Albus', is sometimes available. *G. natalensis* (*psittacinus*), known as parrot gladiolus, is from the Natal region of Africa. Easily recognized by its hooded orange and yellow blooms, it was one of the species used to create the modern hybrid glads, and grows to a height of about 3–4 feet. Foliage appears soon after the last frost, and flowers open on tall, sturdy stems in late April. The plants grow from large, shallow-grown corms that multiply readily and grow well even in heavy soils.

Foliage of both *G. natalensis* and *G. byzantinus* may be cut off just above ground level after it yellows in the summer. Traditionally, gladiolus were planted in rows in the vegetable garden as well as in flower borders. Both species described here were common in Southern cottage gardens of the nineteenth century. They deserve widespread use as perennials in period and modern gardens, though at present are difficult to obtain from commercial sources. This will probably change, but for now botanical garden plant sales, individual gardeners, and a few of the specialty bulb nurseries listed in Sources are the best choices.

Gypsophila paniculata
(jip-SOF-a-la pa-NIK-u-lata)
BABY'S BREATH
Family: Carophyllaceae
Zone: all. Size: 1–3 feet, spring, summer

Baby's breath is a favorite as dried or fresh material. Leaves are small and slender on many branched plants with sprays containing hundreds of tiny white flowers. 'Bristol Fairy' is a double-flowering form with somewhat larger flowers. Baby's breath is not easily grown in the South and requires excellent drainage. Although considered a perennial, the plants are often short-lived. They seem to prefer the dryness and alkaline soils of West Texas gardens to more moist areas of the South. Good specimens are, however,

and remains of the old corms. Dust the new corms with a garden fungicide and store in a well-ventilated, frost-free area until planting time next late winter or early spring. If all this sounds like a lot of trouble, it probably is, and may be avoided by planting either the two species-types described here, or by replanting with new corms each spring.

For mixed borders and cottage gardens, there are two of gladiolus that are excellent perennials requiring little care. *G. byzantinus*, sometimes known as "hardy gladiolus" or "Jacob's ladder," is a delightful plant often found in old cottage gardens in the South. It is a native of southern Europe, where its preference for cornfields has earned it the name "corn lily." It blooms with many of the bearded irises, about April 1, in Central Texas. Flower spikes are a beautiful magenta-purple or rarely white and about 18–24 inches tall. *G. byzantinus* does best in a sunny, well-drained location, but will grow tolerably well in clay soils. Corms are small in comparison to the modern hybrids, but do not require digging and increase nicely each year even in abandoned gardens. *G. byzantinus* responds best to fall planting in Texas and the Gulf South. A rare and somewhat less

Butterfly ginger is probably the best adapted and the most common of the fragrant gingers. NGO

sometimes found in the Middle and Upper South when grown on sunny, well-drained sites.

New plants can be rooted from stem cuttings as well as being grown from seed. Transplants may be set out in the fall in zones 8–10, but should be planted in late winter or spring in cooler areas. *G. elegans* is an annual form of gypsophila grown from seed. Seed should be planted in early spring or late winter in the South. White, pink, or rose forms of *G. elegans* are available. Since each plant produces for only a few weeks, planting dates should be staggered several weeks apart. Baby's breath is easily dried by tying in loose bundles and hanging upside down in a dark, well-ventilated space for several weeks.

Hedychium coronarium
(he-DIK-e-um kor-roe-NA-ree-um
BUTTERFLY GINGER
Family: Zingiberaceae
Zone: 8-10. Size: 3–6 feet, summer, fall

Several genera compose the plants we refer to as gingers. *H. coronarium* is probably the most useful for garden and cut flower use. Flowers are pure white, highly fra-

grant, and resemble butterflies. The handsome foliage is thick with leaves measuring several inches wide and about a foot long. Butterfly ginger should be divided every three or four years to ensure continued flowering. As canes finish blooming in late summer or early fall, they should be cut off at ground level. Where there is ade-

quate water, butterfly ginger may be grown in full sun, but the foliage is more attractive in partially shaded areas. In regions north of zone 8, butterfly ginger may be grown in containers and moved to protected areas during the winter months. Plants perform well in clay soils. *H. flavescens* is similar to *H. coronarium*, except

A close-up of butterfly ginger. WCW

Above: Hidden ginger has long-lasting flowers and attractive foliage. WCW
Below: Variegated alpinia ginger has striking foliage. NGO

sun. *Zingiber zerumbet*, pinecone or shampoo ginger, is naturally deciduous and root-hardy in most of zone 8. The conelike flower head with creamy-yellow florets is a favorite of flower arrangers, especially after the flowers have passed, as the cones turn a rich red. Gingers are usually propagated by dividing clumps in fall or early spring.

Helenium spp.
(hel-in-EE-um)
SNEEZEWEED
Family: Compositae
Zone: 6. Size: 1–4 feet, late summer, fall

Sneezeweed is a common wildflower in Texas valuable for its long-lasting flowers and its ability to grow in wet places. The most common forms available are cultivars of *H. autumnale* such as 'Brilliant' and 'Butterpat'. The center portion, or *disk*, of the 1–2-inch flower is prominent because it is raised and usually contrasts in color to the petals or

they bloom in somewhat larger clusters of yellow-colored flowers with orange patches and cream-colored stamens.

Curcuma petiolata, hidden ginger, is among the most cold-hardy of the gingers. It will survive outdoors through zone 8. The deciduous foliage is light green and thin-textured, somewhat resembling cannas. Typical mature height is 2–3 feet. The foliage normally yellows and begins to die before frost, and is late to sprout again in the spring. Flower spikes appearing in midsummer stay so near the bases of the leaves that they may be overlooked unless the plant is examined closely. Color is rosy-pink with purplish margins. Hidden ginger may be propagated from division in early spring. It is one of the most useful gingers for landscape purposes since it masses well and provides handsome, bold, coarse texture in shaded areas. The foliage tends to burn in full

Maximilian daisies are vigorous fall-blooming sunflowers. NGO

rays. Disks may be brownish-purple, or yellow with rays in a contrasting yellow. *H. flexuosum* is native to Southeast Texas as well as the eastern coast of the United States. Plants may be grown from seed or divisions. Like many native perennials, sneezeweeds tend to be short-lived, but usually reseed in the garden. To maintain specific cultivars, divide existing clumps in the fall or winter.

Helianthus angustifolius
(HE-lee-an-thus an-gus-ti-FOL-e-us)
SWAMP SUNFLOWER
Family: Compositae
Zone: 6. Size: 3–8 feet, fall

Swamp sunflower is a good source of late summer and fall color in the garden or as a cut flower. Like most sunflowers it is fairly aggressive and requires considerable space. Flowers are 2½-inch yellow daisies that begin to open in September. In good soils, where they reach their greatest height, swamp sunflowers may require staking. *H. maximiliana,* the Maximilian sunflower, is also native to the South, but over a broader range. It is a very large plant, sometimes reaching 10 feet tall. Maximilian sunflowers are easily grown and will tolerate con-

siderable abuse. They are best used at the back of the border, since they become quite large and reproduce quickly. A sunny loca-

tion is about the only requirement. Staking may be necessary, especially in good soils. Prune them back several times during

Swamp sunflower provides impressive displays for fall gardens and bouquets. WCW

Heliopsis thrive in the middle and upper South and bloom in later summer and early fall. WCW

bloom at a time when few other plants are at their peak. Cultivar 'Scabra' is the double form and the one I encounter most often in Southern gardens. Plants reach a mature height of 2–4 feet and the bright golden flowers are about 2 inches in diameter in loose clusters. They are drought-tolerant and have a rather long bloom season, beginning in July and sometimes going well into the fall. Clumps should be divided every year or two in spring. Heliopsis tolerate some shade and do well in most soils.

Hesperaloe parviflora
(hes-per-AL-oh par-vi-FLOR-uh)
RED YUCCA
Family: Agavaceae
Zone: 5. Size: 4–7 feet, late spring through early fall

Although native to Texas and Mexico, red yucca is rarely found in the wild. The common name is a bit deceiving, since the leaves are not dangerously sharp like true yuccas. Deer, goats, and cattle have significantly reduced native stands. They are, however, commonly available in the nursery trade in Texas. Plants are composed of long, stiff, gray-green slender leaves that form stemless clumps. The leaves sprout fine white threads from their margins. Gracefully leaning stalks, 5–7 feet tall, bear coral-pink or, rarely, yellow flowers from May through

the summer, until about August 1. This will result in more compact plants. Clumps may be divided in early spring. The yellow daisylike flowers are about 3 inches in diameter, produced on long stems in great numbers.

H. × *multiflorus* cultivars such as 'Flore Pleno' and 'Loddon Gold' are spectacular in late summer. Each plant becomes quite bushy and can fill an area approximately two square feet. Flowers are large and double, somewhat resembling chrysanthemums. Another species of sunflower, *H. tuberosus*, better known as Jerusalem artichoke, grows 6–7 feet tall, bearing yellow flowers. The potatolike tubers are edible and often sold in grocery stores. Because *H. tuberosus* is very prolific, it is best to harvest all but a few of the tubers each year to prevent a complete takeover of the garden.

Heliopsis helianthoides
(he-lee-OP-sis he-lee-an-THOY-dees)
HELIOPSIS
Family: Compositae
Zone: 8 north. Size: 2–4 feet, late summer, fall

Heliopsis are useful sunflowers, excellent as cut flowers. They thrive from zone 8 north, and

Red yucca has long, graceful stems of coral-red flowers. WCW

'Apple Blossom' amaryllis in a Baton Rouge, Louisiana, garden. WCW

early fall. Individual flowers are about 1½ inches long and continue opening for many weeks. Each clump may have numerous flower spikes over the season. Although native to dry areas, hesperaloes are not choosy about soil and tolerate occasionally wet conditions. The flower stalks are useful as cut material. Partially shaded locations are suitable, but sunny sites produce the best clumps and most profuse blooming. Propagation is from seed or division of mature clumps. Landscape uses include accent specimens, masses in borders, or container displays. The only routine maintenance this plant requires is the removal of old flower stalks at the end of the bloom season. An added bonus is the attraction of hummingbirds and butterflies to the flowers.

Hippeastrum x *johnsonii*
(hip-ee-AS-trum jon-SOHN-ee-eye)
HARDY RED AMARYLLIS.
ST. JOSEPH'S LILY
Family: Amaryllidaceae
Zone: 8. Size: 2 feet, spring

Hardy red amaryllis are among the most spectacular spring-flowering bulbs. Their foliage is strap-shaped and long, sometimes to 24 inches, often not appearing until after flowering, then fading away in early autumn. Old clumps can produce dozens of thick flower stems, each topped with six or more funnel-shaped red flowers

with a white stripe on each petal. *H.* x *johnsonii* is the first hybrid amaryllis ever recorded; reportedly, it was produced by an English watchmaker named Johnson about 1790. It is a cross between *A. vittata* and *A. reginae*, the most cold-hardy and vigorous amaryllis for garden culture in the South. It is often found in old cemetery plots and abandoned homesites, where it seems to continue forever with little or no assistance.

Spicy fragrance adds to the value of the plant as a cut flower. Although each flower only lasts a few days, the buds keep opening, even after cutting. Clumps may be divided every three to four years, preferably in the fall. Amaryllis prefer sun and well-drained soils, but also thrive in partial shade and a wide range of soil conditions. They are excellent candidates for pot culture where winter damage is a problem. Hybrid Dutch amaryllis also thrive in the garden,

Hardy amaryllis in a Fredericksburg, Texas, garden. WCW

Fragrant blue Roman hyacinths naturalize in the middle and upper South. WCW

but cold damage during severe winters is common from zone 8 north. My favorite hybrid cultivar is 'Apple Blossom', a huge pink and white form. It has increased and prospered in our Northeast Louisiana garden with only occasional winter damage. We mulch the clumps heavily with pine needles each fall. When planting amaryllis, leave the necks of large bulbs slightly above ground level.

Hyacinthus orientalis
(hi-ah-SIN-thus o-ree-en-TAL-is)
ROMAN HYACINTH
Family: Liliaceae
Zone: 5. Size: 6–8 inches, early spring

Both white and blue forms, and rarely pink, of Roman hyacinths may occasionally be found in old gardens and cemeteries in the South and Southwest. Roman hyacinths resemble their hybrid cousins but have fewer individual flowers and are even more fragrant. Although once commonly sold as cut flowers and pot plants, Roman hyacinths are scarce in today's market. The white form flowers in the middle of winter, usually around January 1, in zone 8, but the blues and pinks wait until March or April for their dis-

play. Allow the foliage to yellow and begin to fade away in late spring before dividing and resetting Roman hyacinths. Select a sunny or partially shaded site with

Dutch hyacinths provide early spring color. NGO

excellent drainage. They seem to increase more freely in areas where they are not irrigated during the summer months. Propagation is by division every three to five

Spider lilies thrive in Gulf South gardens. NGO

abundant moisture is available. The large, dark green foliage and fragrant, white flowers make an excellent accent in the garden or cut flower in the home.

The name 'Tropical Giant' was first coined by Wyndham Hayward at Lakemont Gardens, Winter Park, Florida, in the mid-1940s. Although one of the most common hymenocallis in Southern gardens, this variety has apparently never been properly described botanically. Its flowers are easily recognized by the white petals arranged in two alternating planes, one spreading and the other drooping. 'Tropical Giant' is especially attractive when used as a specimen where its coarse texture contrasts with finer-textured plants. The flowers have a pleasant lilylike fragrance and continue opening their buds over several days, even when cut. 'Tropical Giant' is not hardy beyond zone 8 and is occasionally damaged there. All spider lilies are propagated by division, preferably in the fall. They thrive in just about any soil, even very heavy clay.

years, although old stands seem to go on forever without assistance, if they like their location. Hybrids are relatively easily to grow in the ground or in pots, but usually flower for only one season in the South.

Hymenocallis liriosme
(high-men-oh-KAL-is leer-ee-OS-me)
SPIDER LILY
Family: Amaryllidaceae
Zone: 8. Size: 3–4 feet, spring, summer

The spider lily is an attractive native found in low places in Louisiana, coastal Texas, and sporadically north to Arkansas and east to Mobile Bay. They occur naturally on wet sites. *H. liriosme* 'Tropical Giant' is a popular and impressive selection throughout the Gulf Coast states. It bears large umbrellalike clusters of flowers in late June and early July, and is one of the finest of all-foliage plants available for Southern gardens, growing readily wherever

'Tropical Giant' spider lily has handsome foliage and impressive flowers. WCW

'Cemetery White' irises naturalize all over the South. WCW

Iris spp.
(EYE-ris)
IRIS
Family: Iridaceae
Zone: all. Size: 1–4 feet, spring, summer

Irises are among the most beautiful and diverse perennials. Some groups prefer relatively dry, well-drained locations while others thrive in moist or poorly drained soils. There are good, practical choices among the irises for every area of the South. Irises are generally classified as either bearded or non-bearded. Within these broad classifications are numerous subclasses, a few of which are particularly useful for cut-flower and landscape use. This section will concentrate on the well-adapted irises good for garden and cut-flower use.

Bearded Iris

These are the best-known of all garden iris, and receive their name from the tuft of hair, the "beard," that sprouts from the three lower petals. This class does not thrive in areas adjacent to the Gulf or the ocean, with its excessive humidity and poorly drained soils. Most areas at least a hundred or more miles inland can have some success with bearded iris. They seem to prosper from zone 8 north. The

Above: Hybrid bearded irises are available in a wide variety of colors. NGO
Below: Louisiana irises naturalized at the Rural Life Museum, Burden Plantation, Baton Rouge. NGO

bearded irises are subdivided by flower size and height. Tall bearded irises are those with flower stalks over 27 inches; medians are those under 27 inches. The bearded irises are further divided into miniature dwarfs, standard dwarfs, intermediate, border, and miniature tall. A few are classified as rebloomers because they bloom again in the fall, after having flowered with the others in spring.

Good cultural practices are the best insurance against disease and disappointment with bearded iris. The rhizomes are tough and can withstand considerable heat and drought, but too much water and poorly drained soils invite disaster. Of good substance, too, are the flowers of the modern hybrid types. A single blossom can last

Yellow flag irises are easily grown. NGO

for three to four days, and because each of the plant's many buds opens separately, a single plant may remain in bloom over a long season. Recommended planting time is July through October, although if necessary, iris can be transplanted successfully even while in bloom. Rhizomes dug in mid-summer may be stored in a cool, dry place for many weeks before being placed in their permanent location. Since irises perform best if left undisturbed for two or three years at a stretch, it is logical to prepare the soil well before planting. Bearded irises tolerate soil pH range of 6–9, with a preference for slightly alkaline media (7.0–8.0). Full sun and good drainage are recommended, although locations shaded from the hot afternoon sun may encourage longer-lasting flowers.

When planting, place the rhizomes with their tops barely covered with soil. Spread the roots out as far as possible by forming a mound of soil in the center of the hole and placing the rhizome on top. Place some prepared soil over the roots, compact the soil by hand, and water slowly until the soil settles and no air pockets are likely to remain. If transplanting is the result of division, cut each plant's leaves back to about 6–8 inches; do not prune undivided transplants, however. Though sensitive to fertilizer, irises are heavy feeders and do require regular

feeding. Apply fertilizer with a ratio of 6-10-6 after bloom in the spring or in early fall. Side-dressing with superphosphate improves growth and bloom. Sprinkle the material a couple of inches from the base of each plant in late February or early March. Keep iris plantings free of dead foliage, weeds, and leaves. Water should be applied on the ground and not from sprinklers. Spacing depends upon the ultimate size of the variety and the desired effect in the garden. Place the rhizomes 24–30 inches apart to allow plenty of room for growth. Group several or more rhizomes of the same variety to provide a greater concentration of color.

Place the cut ends of the rhizomes close enough to almost touch, leaves to the outside, to achieve a quick and effective display. When dividing clumps that have been growing for two, three, or more years, it is best to dispose of the old center rhizomes and replant only the best of the outer ones. This reduces disease and ensures healthier and better blooms for the next season. The irises most commonly found growing wild in Texas and the South are sometimes referred to as "cemetery whites." Actually, they are a separate species, *Iris × albicans*, a naturally sterile hybrid. Although their individual blooms may last but a day or two, they are extremely hardy and often mark abandoned homesites and old cemeteries, where for several weeks each spring they command the attention of all passers-by. Originally from Yemen, these irises have naturalized so extensively and become such a part of our rural landscape that many people consider them native. 'Early Purple' irises are also found in abundance on old homesites and cemeteries. These are thought to be a different color form of *Iris × albicans*.

Beardless Iris

The group of iris called Louisiana iris are bred from several wild species in Louisiana, Texas, and Mississippi. They are both cold-

Dutch irises are useful for cutting and garden display. WCW

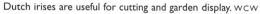

Siberian irises thrive in the middle and upper South. NGO

and heat-hardy, but need considerable moisture during the fall and winter to thrive. They will grow partially submerged, which makes them useful in water gardens and on the edge of streams and lakes. Stalk heights vary from 1–6 feet and flowers from 3–7 inches across. Because all the primary colors are inherent in the various species that contributed to this group, there is no limit to the color range. The Louisianas, for example, include the purest form of red of any iris. Louisianas prefer an acid soil in the range of 6.5 or lower. They like large quantities of fertilizer and water, but their greatest need for these is during the fall, winter, and early spring, when natural moisture is likely to be present. Foliage is lush during the fall, winter, and spring, but goes dormant during the heat of

summer, leaving dead foliage that should be cut back or removed. New foliage will appear again in the fall.

Fall is the best season for transplanting. Beds should be well-tilled and amended with large

amounts of compost, peat, or pine bark. Rhizomes should be planted just below ground level and kept moist until well established. Clumps spread quickly, and individual rhizomes should be spaced several feet apart to avoid need for annual division. Mulching in the summer protects rhizomes against sun-scald. Azalea-camellia fertilizers work well with Louisiana iris, along with water-soluble fertilizers designed to lower the soil pH. After bloom is completed in the spring, stalks should be cut back to the rhizome. Old rhizomes do not bloom again, but increase to produce the following year's crop.

Another iris that does well under wet conditions is *Iris pseudacorus*, a European native that has escaped cultivation and may be found growing in wet ditches and along streams and lakes. It is bright yellow in color and considered by some to be a native plant. The foliage is much like the Louisianas and spurias, tall and almost reedlike. The plant is very hardy, healthy, and aggressive, with clumps becoming very large in time. Although similar to the Louisiana iris, *I. pseudacorus* is not botanically part of that group nor will it cross-pollinate with them. If allowed to set seed, it can colonize large areas.

Siberian irises are another group that is excellent in both the garden and for cutting. Like the bearded iris. Siberians do best a

'Professor Neil' is a new tetraploid Louisiana iris. WCW

Japanese irises in a garden setting. NGO

hundred or more miles inland from the Gulf. They also seem to do better from zone 8 north. Varieties like 'Caesar's Brother' are outstanding in the garden, and their deep purple flowers are beautiful alone or with other flowers in arrangements.

Spurias are still another group of iris excellent for both cutting and garden use. They look a great deal like Louisianas, but are more like bearded iris in their requirements. They often succeed nearer the coasts where the bearded iris may fail. Spurias do well in relatively dry areas and deserve wider use in the South. *Iris ochroleuca* was one of the species used to breed the modern spuria hybrids, and flourishing colonies of it may still be found in old cemeteries and abandoned gardens. Flowers are white with a large yellow spot on the *falls* (the three bottom petals, those carrying the beard in the bearded irises). Like many iris, the spurias are heavy feeders, and even abandoned and neglected specimens can be immediately improved by an application of fertilizer in the fall. Propagation is best done by division in the fall.

Japanese irises are a bit harder

A close-up of Japanese iris. NGO

to handle in the average garden. They require an acid soil, plenty of fertilizer and water, but do not need to stand in water during the fall and winter. Flowers of Japanese iris are the largest of any iris and their forms and color patterns are the most unusual, though they offer less range of color than the Lousisianas. Japanese iris, however, offer more variety of markings. Their bloom date can be a big advantage, since it is late enough in spring to extend the iris season another month. Some gardeners plant them alongside Louisiana iris and treat them similarly. Japanese iris thrive much better from zone 8 north.

Dutch irises are bulbous and quite different from the rhizomatous types described in this section. Dutch irises prefer rich, well-drained soils, and in those conditions will sometimes naturalize.

Top: Shrimp plant blooms all summer and fall. T. E. POPE
Above: Justicia carnea is exotic and colorful, but is not hardy below zone 8B. WCW

They also like sunny locations but can be grown under deciduous trees, where they usually complete their growth and bloom cycles before foliage canopies leaf out in spring. Dutch irises are excellent cut flowers and inexpensive bulbs, although they are not always successful as perennials in the garden. They are available from many sources and are planted in the fall, blooming the following spring. Dutch irises prefer at least a half day of direct sunlight and well-drained soil. Colors range from purple to "wedgewood blue," yellow, white, bronze, and bi-colors.

Justicia brandegeana
(jus-TISS-ee-uh bran-dee-JEE-ah-nuh)
SHRIMP PLANT
Family: Acanthaceae
Zone: 9. Size: 4–5 feet, summer and fall

Shrimp plant is a native of Mexico and very popular in the lower South, where it is used extensively as a garden perennial and often cut for indoor ornament. The dense 3–4-inch floral spikes resemble shrimp in both form and color, with tubular, purple-spotted white flowers extending beyond the showy *bracts* (reddish-brown floral parts). Luxuriant in its

effect, the shrimp plant produces many long-lasting displays through the summer and fall. A chartreuse selection, 'Yellow Queen', is available and attractive. Leaves are egg-shaped and 2–3 inches long. Shrimp plant prefers well-drained soil and some protection from the hottest afternoon sun and winter winds.

The plants are drought-tolerant, once established, and are propagated by division of mature clumps or from cuttings. Winter-damaged top growth should be removed in very early spring. Mulching in the fall can be helpful in providing protection against frost damage. Large, old specimens may sometimes be found in New Orleans, Galveston, and along the Texas coast from Corpus Christi to Brownsville. With winter mulch and a site protected from north winds, shrimp plant may be grown as a perennial into zone 8. *Justicia carnea*, Brazilian plume flower, is an erect, soft-wooded, multi-stemmed perennial with clusters of pink or white tubular flowers on 3–4-foot stems. It performs well in the shade and is attractive as a cut flower, but only fully hardy in zone 10.

Kniphofia uvaria
(nip-HOE-fee-uh you-VAR-ee-uh)
**RED HOT POKER,
TORCH LILY**
Family: Liliaceae
Zone: 6. Size: 2–4 feet, spring

Kniphofias are very popular in herbaceous borders in England and Europe, but not as dependable in the South. They are sometimes worth the effort in gardens a hundred or more miles inland from the Gulf. A sunny location with excellent drainage and good loamy soil is ideal. Foliage is grasslike and should be cut off at the base in fall. The flowers of some varieties are bi-colored yellow and orange; others are solid in ivory, yellows, coral, orange, and scarlet. Kniphofia flowers offer an

Kniphofia, or red hot poker, in a mixed garden border. WCW

flowers are a beautiful accent in the garden and for cutting. Unfortunately, lavenders do not like the humidity typical of most of the South, and tend to be short-lived, often performing poorly. In Central, North, and West Texas, however, they can be useful perennials. The Spanish lavenders, *L. stoechas*, are usually credited with being more tolerant of moisture, but even they tend to perform poorly in the South. For best results, select a sunny site having well-drained, sandy soil. Lavenders are quite drought-tolerant, but excessive winter moisture can be their nemesis, even when grown in sandy soils. Propagation is usually by root division or cuttings, as the seeds are difficult to handle.

Leucojum aestivum
(lu-KO-jum ES-tih-vum)
SUMMER SNOWFLAKE
Family: Amaryllidaceae
Zone: 5. Size: 1 foot, early spring

Snowflakes are among the best naturalizing bulbs in the South, slowly increasing each year if in a suitable location. They are native to the stream banks of southern France and prefer moist locations and heavy clay soil. The small ¾-inch, bell-shaped blossoms appear in February or March, and bear a distinctive green spot on the margins of the petals. They are fra-

excellent contrast in shape to daylilies, daisies, iris, and many other perennials. Clumps are best left undisturbed. Good companion plants include daylilies, coreopsis, and gaura. Red hot pokers are excellent cut flowers. Propagation is by seed or division of mature clumps in the fall. Seedlings require two to three years to flower.

Lavandula angustifolia, L. stoechas
(La-VEN-du-la an-GUS-ti-fol-ee-ah, STA-kas)
ENGLISH AND SPANISH LAVENDER
Family: Labiatae
Zone: 5. Size: 1–2 feet, summer, fall

Lavender has been grown and cherished many centuries by

Europeans for toiletries and sachets as well as medicine. The gray foliage and lavender to purple

Lavender in full bloom. NGO

Liatris elegans
(li-AT-tris EL-ee-ganz)
GAY-FEATHER, BLAZING STAR
Family: Compositae
Zone: 5. Size: 2–3 feet, late summer

Liatris are among our most attractive perennials for cutting. The native form is often found growing along roadsides and hillsides of Texas, Louisiana, Arkansas, Oklahoma, and eastward. Many spikes of frilly rosy-purple or white flowers emerge from clumps in late summer. Liatris grow from curious round, woody corms that can be divided, but seldom become sufficiently thick to require division. New plants are usually started from seed. A problem I have found with the native liatris is that it will not remain erect without staking when transplanted to the improved growing conditions of the garden. Staking can help solve the problem, but I have found *L. spicata* to be a better garden subject than its native cousin. *L. spicata* is considered the most adaptable of the liatris. It grows naturally in deep soils, and is fairly drought-resistant. Staking is not normally necessary and nursery availability is better than for the native species. Liatris are

Top: Snowflakes, or leucojums, are among the best naturalizing perennial bulbs. NGO
Above: Under close examination, individual petals of the snowflake show a dot of green. WCW

green foliage of the snowflakes is among the most attractive of all spring-flowering bulbs. Best landscape effects are achieved with large clumps of bulbs. Leucojums also combine well with other spring-flowering bulbs and thrive in sun or shade of deciduous trees. The foliage is outstanding for several months, and clumps may be left undivided for many years without sacrificing flowers. Mature clumps may be divided in late spring after the foliage has yellowed. Although bulbs can be stored for several months in a dry, well-aerated place, I prefer replanting the divisions immediately after digging them.

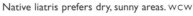
Native liatris prefers dry, sunny areas. WCW

grant and excellent as cut flowers. 'Gravetye Giant', a cultivar that is sometimes available, yields somewhat larger flowers than the more common species-type. Sometimes confusion exists in the bulb trade between *L. aestivum* and *L. vernum*, the latter being a species not adapted to the South. The dark

Cultivated forms of liatris provide outstanding color for late summer and fall. NGO

handsome in combination with *Rudbeckia fulgida* 'Goldsturm', which usually blooms at about the same time. The rosy-purple color of the common form is beautiful, but not easy to combine with other perennials. Foliage is narrow and thin, producing an overall fine texture. As cut flowers liatris are long-lasting.

Lilium candidum
(LIL-ee-um KAN-de-dum)
MADONNA LILY
Family: Liliaceae
Zone: 7. Size: 3–4 feet, mid-spring

Madonna lily is depicted in ruins of Egypt and Crete, and considered the oldest garden flower in cultivation. It is a native of Asia Minor and bears large white flowers in mid-spring. Madonna lilies do well in North Texas and the Hill Country of Texas, as well as other areas where limestone soils are common. Their shallow-growing bulbs produce attractive rosettes of foliage much like hosta through the winter, before bolting in spring to produce their sweet-scented flowers. The foliage dies down soon after flowering, and remains dormant until early fall, when the growth cycle begins anew. Transplanting and dividing

should be done in late summer or early fall. Bulbs should be set in a sunny location, only 1–2 inches below the soil surface. Few other garden lilies available to the gardener return as perennials in the South. Many cultivars are late-blooming and last only a few days in our intense late spring and

summer heat. In addition to *L. candidum*, *L. tigrinum* (tiger lily), *L. regale* (regal lily), *L. formosanum* (Easter lily), and some of the Aurelian hybrids such as 'Golden Splendor' and 'Thunderbolt' are successful in our area.

L. tigrinum grows to 4 feet

Easter lilies are favorites in Southern gardens. WCW

Tiger lilies bloom in midsummer. WCW

Philippine lily naturalizes well in Southern gardens. WCW

aged by hoeing or other cultivation in their immediate vicinity. Flooding is better than sprinkler-irrigation, especially once the plant starts flowering, since it does not damage the flower or spread spores of disease.

L. formosanum is known to most of us as the Easter lily, though it blooms in late spring when grown in the garden. Bulbs should be set 5–6 inches deep to allow for development of the extensive stem rooting system. Modern hybrid Easter lilies should not be confused with *L. formosanum*; they differ in having dark green instead of lime green foliage and will not often succeed as garden plants. Philippine lilies (*L. formosanum* 'Philippinense') are wonderful mid- to late-summer flowering lilies that have naturalized from seed in parts of the South. Their thin, grasslike foliage makes clumps from which tall spikes (3–7 feet) of magnificent and fragrant white trumpets open in mid- to late summer. I like to use them near the back of a border, where their graceful height is a real asset. A more compact form growing only 3–4 feet tall is also sometimes available. They prefer well-drained, acid soils and partial shade. Seed started in early fall will usually provide blooming plants by the next summer, if wintered in a greenhouse or cold frame.

L. regale is probably the most famous of all lilies. It was discovered by Ernest Wilson growing on

or more to bear many pendulous flowers of orange spotted with black. The tiger lily is believed to be a natural hybrid, reproducing by bulblets formed at the point where the leaves meet the stems, rather than by seed. It is a very vigorous garden lily, thriving in acid soil areas of the South. In the Far East, tiger lilies have been cultivated for many centuries. Garden lilies require well-drained soil, and their flowers last longer if they receive protection from the hot afternoon sun. Remove faded flowers, but wait until stems and leaves have turned yellow before cutting them back nearly to the ground. With care, lilies can be transplanted at any time, even when in flower, but spring and fall are ideal. They need constant

moisture while growing and blooming, but withstand dry periods after they have flowered. Mulch is advised, to keep moisture even, reduce weed growth, and keep the soil cool. Roots are near the surface and may be dam-

Surprise lilies provide garden display and cutting material in midsummer. WCW

Lycoris incarnata is a rare and beautiful species. D. GREG GRANT

Bouquet of assorted lycoris: *L. radiata, L. aurea,* and *L. albiflora.* D. GREG GRANT

Red lycoris is the most common and easily grown form. D. GREG GRANT

limestone soil in Western China. The white trumpets on tall stems resemble Easter lilies, but are much more cold-hardy. They are parents of the Olympic and Aurelian hybrids, and are well-adapted to the Central South; this is a versatile and adaptable garden lily. Garden lilies are an elegant addition to the perennial border or flower arrangements, but well-adapted varieties are few for the South.

Lycoris radiata
(Lie-KORE-is ray-dee-AH-tuh)
SPIDER LILY, GUERNSEY LILY
Family: Amaryllidaceae
Zone: 7. Size: 12–18 inches, fall

The common red spider lily, found naturalized in the South, has been researched at the United States National Arboretum at Beltsville, Maryland, and found to be a *triploid*—which means it has three sets of chromosomes, rather than the usual two, and so cannot reproduce from seed. Even if slower to propagate, it is stronger to grow—more vigorously than the type currently being imported from Japan. The foliage appears in the fall and dies down in spring. Following the first good rains in September, the bloom spikes quickly come forth with their beautiful red, spidery blossoms on 1½-foot stems. They are excellent

as cut flowers and good to mix with non-aggressive ground covers such as English ivy and vinca, and for naturalizing in partially shaded or sunny sites. They grow well in heavy clay soils with abundant winter moisture, and are especially fine for planting under deciduous trees. Dividing every fourth or fifth year soon after the foliage dies in spring is helpful. If left undivided, the bulbs become so thick they push themselves out of the ground. The strap-shaped foliage is somewhat similar to liriope, but has a silver stripe down the center. It remains lush and green all fall and winter, at a time when few other garden plants are in good foliage.

L. albiflora, the white spider lily, is similar to *L. radiata* except for the white or cream color of the flowers. It is believed to be a natural hybrid of *L. africana* and *L. radiata,* but is less cold-hardy than the red form. *L. africana.* St. Augustine lily, is a yellow form of lycoris that was reportedly brought to Florida by early Spanish settlers. It blooms at a similar time to the other fall spider lilies, but with a somewhat larger flower. It also has a much broader leaf and does not bloom dependably west of East Texas or north of Central Louisiana.

L. squamigera (Amaryllis hal-lii) is the hardiest of all lycoris,

Lythrum 'Morden's Pink' blooms intermittently from spring to fall in Southern gardens. NGO

blooming in July or August with large, fragrant, lavender-pink flowers. It does not thrive close to the Gulf, but for gardens in Central East Texas, east, and northward, it is a good garden plant that blooms at a time when few other perennials are at their peak. Mature clumps are best divided in late spring, when the winter foliage has yellowed. My friend Cleo Barnwell of Shreveport, Louisiana, shared bulbs of *Lycoris incarnata* with me about ten years ago. She obtained them from Sam Caldwell of Tennessee. They are a beautiful cream color with pink stripes—rare, but very beautiful and well-adapted to Central Texas and Louisiana, as well as possibly other areas. Lycoris are wonderful and relatively carefree garden perennials exciting as cut flowers.

Lythrum virgatum
(LITH-rum vir-GAH-tum)
PURPLE LOOSESTRIFE
Family: Lythraceae
Zone: 5. Size: 2–5 feet, summer, fall

Lythrum was introduced into the northern and eastern United States from Europe and Asia, and has become a pest in some areas. In the South, however, the cultivated varieties have not become a problem. They are valued for their long season of spring and summer bloom in the garden and as cut flowers. Varieties such as 'Morden's Pink' and 'Morden's Gleam' have continuous spikes of magenta-pink 3/4-inch flowers from many-stemmed 2-foot clumps during the warm seasons. They do best from zone 8 north, and perform poorly in coastal areas of zones 9 and 10. Lythrum

will tolerate wetness, but will also handle periods of dryness in the garden. Their bright color may be softened in border plantings by combining with silver foliage and white flowers. Propagation is from division of mature clumps or cuttings. Some cultivars are listed as L. salicaria, which is sometimes listed as the native species from Europe and quite similar to L. virgatum.

Mascagnia macroptera (Stigmaphyllon ciliatum)
(Mass-CAG-nee-ah ma-CROP-ter-ah)
BUTTERFLY VINE
Family: Malpighiaceae
Zone: 9. Size: 10–20 feet, summer, fall

Butterfly vine is distinguished by its fruit, which resembles 2–3-inch chartreuse butterflies. The vine flaunts clusters of small, bright yellow, orchidlike flowers from late summer through early fall. These mature into the unusual fruit, usually arranged one to three per stem. The chartreuse coloring of the "butterflies" changes to brown as they dry. They are beautiful and useful fresh or in dried arrangements that can last for many months. Leaves are shiny, dark green, lance-shaped, and about 3 inches long. Butterfly vine is a vigorous plant usually contained by freezing temperatures. Once established, the plant returns reliably and promptly each spring, but a mulch should be provided and care taken to provide protection from winter winds. Sunny locations such as south or east exposures are best. The vines are rather drought-tolerant, once established. *M. macroptera* is fairly common in South Texas, the Rio Grande Valley, New Orleans. South Louisiana, Florida, and other semi-tropical areas. Because of its susceptibility to cold, this plant is sometimes cultivated in greenhouses and other enclosed structures outside its range. Most garden soils are adequate for butterfly vine, but extremely alkaline

Cultivated monarda thrives in the middle and upper South. NGO

conditions result in yellowing from iron chlorosis, which results when the soil is too alkaline for iron to be available to the plant. This can usually be corrected by adding organic material such as composted pine bark or peat moss to the soil. Propagation is from cuttings, seed, or the layers that spring up naturally in the vicinity of mature plants. Another easy technique for starting new plants is to bury a length of the vine, weighing it down with a brick or stone, but making sure to leave the vine's tip exposed. After several months, the buried portion of the vine will usually have developed enough roots to be separated from the parent plant.

Monarda didyma
(mo-NAR-da Di-DEE-muh)
BEE BALM
Family: Labiatae
Zone: 4. Size: 3 feet, spring, early summer

Bee balms are staples in perennial gardens outside the South, but marginal in our area. Individual flowers surround a rounded head attractive even after the flowers have faded and sometimes used as dried floral material. Many colors are available, but two of the most popular are the soft pink 'Croftway Pink' and bright red 'Cambridge Scarlet'. Bee balm grows best where it enjoys protection from the hottest afternoon sun, and is easily propagated by division of spreading clumps.

Powdery mildew is a frequent problem affecting the foliage of monarda in our area. Applications of fungicides will control it, but the problem limits the usefulness of the plant. *M. fistulosa*, wild bergamot, is native and a common wildflower of Texas and the Gulf South. When moved into the garden, it often outgrows the typical 2-foot stature it adheres to in the wild. If cut to the ground after it flowers, wild bergamot will produce an attractive mound of new foliage that persists through the remainder of the growing season. The lavender flowers are prominent in May and early June. *M. fistulosa* is also sometimes known as Oswego tea, which refers to the Native American use of the plant for a beverage.

Narcissus
(nar-CISS-us)
DAFFODILS, JONQUILS, PAPER WHITES
Family: Amaryllidaceae
Zone: 5. Size: 12–18 inches, winter, spring

Daffodils are among the first flowers of spring and can create memorable displays in Southern gardens. Some types will naturalize, a few even in coastal areas of the

Naturalized narcissus near Shreveport, Louisiana. WCW

An early spring bouquet of campernelles, 'Grand Primo', Lent lily, and *N. jonquilla*. WCW

South. Fragrance adds to the garden and cut-flower value of these plants, which mark many abandoned homesites and cemeteries in our region. Some bloom as early as December, while others are as late as May. Since the later-flowering types are exposed to the heat of late spring, their flowers don't tend to last as long. From a scientific viewpoint, all daffodils belong to the genus *Narcissus*. This can be confusing, since the name "narcissus" also functions as a common name when it isn't underlined or italicized, and the first letter isn't capitalized. So, *Narcissus* is the genus or generic name for all daffodils, while "narcissus" is a common name for only certain types. In common usage, the large, trumpet-shaped types are often referred to as daffodils and the small, cluster-flowering sorts as narcissus, though even this varies in different parts of the country.

Daffodils prefer a sunny location. They will, however, bloom fairly well in open shade, under deciduous trees that allow the sun to reach the plants during late fall, winter, and early spring. Good drainage is essential. Raised beds should be constructed in areas where surface or internal drainage is inadequate. Ideally, prepare the beds a month or more in advance of planting the bulbs, to give the soil a chance to settle. If the soil is heavy clay, it should be loosened by tilling in gypsum or builder's sand. A mixture of organic materials such as peat, pine bark, or compost can be then applied as the next step in improving a heavy clay, but should only be added once drainage has been improved; otherwise organic additives may only increase the bulbs' tendency to rot. Generous amounts of organic material do improve sandy soils, though many fine displays of daffodils persist on land of very low organic content. Daffodils prefer a neutral pH in the range of 5.5 to 7.5. They should be planted in the fall. Unlike most tulips and hyacinths, narcissus normally require no artificial chilling in the refrigerator to succeed. Most daffodils may be planted 6 inches deep (to the base of the bulb) and 6 inches apart. Small types and miniatures may be planted as close as 1 inch apart and covered with as little as an inch of soil. After planting, beds should be lightly mulched with pinestraw, wheat straw, coastal Bermuda grass hay, or similar material. This also keeps down weed growth and prevents dirt from being splashed on the open flowers.

High-nitrogen fertilizers and fresh manures are not suitable for use with daffodils since they are sometimes associated with bulb rot. A pound to a pound and a half of low-nitrogen fertilizer, such as 8-24-24, may be broadcast over every 100 square feet of bed right after planting or just as the first leaf tips begin to emerge from the ground—a pint jar contains approximately one pound of granular fertilizer. Bone meal is a popular fertilizer for daffodils and other bulbs, though super-phosphate is preferred by some daffodil experts. Both materials are good sources of phosphorus, which may, however, be more economically available in standard fertilizer mixes.

After flowers have faded, it is

'Grand Primo' narcissus line an entrance walk in College Station, Texas. WCW

'Delibes' daffodil in a garden setting. NGO

always a temptation to tidy up by removing the daffodils' foliage. Resist this urge; controlled experiments have shown that cutting daffodil foliage shortly after blooming may kill the bulb, or at least weaken it so that it will set fewer blooms in subsequent years. Next year's flowers begin to form in the bulb immediately after bloom, and by interrupting the growth cycle of the plant, the removal of foliage at this critical time can abort the following season's bloom. Allow at least six weeks after the last flowers have faded before removing daffodil foliage.

Varieties Known to Naturalize in Texas and the Gulf South

Many daffodils will grow and bloom for a year or two in the South, but the ones found marking old homesites, cemeteries, and roadsides, the varieties unsurpassed for their reliability as naturalizers, are relatively few. All the varieties described are quite fragrant and work well as cut flowers. *N. jonquilla* is the true jonquil. It bears clusters of small, yellow, fragrant flowers held above deep green, rushlike foliage. Jonquils

bloom around February and naturalize prolifically by bulb and seed. *N. pseudonarcissus* is known as the Lent lily in Europe, but usually goes by "early daffodil" here since it usually blooms in February. It is the forerunner of modern varieties such as 'King Alfred'. Lent lilies are yellow, somewhat smaller than most modern daffodils and naturalize over most of the South.

N. × odorus is a delightful plant often known as 'Campernellii'. It is a natural hybrid cross between *N. pseudonarcissus* and *N. jonquilla* and has characteristics intermediate between its parents. 'Campernellii' flowers are borne in twos and threes above foliage that looks like very vigorous jonquil foliage. The flowers are bright yellow and very fragrant. It is a strong grower and naturalizer, but like many first generation hybrids, sets no seed. *N. tazetta* is considered the oldest of the cultivated narcissus. There are many forms of tazettas, which are also sometimes called polyanthos narcissus, or simply narcissus. Most bear white, cream, or yellow, small, cupped flowers that are extremely fragrant. Paper-white narcissus are in

the class and are often forced for early flowers. 'Grand Primo' is a very commonly found tazetta having large clusters of small white flowers on strong healthy stems, usually during February or early March. 'Grand Primo' often naturalizes all the way to the Gulf Coast. 'Golden Dawn' is a fairly recent tazetta that blooms later in the season and has large clusters of bright golden flowers. Large-flowering daffodils are quite popular as cut material and some naturalize quite well if they are inland a hundred or more miles from the coast. Varieties such as 'Ice Follies', 'Carlton', and 'Buccaneer' are among the best. No garden should be without the beauty and fragrance of narcissus. Whether massed in large bouquets or displayed singly in a bud vase they are indispensable for the Southern garden.

Special Note: Narcissus emit a gummy material from their stems that is harmful to other flowers. It is recommended to keep daffodils separately in water for 24 hours before combining with other flowers in fresh water. Do not cut any more of the stem before arranging.

Brazos penstemon reseeds easily and provides airy spikes of bloom. WCW

Penstemon spp.
(PEN-steh-mon)

BEARD-TONGUE, WILD FOXGLOVE

Family: Scrophulariacea
Zone 5. Size: 1–2 feet, spring

Penstemons may be found growing naturally from Central Texas to Kansas. They prefer open, sunny areas having well-drained, alkaline soils. *P. cobaea* is among our showiest native perennials. Its flowers resemble snapdragons and emerge in mid-spring. They are usually lavender, but may be white, purple, or any shade in the range between. The evergreen foliage forms small clumps of relatively large, simple leaves. Individual plants increase slowly, but may sometimes be divided in the fall or early spring. Seed propagation is reported to be successful, although my limited attempts have not been so. Wild foxglove is a plant of considerable landscape value, but a lack of commercial sources is limiting its use.

P. tenuis, sharp-sepal or Brazos penstemon, is a small-flowering species native to coastal areas of Texas and Louisiana. Individual flowers measure only about 3/4-inch, but they bloom profusely in loose, showy terminal clusters from mid-spring until early summer. The only color I have grown is a lavender-pink, but pale pink to dark rose forms are reported in the literature. P. tenuis is a good garden plant that creates an almost ethereal effect for many weeks. Its color is soft and combines well with other perennials in the garden and the vase. Mature height is about 2 feet. When blooms fade they should be cut back to near ground level, unless production is desired. They often respond to this pruning with another, but less showy, round of blossoms. They seem to prefer slightly acid soils but are not very particular about drainage. Culture is very easy and new seedlings often volunteer in the garden.

P. murrayanus, cup-leaf penstemon, is a brilliant red-flowering species native to the acid sands of East Texas. Foliage is distinctively blue-gray; 1¼-inch flowers open in pairs on showy terminal clusters that can be 3–6 feet tall. Seed sown in early fall or division of mature clumps at that time is usually successful, but good drainage is a must. I also grow a lovely pure white penstemon from a friend's garden in Beaumont. Individual flowers are not as large as *P. cobaea* but considerably larger than *P. tenuis.* Penstemons are beautiful spike flowers in the garden and for cutting.

Wild foxglove (Penstemon) may be used in the border and for cut-flower plantings. NGO

Peonies are excellent for garden and cutting use in the upper and middle South. WCW

Paeonia spp.
(PEE-an-ee)
PEONY
Family: Paeoniaceae
Zone: 8. Size: 1–2 feet, spring

One of the best-loved—and most beautiful—of cultivated flowers, peonies have played an important role in American gardens for more than a century. Unfortunately, they are not well adapted to the climate of the Deep South. But a number of older cultivars flourish in the Upper South, and peonies are an important element of perennial borders and cut-flower gardens in that region. The older peonies found in Southern gardens are usually varieties of either *P. officinalis* or *P. lactiflora*. *P. officinalis* in particular is a venerable garden plant. First described around 300 B.C. by the Greek scientist Theophrastus in his *Enquiry into Plants*, *P. officinalis* had trav-

eled as far as England before the beginning of the sixteenth century, when a double-flowered form was cultivated. These flowers were greatly admired because of the luminescent quality of the blossoms. Probably the most frequently found form of peony in old Southern gardens is 'Festiva Maxima', a cultivar of *P. lactifolia*.

Best results with peonies in the South are when they are planted on a site away from competing roots of heavily feeding trees, shrubs, and hedges, where the peonies can receive a half to a full day's sun. Some afternoon shade, however, results in longer-lasting flowers.

Peonies perform best when they are planted in well-prepared and drained soils and not transplanted for many years. Holes should be prepared 3 feet in diameter and 2 feet deep. Any good topsoil excavated from the hole

should be saved, but any hardpan or subsoil should be replaced with good, loamy soil. Mix the soil with about 1 pound of bone meal before refilling the hole to within 8 inches of its top, and tamp the soil fill down thoroughly. If necessary, more soil should be added and packed in sufficiently so winter rains will not cause settling. The next step is to mound soil in the center of the hole, so that when the dormant peony is set on the mound's top, the peony's "eye," or "crown," rests 1–2 inches above ground level. Fill the remainder of the planting hole, gently shaking the peony from time to time, to make sure that the soil settles in around the roots and fills any air pockets. When planting is completed, the top of the peony plant should be covered with about 1 inch of soil. Water well, and after the water has drained away, add soil if necessary to recover the peony's eyes. Do not mulch at this time, since in the South peonies relish exposure to winter cold. In the summertime, however, a mulch of pinestraw or bark helps to conserve moisture and prevent weeds. Remove the mulch in the fall and any dead stalks when the plant goes dormant. Otherwise, the only care necessary is to water occasionally during dry spells and to administer an annual feeding of one cup of bone meal per plant in the fall. Varieties that flower early or mid-season are usually more successful than late-flowering sorts in the South. Planting in the fall or winter is best.

Phlox spp.
(FLOX)
PERENNIAL PHLOX
Family: Polemoniaceae
Zone: 5. Size: 1–3 feet, spring, summer

Several of the perennial phlox have sufficient stems to make them useful as cut flowers. *Phlox divaricata* is valuable for its long season of bloom, compact form, and adaptability to many garden

situations. Showy clusters of flowers stand on erect stems well above the foliage in March and April. In addition to the common blue-lavender form, a creamy white cultivar, 'Fuller's White', and a violet-blue, 'Laphamii', are sometimes available. Flower stems range from 12–15 inches tall and the foliage is semi-evergreen, although of little landscape impact when not in bloom. *P. divaricata* is sometimes known as Louisiana phlox, and is native to the eastern United States and from Florida to East Texas. It grows best with morning sun and at least partial shade in the afternoon. Soil must be well-drained, and contain large amounts of organic material such as composted pine bark, peat, or

Top: Phlox paniculata in a Williamsburg, Virginia, border. NGO
Above: Phlox pilosa in the author's Mangham, Louisiana, garden. WCW
Bottom: Phlox paniculata in the magenta form is the hardiest of the phloxes. WCW

compost, if the phlox are to thrive. Apply a balanced fertilizer immediately after flowering. Phlox are not very drought-tolerant and benefit from a summer mulch and fairly frequent irrigation during dry spells. Propagation is by division, cuttings, or seed. Division is best done in the fall.

P. pilosa is better known as prairie or downy phlox, and is native to the pine woodlands of our region. It is similar to *P. divaricata* but bears pinkish-blue or, rarely, white spring flowers on 15-inch stems. Its flower season starts about two weeks after *P. divaricata* and usually extends into May and June. It is nicely scented and a wonderful landscape plant in my garden. My original start came from Ruth Knopf in South Carolina, who obtained it

Balloon flower, or *Platycodon*, does best in the middle and upper South. WCW

flowers open from the round buds in blue, pink, or white. There are also handsome, semi-double forms, as well as dwarf and large-growing cultivars. Though the balloon flower is a late spring bloomer, by removing spent flowers the gardener can extend its flowering into the summer. Well-drained and well-prepared soil is preferred, along with some protection from hot afternoon sun during the summer months. In wintertime, the balloon flower enters a deep dormancy from which it is slow to emerge in spring. Transplanting should be left to fall or early spring, with care being taken not to damage the plant's carrotlike tap root. Seedlings usually bloom the second year from sowing. Mature clumps may be divided, but it is not necessary to do so for the well-being of the plants. Balloon flower stems are sufficiently long to be practical and useful as cut flowers.

from the late Elizabeth Lawrence. No one knows for sure where Miss Lawrence obtained it, but it appears to be a superior clone. I have shared it with Petals from the Past Nursery in Jemison, Alabama, and other nurseries interested in propagating it.

    P. paniculata, summer phlox or border phlox, blooms for prolonged periods in summer. If kept well watered and spent flowers are removed, they often repeat in late summer and early fall. Staking may be necessary since normal height is 3–4 feet and stems are sometimes weak. Propagation is by division of clumps in fall or early spring, or from cuttings. Numerous colors are available, but by far the hardiest is the bright lavender-pink so often found in old Southern gardens. A white form is sometimes available and seems to persist in some gardens. *P. paniculata* prefers sandy loam soils and at least a half-day of direct sunlight. Flowers are fragrant and may be long-stemmed, making them useful as cut flowers.

Platycodon grandiflorus
(plat-ah-KOE-don)
BALLOON FLOWER
Zone: 4. Size: 1½–3 feet, late spring

Balloon flower receives its name from the shape of its buds. It is marginally adapted to the Gulf South, succeeding much better in areas a hundred or more miles inland from the coast. Star-shaped

Polianthes tuberosa
(pol-ee-AN-theez too-buh-ROE-suh)
MEXICAN TUBEROSE
Family: Agavaceae
Zone: 9. Size: 2–4 feet, late summer

Tuberose is among the most fragrant flowering plants of summer. Like corn and dahlias, the

The single Mexican tuberose is easier to grow than the double form for the South. WCW

Giant coneflower *(Rudbeckia maxima)* provides tall accents for gardens and for cutting. WCW

tuberose was domesticated by pre-Columbian Indians of Mexico, and not known as a wild plant. The tuberose is still popular in Mexican gardens, where it is called "Nardo" or "Azucena." *P. tuberosa* has been grown commercially for florists and bulb distributors in the San Antonio area for many years. It is also grown commercially in the south of France as a cut flower and as a source of perfume. Flowers are white, tubular, and loosely arranged on spikes that can reach 3–4 feet in height. The season of bloom is late summer to early fall. Foliage is long, slender, and grasslike, with little landscape value. 'Mexican Single' performs best in hot climates; double 'Pearl' sometimes fails to open properly, except in cooler fall weather. The plants grow from elongated tubers planted in mid-spring. These may be left in the ground year-round when grown in sunny, well-drained areas of zones 9 and 10, but in more northern locations the tubers should be lifted and stored like gladiolus after the foliage has yellowed. The tubers always show a point of green if they are alive and healthy. For a mass effect in the border, tubers should be planted 4–6 inches apart and 2 inches deep in well-prepared garden soil. Sunny locations with some protection from hot afternoon sun are ideal.

Rudbeckia maxima
(rood-BECK-ee-uh MAX-i-ma)
CONEFLOWER, BLACK-EYED SUSAN
Family: Compositae
Zone: 7. Size: 5–6 feet, summer

Coneflower is native to much of the Gulf South. It prefers moist soils and sunny locations where generous yields of 4-inch, black-eyed, yellow flowers appear during June and July. These blossoms are ray-type; the yellow petals center on the black cone that gives this flower its name. Foliage is a dense rosette of grayish-green leaves, 6–8 inches long, and 2–3 inches wide. Propagation is by seeds and division. Young seedlings may sometimes be found in the vicinity of parent plants, but *R. maxima* is not overly aggressive in the garden. Flower stems can be 4–6 feet tall, which makes them most impressive in the garden or as cut flowers. *R. maxima* is a striking plant to combine with ornamental grasses in perennial borders.

R. fulgida 'Goldsturm' is a compact selection that is fast becoming a favorite in Southern gardens. It blooms from mid- to late summer with masses of golden-yellow, black-eyed daisies and must be propagated by division, since it does not come true from seed. Seedlings are likely to be good garden plants, but not exactly like the parent. Since it is very vigorous in most of the South,

Rudbeckia 'Goldsturm' thrives in the middle and upper South, providing large masses of summer color. NGO

Mexican bush sage blooms in fall. WCW

'Goldsturm' may be divided each year in early spring or fall. It is much more successfully grown in areas a couple of hundred miles inland from the Gulf Coast. Stems are relatively short on 'Goldsturm', making it marginally useful as a cut flower.

Salvia leucantha
(SAL-vee-uh loo-CAN-tha)
MEXICAN BUSH SAGE
Family: Labiatae
Zone: 8. Size: 3–5 feet, late summer, fall

Mexican bush sage is one of the many useful salvias for Southern gardens. Even where it cannot be grown as a perennial due to sensitivity to cold, it is well worth growing as an annual. Individual plants can become rather large 5- to 6-foot mounds, but are more typically 3–4 feet. For a salvia the foliage is large and grayish-green in color. It blooms only in the fall, but is quite spectacular during late September, October, and November, when it sends up long, slender, rose-purple spikes studded with small white flowers. There are clones of this plant that bear flowers of other colors, my favorite being one that produces 6- to 10-inch spikes and flowers of a uniform deep rose-purple. Mexican bush sage furnishes good cut flowers and is very drought-tolerant. It is probably not reliably

Above: Salvia 'Indigo Spires' is excellent for cutting or garden display. WCW
Below: 'Mealy Sage' is a drought-tolerant source of blue color. NGO

root-hardy north of zone 9, but on sunny, well-drained sites has been reported to make it through some winters as far north as zone 7. Propagation is from cuttings, or by division of mature clumps in spring. Occasional pruning during the summer helps to keep the plant compact.

Salvia × 'Indigo Spires' is a fairly recent release from the Huntington Botanical Garden in California. It is reported to be a cross between *S. farinaceae* and *S. longispicata*. 'Indigo Spires' much resembles our native *S. farinaceae*, but instead of 4- to 6-inch flower spikes, 'Indigo Spires' spikes are much longer (up to 15 inches) and the color a more intense blue-purple. Each plant can be 3–4 feet tall, with a similar spread. Cold-hardiness does not extend much beyond zone 9, but this is another salvia well worth growing as an annual. Flowers appear from mid-spring through fall. Pruning during the growing season helps keep the plants compact and in nearly continuous flower. *S. madrensis*, forsythia sage, is a spectacular yellow-flowering species not usually cold-hardy north of zone 9. It is, however, worth growing as an annual in other areas where its 12- to 18-inch spikes of soft yellow flowers are prized for garden display and cut-flower use. Give it plenty of room since the clumps

Forsythia sage (*Salvia madrensis*) in the Broderson Garden, Tallahassee, Florida. WCW

can be 3–5 feet wide and as tall. Few plants offer so many flowers for such little attention. Propagation is from cuttings taken during the growing season.

Solidago altissima
(so-li-DAY-go al-TISS-a-ma)
GOLDENROD
Family: Compositae
Zone: 4. Size: 3–5 feet, early to late fall

There are many goldenrods common to our region, both in the garden and in the wild. For years they had a reputation for causing hay fever, but experts tell us that their pollen is heavy and not easily wind-borne. The culprit is usually the pollen of the far less attractive ragweed, which blooms at the same time. Goldenrods of this species grow larger and more vigorously in the garden than they do in their natural state, so allow them plenty of room. Some of the more dwarf cultivars are appealing, but even they border on the invasive in our climate. Flower heads are large and pyramidal in shape and golden-yellow in color. Leaves are lancelike and 3–5 inches long. Propagation is by seed or division of mature clumps, which should be cut back to the ground after the first hard freeze. Goldenrods prefer well-drained locations and full or nearly-full sun. They adapt to a wide range of growing situations, and provide color and cut flowers at a time of year when few plants are at their peak. Early spring is the ideal time to set out transplants.

Stokesia laevis
(sto-KEE-zee-uh LAY-vis)
STOKE'S ASTER
Family: Compositae
Zone: 7. Size: 1–2 feet, spring, fall

Sometimes known as "cornflower aster," stokesia is native from South Carolina to Florida, and west to Louisiana. In her book *A Southern Garden*, Elizabeth Lawrence extols its virtues, rating it "one of the best perennials for the South." Stoke's aster occurs naturally on moist but well-drained soil. Flowers are many petaled, 2–5 inches across, and an unusual wisteria-blue. Foliage is smooth and of a medium texture, with toothed, medium-green leaves 2–8 inches long. Stokesia prefer a sunny location but will tolerate filtered light. Several cultivars are available: 'Blue Danube' is a soft blue; 'Silver Moon' is not a pure white, but a nice color, and 'Blue Moon' tends to be more mauve. *S. laevis* blooms all summer in cooler climates, but for the South it more often yields a heavy spring bloom, followed by a summer's rest, then sometimes a rebloom in fall. Stems range from 10–15 inches long and the flowers are useful for cutting. Mature clumps may be divided in the fall. Seeds planted in the fall usually bloom the following summer.

Tagetes lucida
(ta-JE-tez loo-SEE-da)
MEXICAN MARIGOLD MINT
Family: Compositae
Zone: 8. Size: 2–3 feet, fall

T. lucida is native to Mexico and Guatemala, where its foliage is used for teas, seasoning, and medicinal purposes. When not in flower, this plant would be difficult to identify as a marigold since it has simple, lance-shaped leaves with slightly serrated margins. Another important, if less visible, difference is that *T. lucida* does not seem susceptible to spider

Goldenrod provides late-summer color for gardens and bouquets. WCW

Mexican marigold mint has become a favorite for its spicy foliage and bright fall flowers. WCW

mites, a pest that limits the use of common garden marigolds in the South. Mexican marigold mint bears clusters of golden-yellow, single flowers occurring from mid-fall until frost. Plants form attractive many-branched mounds, if grown in well-drained soil and sunny exposures. The leaves have a distinctive and pleasing aniselike scent somewhat like licorice, and are popular as a substitute for tarragon in seasoning vinegars. New plants root readily from cuttings taken during the growing season, and mature clumps may be divided in spring. Mexican marigold mint is impressive when combined with fall-blooming *Aster oblongifolius*, and Mexican bush sage (*S. leucantha*). It also contrasts nicely with *Eupatorium*

coelestinum, the fall-blooming ageratum or mist flower. Although they freeze back in late fall, my plants have always returned in spring, bigger and better than before. *T. lucida* is a good plant for sunny exposures in the South, where it appears to be drought-tolerant. The flowers are born on 12–18-inch stems, and are attractive for cutting. Pruning the plants lightly several times during the summer helps keep them compact.

Tulipa clusiana
(TOO-lip-uh cloo-see-AN-uh)
LADY TULIP
Family: Liliaceae
Zone: 9. Size: 1 foot, spring

Most gardeners in our region have found hybrid garden tulips to be annuals. *T. clusiana* is a small, beautiful species tulip that naturalizes in all of our region, with the possible exception of zone 10. The medium-sized flowers bloom about April 1. Exterior petals are a

Dutch tulips in a garden setting. JO KELLUM, ASLA

Clusiana tulips often naturalize in Southern gardens. WCW

Top: Masses of yellow tulips at Biedenharn Garden, Monroe, Louisiana. NGO
Above: Mixed beds of hybrid tulips. JO KELLUM, ASLA

Yucca filamentosa
(YUK-kuh fill-uh-men-TOW-sa)
ADAM'S NEEDLE
Family: Agavaceae
Zone: 7. Size, 3–4 feet, spring, summer

boldly colored red, and the inner petals white, a combination that results in a gay, candy-striped effect. Flowers exhibit daily sleep movement, expanding to flat white stars at noon, but closing to tight red buds each evening. Best performance occurs in sunny exposures and well-drained soil. The best plantings I have observed are in Central and West Texas, where they receive little or no irrigation during the summer months. Clumps may be divided and reset after the foliage yellows in late spring. *T. chrysantha* is similar to the lady tulip, and blooms about two weeks later to bear somewhat smaller flowers of yellow and red. It is a native of Iran

and thought by some to be merely a variety of *T. clusiana*. Hybrid tulips are well worth planting as annuals in the South but perform best if given an artificial cold treatment prior to planting. The lower part of the refrigerator is a good place to provide this chilling, but keep your tulips away from ripening apples and other fruit since the ethylene gas given off in their ripening process is damaging to the tulips. About six weeks of cold treatment at 40° F is sufficient for most tulips. Plant them in well-prepared and drained soil 6–8 inches apart and 4–6 inches deep with sunny exposure. Tulips continue to open and grow after cutting and are excellent cut flowers.

The yuccas best suited for perennials are almost without trunks and form mounding rosettes of a pointed-leaf foliage that is flexible, and not a major danger to passers-by. *Yucca filamentosa* is native from South Carolina to Mississippi and Florida on dry, infertile soils. It is fairly common in the nursery trade. Foliage is gray-green and flexible. Flowers make a real spectacle in the landscape. Fragrant, white, pendulous blossoms cluster in large masses atop slender spikes 4–8 feet tall. Yuccas do best in sunny exposures with well-drained soil. Once established, irrigation is rarely necessary. Propagation is from seed, by division of offsets, or from root cuttings. Trunkless yuccas are not easily transplanted, and are best purchased as container plants. They are valuable as specimens or masses in the border. Flower spikes are impressively large and popular for cutting.

Yuccas provide interesting foliage texture for the garden and impressive spikes for cutting. NGO

should be allowed to go semi-dormant during the winter and put on a low-water, low-fertilizer diet. Container-grown specimens bloom better after becoming somewhat crowded and root-bound. Callas are elegant as cut flowers or in the garden. They require a special location and some attention to reach perfection.

WCW

Calla lilies prefer partially shaded locations in the lower South. NGO

Zantedeschia aethiopica
(zan-tay-DES-key-uh ee-thee-OH-pi-kuh)
CALLA LILY
Family: Araceae
Zone: 9. Size: 2–3 feet, spring

Calla lilies prefer semi-shaded locations having rich, moist, well-drained soil that is slightly acid. They also prefer morning sun, afternoon shade, and a location adjacent to the south or east side of a structure. Callas are not very cold-hardy and may be lost during cold spells even in zone 9, although I have grown them for many years as perennials in zone 8. Foliage is large and heart-shaped, borne on long stems, and rich, dark green in color. Flowers are large, creamy-white, semi-funnel shaped spathes with prominent yellow centers.

Callas are traditional flowers of New Orleans and other Gulf Coast areas. Other species are *Z. albomaculata*, with white spotted foliage; *Z. elliottiana*, with yellow flowers and white-spotted foliage; and *Z. rehmannii*, a dwarf plant that produces small, pink flowers. Callas grow from thick, tuberous roots that should be planted in early spring. They are often culti-vated in containers, where they

Five

Flowering Trees, Shrubs, Vines, and Ground Covers of Merit

There has never been a time in the history of American landscape design when color was more important in public plantings than it is today. Drive the streets and roadways of the country and observe the level of interest devoted to flowering plants at corporate headquarters, local business establishments, service centers, fast food outlets, and recently designed residential plantings—nearly all are including in their plantings a lot of color, and they are not only featuring herbaceous bedding plants, but an increasing quantity of flowering trees and shrubs.

will be one that exhibits a lot of life and vitality at all seasons of the year.

Trees and shrubs, in addition, provide a degree of permanence to the landscape that bedding plants, even perennials, cannot do. As these woody elements grow, spread, and take on the characters that are uniquely theirs, the periods of their flowering become ever more significant.

Those who design gardens for individuals are also including a wide assortment of flowering trees and shrubs. Clients are urging designers to work into the design those plants which will provide color throughout the year. Nurseries, garden centers, and other suppliers of plants are recognizing the increased interest in flowering trees and shrubs, as reflected in the types of plants being featured in their sales yards.

In the South, in particular, flowering trees and shrubs have an important role to play. One of the best ways to emphasize the change of seasons where there is always a dominance of greens is by the introduction into planting schemes a significant number of woody flowering plants. A landscape punctuated with carefully selected flowering trees and shrubs

Flowering shrubs and perennials dominate this Atlanta shade garden. NGO

Where does one start to highlight the array of choices in these two major groups? Surely this region rivals any other part of the country for its distinctive and diverse assortment of trees, shrubs, vines, and ground covers that have special merit for cuttings to be used indoors. Included in the group that follows are many of the old favorites and several less familiar but equally exciting flowering woody ornamentals.

As with other plants to be cut for indoor uses, the best time to make cuttings of woody materials is either in the early morning or late afternoon. Trees and shrubs have very hard, woody stems. Sometimes the uptake of water is relatively slow. Most people who do a lot of arranging with woody plants advocate lightly crushing the ends of the stems, so as to encourage a faster uptake of water. Use tepid water—water that is sufficiently hot to the touch, and which will stay warm for about an hour after placing the plant material stems in the water. Strip all foliage from the lower one-third to one-half of the stems, so that foliage will not be in the water. Three to four inches of water in a container is sufficient. Studies indicate that plants do not benefit from having water up to the floral heads over those with their stems in a small amount of water. Always use a floral preservative at the prescribed rate on the packaging. Large containers of water require a correspondingly large amount of preservatives. However, it is wasteful to use more than is needed. If a floral foam is to be used in a container, soak it in water with the prescribed amount of preservative dissolved in it. Plants with milky saps should have their stem ends burned or placed in hot water to coagulate the oozing sap. Other plants requiring this special treatment are noted in sections of the book devoted to individual plants.

Cross vine cultivar 'Apricot Beauty', a mannerly climber and an excellent choice for garden structures. T. E. POPE

GARDEN PLANTS

Bignonia capreolata
(*Anisostichus capreolata*)
(big-KNOWN-i-a kap-rae-o-LAY-ta)
CROSS VINE
Family: Bignoniaceae
Zone: 6–9. Size: 40–50 feet, climbing vine

The cross vine is a strong, vigorously-growing, native vine occurring over most of the region. This woody, high-climbing vine produces beautiful, orange-red, funnel-shaped flowers often hidden in the canopies of trees and other vegetation. It is an excellent vine to use on garden structures. The cultivar 'Tangerine Beauty' produces a huge number of flowers in spring and early summer. This vine is particularly useful to cover chainlink and other wire fencing. Flowering shoots can be cut, placed in water with a floral preservative, and conditioned for arranging. Open flowers drop in a couple of days, but buds persist for several more days. This vine has beautiful line quality and handsome bark. Turtles relish the fallen blossoms of cross vine.

Buddleia spp.
(BUD-lea-a)
BUTTERFLY BUSH, FOUNTAIN BUDDLEIA
Family: Loganiaceae
Zone: 5–9. Size: 6–12 feet by 10 feet

As the name implies, a specimen of butterfly bush is a choice plant for attracting butterflies and other beneficial insects to the garden. The large, gangly, deciduous shrub with velvety, willowlike foliage produces a profusion of long, somewhat drooping conical-shaped, lilaclike flowers in early summer and will produce other blooms sporadically throughout the season. Colors include blue, purple, pink, and white. Provide full sunlight and a well-drained soil for the butterfly bushes. The old-fashioned butterfly bush, *B. alternifolia*, should be thinned annually of old, non-productive canes, while the many new cultivars of *B. davidii*, grown primarily for their very prominent spike flowers, should be pruned back nearly to the ground every late winter just before new growth begins. Some popular garden

Butterfly bush in full bloom. NGO

choices in this group include 'Black Knight' (deep purple), 'Charming' (deep rose-pink), 'White Bouquet' (white), and 'Royal Red' (red). Condition cut flowers in warm water for a couple of hours before placing them in an arrangement. Depending on the maturity of the flower heads, the tall spikes of flowers can be expected to last for about three days in a cut state.

Callistemon rigidus
(kal-lis-TEA-mon RI-ji-dus)
BOTTLEBRUSH
Family: Myrtaceae
Zone: 8-10. Size: 6-10 feet by 6 feet

Bottlebrush is an evergreen, upright-growing shrub with narrow, rigid leaves grown primarily for its showy, dense, bottlebrush-shaped clusters of bright red flowers produced in early summer and sporadically at other times during the summer months. It is relatively cold-tender in landscapes away from the coast, and should always be planted in protected places

with full sunlight and very well-drained soil that contains a generous amount of sand. Because the flowers are so bright and showy, it is tempting to cut flowers for arranging, and they do well for a day or two before they begin shedding, but this plant is not noted for its longevity as a cut flower.

Camellia japonica
(ka-MEL-i-a ja-PON-i-ka)
CAMELLIA
Family: Theaceae
Zone: 7–10. Size: 8–15 feet by 6 feet

The queen of the winter landscape across the South is surely the camellia. With careful cultivar selection, camellias can bloom from late November through April. This dense evergreen shrub with glossy, leathery foliage grows slowly, but produces an abundance of flowers from the beginning of its presence in the garden. In fact, it is wise to remove some of the flower buds to encourage

more growth, before allowing a plant to come into full flower production. A great feature of the camellia is the diversity in bloom color and type. Pink, red, and white are common colors in both single and double flowers. Blooms are subject to damage during hard frosts and freezes. Camellia plants must have a well-drained, acid soil and do best if protected from direct sunlight during the hot part of the day in summer; this is particularly true for young plants. Old, mature specimens seem to fare reasonably well in direct sunlight. They are relatively easy to grow in containers, if ground bed conditions cannot otherwise be met.

There is an old adage which holds that a cut camellia flower out of water will last just as long as those with stems in water. This is not true. Blooms will last considerably longer if their cut stems are in water. Camellias are often cut with very short stems.

Sasanqua camellia (*C. sasan-*

Bottlebrush thrives in hot, dry, sunny locations. T. E. POPE

Well-chosen cultivars of camellias can produce flowers from late autumn through winter. T. E. POPE

'Madame Galen' is an excellent cultivar of the trumpet vine. NGO

qua), a close relative, produces an abundance of small flowers and begins blooming six weeks or more before most japonicas. Entire branches laden with sasanqua flowers are often cut for indoor use, whereas single flowers of the japonicas are normally cut for indoor exhibition.

Campsis radicans
(KAMP-sis RAD-i-kanz)
TRUMPET VINE
Family: Bignoniaceae
Zone: 5–9. Size: 20–30 feet, vine

The trumpet vine is found growing over virtually the entire South. Unfortunately, many people miss seeing its clusters of large, bright orange, trumpet-shaped flowers because they are often out of view—growing high in treetops or over masses of volunteer vegetation. This woody, deciduous climbing vine is relatively easy to manage, but the aerial rootlets do cling to virtually any surface in its path. The fast-growing trumpet vine is great for providing quick cover for garden structures. Bright, showy flowers throughout the summer months are an additional reward for those who give it a home. It also grows and blooms well when planted adjacent to the trunks of rough-barked, high-branched trees, like pines and pecan, that can provide tall structural support. Two exceptionally fine cultivars include 'Madame Galen' and 'Crimson Trumpet.' Both produce intensely shocking, orange-red flowers. Flowers are produced in clusters that can be cut for indoor use, but blooms persist for only a few days.

Cercis canadensis
(SIR-sis kan-a-DEN-sis)
REDBUD, EASTERN REDBUD
Family: Leguminosae
Zone: 4–9. Size: 20–30 feet by 20 feet

The redbud is one of our most prized Southern flowering trees that produce an abundance of rosy-pink, pealike flowers. This broad-spreading, deciduous tree comes into bloom very early and blooms persist for a relatively long period because temperatures are generally still low in early spring. Redbud self-seeds freely in parts of the region where it thrives and where soil is well-drained. Like dogwood, the redbud can grow beneath pines and adjacent to

Two colors of redbuds brighten a spring garden at Biltmore Estate in Asheville, North Carolina. USED WITH PERMISSION FROM BILTMORE ESTATE, ASHEVILLE, NC; JO KELLUM, ASLA

other high-branched trees. While individual specimens can live for thirty years or more, as a general rule redbuds are relatively short-lived trees. Their branches have beautiful line qualities. Nearly every one, with its zigzag pattern, makes a unique cut specimen. Consequently, redbud branches are very popular in Japanese flower arranging.

One caution: flowers must have very strong light if they are to make a commanding presence indoors. The dark, rosy-pink to magenta color is quite recessive, because of the dominance of blue in their color. This condition becomes particularly noticeable indoors under artificial light, but is even apparent when trees bloom in shade. The cultivar 'Alba' is a delightful white-flowering form. The Texas star redbud is a smaller, more shrublike tree, but is a prolific bloomer. 'Forest Pansy' is noted for its handsome scarlet-purple foliage.

Chaenomeles speciosa
(ke-NOM-e-lez spee-si-O-sa)
FLOWERING QUINCE
Family: Rosaceae
Zone: 4–9. Size: 6–10 feet by 6 feet

Flowering quince is among our earliest spring-flowering shrubs. Quince can begin flowering with a

Flowering quince is among the earliest of the spring-flowering shrubs. T. E. POPE

The Chinese white fringe tree, an excellent flowering tree for small spaces. WCW

bloom here and there as early as late December and early January, followed by its big show of color coming just after the danger of frost has past in late winter. Flower colors include the common orange-red, red, pink, and white. Green, apple-shaped fruit are somewhat common on old specimens growing in the upper South. A large, broad-spreading flowering quince can live for many years with virtually no care, but performs best if old, gray-colored canes are removed periodically to promote new growth on which flowers will appear the following year. Provide well-drained soil and full sunlight, although this ornamental will grow in rather poor, dry soils.

The flowering quince has beautiful line qualities in its branches. A carefully selected

branch can stand alone, or stems can be cut to give an arrangement more height and a stronger presence. Stems of quince have been mainstays in Japanese arrangements for centuries because of their exquisite branching patterns and delicately positioned flower buds and open blossoms along the thin, shiny, bare stems. Although the individual flowers do not persist for a lengthy period, stems remain handsome for weeks in an arrangement.

Chionanthus spp.
(ki-o-NAN-thus)
WHITE FRINGE TREE
Family: Oleaceae
Zone: 4–8. Size: 15–25 feet by 15 feet

There are two delightful spring-flowering fringe trees. One is the white fringe tree, or grancy gray-

Native white fringe tree blooms in early spring. T. E. POPE

Citrus in flower and fruit. CHARLES F. FRYLING JR.

normally cut only for special occasions like weddings, have a delightful fragrance, but are relatively short-lived as a cut material. The range of their growth is drastically limited by temperature, although they can tolerate a wide range of soil types and sunlight exposure. Temperatures in the low twenties will injure the foliage, and low-teen temperatures over a few days and nights will kill plants, roots and all.

Kumquats and lemons make handsome tub specimens for patios, terraces, and other outdoor living areas. The sweet scent of their blooms, which appear over a long period, is a delight. The wild orange, *Poncirus trifoliata*, produces small fragrant flowers and a colorful lemonlike fruit in late autumn, but it is heavily armed with long pointed thorns which make it a very unfriendly specimen to work with. In early days branches were popular as gumdrop trees. Fruit emit a wonderful fresh-fruit fragrance when placed in a warm, humid room.

beard, *C. virginicus*, that is native to the southeastern United States; the other is an introduced species, the Chinese fringe tree, *C. retusus*. Both are relatively small-growing, deciduous trees that are of ideal size for small gardens. The native tree produces very showy *panicles* (loose, irregularly formed flower clusters) of fleecy-white, fringelike petals, while the Chinese form produces relatively dense clusters of snow-white flowers at the end of new shoots. The Chinese species has a very interesting trunk form, while the native species is more shrublike before it eventually grows into its mature tree form. Branches of both species hold up relatively well in water with a floral preservative added to it to extend the life of the flowers.

Citrus spp.
(SIT-rus)
CITRUS—SATSUMA, LEMON, and KUMQUAT
Family: Rutaceae
Zone: 9–10. Size: 8–12 feet by 8 feet

For a sweet fragrance that fills the air, members of the citrus family are unsurpassed. Citrus blossoms,

Clematis spp.
(KLEM-a-tis)
CLEMATIS
Family: Ranunculaceae
Zone: 4–9. Size: 10–15 feet, vine

This is a large and complex genus comprising hundreds of introduced cultivars of delightfully-colored flowering vines. One of the true treasures among the species is the native autumn clematis, *Clematis paniculata*. It is

White-flowering sweet autumn clematis perfumes the late summer and autumn landscape. WCW

Clematis 'Nelly Moser' has large, impressive, long-lasting flowers. JO KELLUM, ASLA

Cornus florida
(KOR-nus FLOR-i-da)
FLOWERING DOGWOOD
Family: Cornaceae
Zone: 4–9. Size: 20–30 feet by 20 feet

a vigorously growing evergreen throughout most of the region, and it will cover virtually everything in its path. A special feature of this clematis is the fact that it blooms when few other plants are in flower. It produces a blanket of tiny, white, fragrant flowers in late August and early September, thus the name autumn clematis. Although it grows well as a cultivated vine trained on garden structures, this native vine can also be seen growing on volunteer vegetation over most of the region. Many of the hybrids are twining, deciduous vines grown primarily for their showy blooms in white, blue, pink, and purple. Some produce large saucer-shaped blossoms

up to 8 inches in diameter. The hybrids are relatively tame growers, and are easily trained to grow on small garden structures. They can be allowed to grow over other choice garden plants because they do not pose a threat, as do many of the more aggressively growing vines.

Cuttings of the autumn clematis last several days in water. It is a special treat for use at autumn weddings. Many of the hybrid clematises produce very large decorative seed heads that can also be used in arrangements. They should be sprayed with a hair spray to keep them from shedding.

There are few trees more beloved than the flowering dogwood. Across the entire region people of all dispositions and attitudes toward gardening long to have this small flowering tree in their gardens. However, few trees are more temperamental in their growth requirements than dogwoods. Where soils and light exposure are just right, they flourish. There are places in the South where the white of dogwood blossoms cover virtually entire neighborhoods like patches of snow. Such is the case on the rolling hills of Atlanta. On the other hand, most attempts to make this tree grow in "foreign," amended soils are met with disaster. As a general rule, dogwoods grow well where the general topography of the land is slightly rolling, and soils are moist but well-drained—in other words, those locations where pines grow. Pines are good companion plants for dogwoods because they are high-branched and can form a

An impressive grove of flowering dogwoods growing at the Governor's Mansion, Columbia, South Carolina. NGO

A branch of the flowering dogwood lasts well as a cut specimen. NGO

Pearlbush, a large flowering shrub for the upper South. NGO

protective canopy from the hot, searing, direct noon-day sunlight. The best general exposure for dogwoods is a south to southeastern orientation, since the tree responds quite favorably to morning sunlight, but needs protection from the hot western sun. There are numerous cultivars, with white being the most popular, but pink-flowering selections are equally spectacular in the landscape. Two troublesome diseases, *anthracnose* and *discula*, are severe problems of dogwoods, especially in the southeastern part of the region.

Cut branches of dogwoods hold up relatively well if cut ends are crushed and immediately placed in hot water and then in a floral preservative. Because dogwood branches grow horizontally on the tree, they are difficult to position in a vertical container. Try to exhibit them in the same position that they grow on the tree. Cut stems of the flowering dogwood are especially handsome at night under artificial light.

Deutzia scabra
(DOOT-zi-a SKAY-bra)
DEUTZIA
Family: Saxifragaceae
Zone: 4–8. Size: 8–12 feet by 8 feet

Deutzia has been a popular, large, white-flowering shrub in Southern gardens since colonial days. It is a tough, persistent deciduous shrub which blooms just after the big spring show of color from other spring-flowering shrubs and trees. Its moment of prominence is quite noticeable, because it comes at a crucial time in the garden when few other shrubs are in bloom. This shrub works nicely tucked into an established shrub border, but needs considerable

space to develop fully. The tan-colored, exfoliating bark is a nice winter feature of deutzia. White flowers are produced on long, ascending stems, thus making deutzia a fine choice for cuttings where tall, elegant stems of white flowers are needed. Unfortunately, the blooms begin shedding after a couple of days in water. This old-time favorite needs good drainage and preferably full sunlight for most of the day. It is subject to root rot in poorly-drained soils, but otherwise has few troublesome pests. Specimens have been known to survive in old plantings for over fifty years. Long, slender branches of deutzia are wonderful for late spring arrangements, even if the flowers do not last for a long period.

Exochorda racemosa
(ek-so-KOR-da ra-se-MO-sa)
PEARLBUSH
Family: Rosaceae
Zone: 5–8. Size: 8–12 feet by 8 feet

Pearlbush is one of the lesser-known deciduous shrubs of the region and grows best in parts of the South where it can receive sufficient cold temperatures to satisfy

A large specimen deutzia at the Hermitage in Nashville. NGO

Above: A mass of forsythia in a meadow of naturalized spring bulbs. NGO
Right: Forsythia, a popular spring-flowering shrub. NGO

its special dormancy needs. Otherwise, plants bloom sporadically in the spring. It is a shrub that produces pure white flowers, but is rather nondescript at other times of the year. A fine specimen of this old garden favorite can produce a mass of pearllike buds that open into pure white flowers in spring. Provide pearlbush full sunlight and well-drained soil. Remove old, non-productive canes near the base of the plant periodically to encourage new growth and more consistent flowering on previous season's growth. Stems of the pearlbush in bud and full bloom are especially effective in large arrangements, but open flowers begin shedding petals in a day or so after being cut.

Forsythia x *intermedia*
(for-SITH-i-a in-ter-MEED-di-a)
FORSYTHIA, GOLDEN BELLS
Family: Oleaceae
Zone: 5–8. Size: 6–10 feet by 6 feet

Forsthyia may stand alone as the favorite of all the spring-flowering shrubs because of its dramatic display of bright yellow, bell-shaped flowers on bare branches. It comes into glorious color while most other plants are still in full winter dormancy. Plants require cold temperatures to bloom profusely. In parts of the region with mild winters and hot summers, forsythias are not very dependable, and blooms occur sporadically over a long period. On the other hand, specimens growing in the northern part of the region make a dazzling display of yellow color. Its color is so intense that flowering

specimens can be spotted in gardens from the air as planes approach cities for landing in late winter. Forsythia is a great companion plant with spring-flowering bulbs. This is a woody shrub grown commercially for its striking yellow flowers tightly arranged on long slender canes. It is a late winter and spring favorite for making huge, mass arrangements or using a single cutting of a stem to place on a small table.

Gardenia jasminoides
(gar-DE-ni-a jas-min-OI-dez)
GARDENIA, CAPE JASMINE
Family: Rubiaceae
Zone: 8–9. Size: 5–8 feet by 6 feet

For fragrance there are few plants that can rival this powerfully-scented old garden favorite. The fragrance of the gardenia is so strong that it is offensive to some people. It has been a mainstay for Southern gardens since it was introduced into this country from China during colonial days. A single specimen will produce an abundance of blooms and can make a significant presence in a planting, so there is seldom a need for mass plantings of gardenias, although they are effective in hedge plantings. They also com-

Top: Gardenias are an old favorite, fragrant-flowering Southern shrub. NGO
Above: The lesser-known hip gardenia bears colorful fruit in autumn and winter. NGO
Right: Carolina jessamine, a fragrant-flowering evergreen, vine is prevalent over the entire South. T. E. POPE

and attractive red fruit (*hips*) during the winter months. This relatively rare species has received considerable recognition at Rosedown Gardens in St. Francisville, Louisiana.

Unfortunately there are several insect pests that attack gardenia foliage and tender stems, and plants turn yellow when soils are deficient in iron. An insecticide spray can take care of the insects, and a soil-amending chemical can be applied to bring back a strong, deep green color. Cut blooms turn brown relatively soon, but they are still one of our most popular flowers for weddings bouquets and for Mother's Day corsages in late spring and early summer. To keep cut blossoms from turning brown, handle them with wet hands or with soft, moistened cotton gloves. Try working with the flower without touching the petals.

Gelsemium sempervirens
(jel-SE-mi-um sem-per-VI-renz)
CAROLINA YELLOW JESSAMINE
Family: Loganiaceae
Zone: 7–9. Size: 20–30 feet, vine

Carolina yellow jessamine, often called "yellow jasmine," is a prolific native vine frequently seen growing throughout the South along woodlands edges and into and over other volunteer vegetation. It also has many virtues as a tamed vine. It thrives in full sun-

bine well with other plants in shrub borders.

It is essential to provide this shrub with moist, fertile, well-drained, acid soils and direct sunlight for several hours of the day for best performance. Gardenias do well near buildings, where soils tend to say cool and moist. Several special cultivars that have been introduced because of their outstanding floral and foliage qualities include 'August Beauty', 'Mystery', and 'Veitchii'. The hip gardenia, *G. thunbergia*, produces a profusion of small, single white flowers

Native witch hazel blooms in late autumn when very little else is in flower. T. E. POPE

ing shrub that produces showy, yellow flowers in late winter and downy, dull green foliage that turns bright yellow in autumn.

Witch hazels are excellent for cutting and displaying indoors. Branches have beautiful, striking lines all year. In autumn, yellow flowers brighten interiors that are becoming darker as the days become shorter. The flowers persist for a week or more on cut branches.

light, but is not particular about soils or other growing conditions. This vine begins flowering in mid- to late winter and reaches its peak of bloom in early spring, when it produces a mass of yellow, trumpet-shaped, sweet-scented flowers. Yellow jessamine is especially well adapted for growing on garden structures like pergolas, arbors, trellises, and garden fences. Because of its rampant growth, prune in mid-spring after bloom to keep growth controlled. 'Pride of Augusta' is a double-flowering cultivar. The long, wiry vines make excellent cuttings in the bud and full-bloom stages. Cuttings remain fresh for about a week in water.

er trees) species, native throughout the eastern United States to Texas, and is especially prevalent along sandy streams in the South. Companion plants include the native azaleas, maples, dogwood, beech, yellow poplar, red oaks, and several species of viburnum. Witch hazels perform well in a wide range of soils, provided they are well drained. An outstanding characteristic of this native is its gracefully-growing horizontal branching. A close relative, *H. × intermedia* 'Arnold Promise', grows well in the upper South and produces very prominent yellow-green flowers. The Chinese witch hazel, *H. mollis*, is a broad-spread-

Hydrangea spp.
(hi-DRAN-je-ah)
HYDRANGEAS
Family: Hydrangeaceae
Zones: 7–9. Size: 4–10 feet by 6 feet

This genus comprises some of the most important plants in Southern gardens. They include natives like the oakleaf hydrangea (*H. quercifolia*) that produce conical-shaped white flowers in spring. The popular common garden hydrangea (*H. macrophylla*) received a sensational welcome when it was introduced to England and finally to this country from its native China in the nineteenth century.

Hydrangeas grow best in exposures that receive morning

Hamamelis virginiana
(ham-a-ME-lis ver-jin-i-A-na)
WITCH HAZEL
Family: Hamamelidaceae
Zone: 4–9. Size: 12–15 feet by 8–10 feet

Witch hazel is a large native, deciduous, spreading shrub to small tree that produces rather striking sulfur-yellow flowers with crimped, ribbonlike petals, and wavy-edged foliage that turns golden-yellow in the autumn. The flowers are especially noticeable because witch hazels come into bloom in late autumn, when most other woody plants are going into their winter dormancy. The leaves are two to four inches long and three inches wide. It is a relatively common *understory* (a plant that grows beneath the canopy of larg-

A closeup of hydrangea blooms. NGO

Hydrangeas along a garden path. NGO

Oakleaf hydrangea is native to our Southern woodlands near streams and on bluffs.
T. E. POPE

sunlight and are protected from the hot sunlight during other parts of the day. The common hydrangea does exceptionally well on the north side of buildings, where soils stay moist and the plants receive only indirect sunlight. Hydrangeas do not generally last long beneath the canopy of large trees because the shallow roots have difficulty competing for moisture with the extensive root system of most trees.

Soil pH affects the color of the garden hydrangea. An acid condition (low pH) results in blue color, while an alkaline soil reaction will cause blooms to become pink. Prune hydrangeas after they bloom in mid- to late summer. Caution: winter pruning of the dormant, dead-appearing canes will remove next year's blooms! The garden hydrangea produces large, globular floral heads of mostly showy, sterile flowers, while lacecap hydrangeas produce flat, round heads of both fertile and infertile flowers.

New, very showy double-flowering cultivars of the native oakleaf hydrangea are becoming very popular for garden plantings. These include 'Harmony', 'Roanoke', and 'Snow Flake'. These larger-flowering forms may

be gradually taking the place of the smaller, single-flowering native plants.

Two other species of hydrangeas increasing in popularity are mountain hydrangea (*H. arborescens* 'Annabelle'), a mounding, deciduous shrub that produces large 12-inch, white, densely-packed rounded flower heads in mid-summer; and the panicle hydrangea (*H. paniculata* 'Grandiflora'), oftentimes referred to as the "Peegee" hydrangea, a very tall-growing deciduous shrub that produces lacy, white flower heads to 18 inches tall in late summer. Because white-flowering

plants are so popular in warm, Southern landscapes, the white-flowering hydrangea species and cultivars are in great demand. Strong contrast with the dominant greens in most gardens really makes them powerful accents in both garden plantings and when cut for indoor arrangements.

Hydrangeas have many stages of development when they are useful as cut flowers. The large, rounded bloom heads of the common hydrangea can be used in arrangements when they are in the chartreuse-colored bud stage in late spring; the full-blown bloom stage in later spring through early

The snowball hydrangea produces huge white blooms in summer. NGO

summer; an intermediate chartreuse green to pinkish mature stage that occurs during mid- to late summer; and as dried blossoms in late autumn. Hydrangea flowers at varying stages of development are prized as naturally dried plant material. Fresh-cut flower stems should be slightly crushed and placed in hot water a couple of hours before placing them in a floral preservative in the arrangement container. Most stay very turgid after being cut. However, even after recommended conditioning practices are followed, some blooms go to "sleep" and become limp. These are normally blossoms on very tender

shoots. Recutting the tender stems and repeating the warm water conditioning process will sometimes bring them back to a turgid condition.

Dried flowers that occur naturally in late summer and autumn make great cuttings for holiday season arrangements. Delay harvesting until flowers are mature (green stage and in a semi-dried condition), remove all foliage, and hang flowers in an upside down position in a warm room to complete the drying process prior to arranging. Drying has occurred when the flowers rattle like paper when touched or shaken. Some people hang stems of flowers in

brown bags for drying. Flowers dried in this manner tend to retain their beautiful natural colors, lasting for months in dried arrangements.

Kerria japonica 'Pleniflora'
(KER-ri-a ja-PON-i-ka)
JAPANESE ROSE, KERRIA
Family: Rosaceae
Zone: 5–9. Size: 6–8 feet by 6 feet

The Japanese rose is a vigorously growing, heavily *suckering* (new plants formed from the underground stems of the parent plants), deciduous shrub that has been an old garden favorite survivor which blooms year after year with relatively little attention. It performs best in a well-drained soil and full sunlight, but is not as temperamental as other members of the same family. Bright, golden-yellow, double flowers appear on tall, ascending green canes in early spring. A few blooms appear sporadically throughout the summer, but they do not make a big show. The Japanese rose does surprisingly well under partially shaded conditions. Blooming is more profuse in the upper South, where moderately cold temperatures occur. Cuttings of the green flowering canes can be quite dramatic in arrangements, but blooms last for a relatively short time before petals begin shedding. This is one member of the rose family with no major plant pests.

Kolkwitzia amabilis
(kolk-KWIT-zi-a a-MAB-a-lis)
BEAUTYBUSH
Family: Caprifoliaceae
Zone: 5–9. Size: 8–10 feet by 8 feet

The species name, *amabilis*, meaning lovable or pleasing, is a good description of beautybush, a mainstay in old gardens of the upper South, where temperatures are moderately cold. It is a very large, fast-growing, deciduous shrub that performs well in a wide range of soil conditions, even those which are relatively dry. It is a sun

Kerria, or Japanese rose, has green stems and single or double flowers and an open, airy form. NGO

Kolkwitzia, or beautybush, a very large-flowering shrub best adapted to the upper South. NGO

plant and should be given ample space to grow, so it can express its commanding, broad-spreading, vaselike form. A typical shrub is covered with a mass of off-white to pinkish-colored, bell-shaped flowers in spring. As with most spring-flowering shrubs, periodically remove some of the old, non-productive canes in the center of the plant to encourage the formation of new, productive flowering wood. Long, arching, bloom-laden stems make handsome cuttings, but flowers last for only a few days indoors.

Lagerstroemia indica
(la-ger-STRE-mi-a IN-die-ka)
CRAPE MYRTLE
Family: Lythraceae
Zone: 7–9. Size: 15–25 feet by 12 feet

Few flowering trees are held in higher esteem in the South than are the crape myrtles. It is virtually a tree for all the seasons—tall, loose panicles of beautiful flowers for over three months during summer, striking autumn color, and smooth, silky sculptural trunks in winter. Northerners who migrate to the South are often dismayed to find that they dare not plant their beloved lilacs, but find some degree of solace by planting

Above: A close-up of the popular watermelon-red crape myrtle. T. E. POPE
Bottom: 'Near East' crape myrtle is noted for its prolific, flesh-pink clusters of flowers. T. E. POPE

crape myrtles, the "Southern lilac." In recent years, there have been many new cultivars that provide a broad range of color options, including pink, lavender, peppermint (red and white mixed), red, and several whites, to name a few. Provide crape myrtles full sunlight and well-drained soil for satisfactory performance, but they are actually quite tolerant of a wide range of growing conditions. They have traditionally been among our toughest and most enduring flowering trees.

Unfortunately of late, several plant pests are causing premature leaf drop during the hot, humid days of late summer. *Aphids* (leaf insects) and *sooty mold* (leaf fungus) appear to be reducing the

Top: Lonicera americana, a handsome honeysuckle and an excellent vine for growing on garden structures. WCW

Above: The coral honeysuckle is a prolifically growing vine, but is quite manageable when compared to some other honeysuckles. This one attracts large numbers of hummingbirds. T. E. POPE

shed rather freely soon after being cut. Because flowering occurs during a part of the summer when few other garden plants are in flower, they are most effective for short periods.

Lonicera spp.
(lo-NIS-er-a)
HONEYSUCKLES
Family: Caprifoliaceae
Zone: 6–9, Sizes: varying

The honeysuckle family comprises a large and complex group of wonderful ornamental plants of all types from the woody, twining, climbing vines to large shrubs. One of the introduced exotics, the Japanese honeysuckle that was brought to this country many years ago, has escaped cultivation, and is today quite pesky in our native landscapes. Others are among our most prized ornamentals. Several of the somewhat nondescript plants are included in the list of garden honeysuckles, but their claim to fame among gardeners is their delightfully sweet-scented flowers. The winter honeysuckle (*L. fragrantissima*), an old garden favorite, has been in this country for over 150 years. It blooms in late winter, at the earliest sign of warm weather. The lemon-scented fragrance from the small, creamy-white flowers fills the garden air. This plant performs well in full sunlight to partial shade and will grow in most soils. A semi-evergreen shrub, it does well tucked into an established shrub border. Periodically remove old woody canes at the bottom of a large shrub mass to keep it thrifty. In the more northern part of the region, belle honeysuckle (*L. × bella*) is a deciduous shrub that produces a mass of white to off-pink flowers. The flowers are followed by very attractive red fruit in mid- to late summer.

Coral honeysuckle (*L. sempervirens*) is a very manageable flowering vine with orange-red trumpet-shaped blooms. People who

overall vigor of this great Southern tree. It is too early to tell to what extent the long-range implications of these pests will be. Leaves and flowers falling on paved surfaces like terraces and patios can be very troublesome. Never cut back the primary trunk or trunks of a crape myrtle. Drastic cutting back of the main trunks destroys the clean-sweeping, sculptural lines, a classic feature of this delightful summer-flowering tree. If necessary, entire trunks can be removed to reduce mass, and removal of fast-growing "water sprouts" around the base of mature plants is a recommended practice. Through the years, crape myrtle flowers have been used for many functions where flowers are needed for short periods, like in church and wedding arrangements, because blooms

Chinese witch hazel, or Loropetalum, is available in green and this purple leaf form, 'Rubrum'. T. E. POPE

love hummingbirds always place this vine at the top of their list of plants to include in the hummingbird garden. Other honeysuckle vines of merit include the gold-flame honeysuckle (*L.* x *heckrottii*); Hall's honeysuckle (*L. japonica*), a good ground cover for the dry parts of the region; and *L. americana* produces a profusion of beautiful pink and cream-colored flowers. Do not overlook the delightful fruit that several of the honeysuckles produce. Two favorites include amur honeysuckle (*L. maackii*) and tatarian honeysuckle (*L. tatarica*). Birds relish the fruit of honeysuckles.

Cuttings of honeysuckles hold up quite well in arrangements, and some woody branches root while in water. It is worth having a clump of the winter honeysuckle if for no other reason than the flowering branches in January and early February, when there are few other plants in bloom. Tall honeysuckle branches are excellent material for achieving ascending lines and height in an arrangement.

Loropetalum chinense
(lo-ro-PET-a-lum chi-NIN-se)
CHINESE WITCH HAZEL
Family: Hamamelidaceae
Zone: 8–9. Size: 6–15 feet by 8 feet

The Chinese witch hazel and many of its recently released cultivars have become all the rage in Southern gardens in recent years. Often referred to by its generic name, *Loropetalum*, this multi-stemmed, open-structured, evergreen shrub produces a mass of thin, strap-shaped petals making up creamy-white flowers on tall, arching canes in early spring. For best growth, provide a fertile,

well-drained soil in full sunlight to partial shade. Gardeners have been very surprised by how well this tall shrub does in shade. To maintain a thrifty specimen that will continually produce a profusion of flowers, remove old, non-productive canes periodically. Several of the new cultivars produce attractive burgundy-colored foliage and rosy-red flowers. Two of these are 'Rubrum' and 'Plum Delight'. Tall, thin canes covered with flowers make excellent cuttings for indoor use. They hold up quite well, if conditioned with a floral preservative.

Magnolia spp.
(mag-NO-li-a)
MAGNOLIAS
Family: Magnoliaceae
Zone: 5–9. Size: 12–40 feet by 20 feet

Virtually every garden in the South will include one or more magnolias because of their many and diverse attributes. There are none to equal the great virtues of the grand madam of all Southern evergreen trees, the Southern magnolia (*M. grandiflora*). It is surely among our great favorites for both private gardens and public grounds, as recognized by two Southern states, Mississippi and Louisiana, which have adopted it as their state tree or state flower. In late spring and early summer, terminal shoots bear large ivory-colored buds and magnificent, cup-shaped open blossoms. These beautiful specimens often find

The Japanese or saucer magnolia, among the earliest of our flowering trees, is wonderful for cutting. DAVID AGER

The Southern magnolia produces impressive flowers, foliage, and fruit. NGO

their way into decorations for all types of celebrations like graduation parties, receptions, weddings, and other social gatherings that take place in early summer. The sweet fragrance from these mammoth-sized flowers fills a good-sized space.

The Oriental magnolias (*M. × soulangiana*, *M. denudata*, and *M. liliiflora*), all introductions from China, are sometimes referred to as the tulip or Japanese magnolias. These trees, which are much smaller than the Southern magnolia, produce masses of exotic, fragrant, tulip-shaped flowers in shades of pink, dark purple, lavender, and white. They are among our earliest spring-flowering trees to burst forth in bloom. The gradations of color among their flowers, even their individual petals, are sufficiently enchanting that a single branch is enough to grace a table setting for any occasion. A magnolia that has a smaller, star-shaped flower made up of many thin petals is the star magnolia (*M.*

stellata). It tends to be more shrublike in its overall form in its youth, but will ultimately grow into a sizable tree.

No discussion of the magnolias is complete without mentioning the marvelous group of native species that grow in our woodlands across the South. The grandest of all is the bigleaf magnolia (*M. macrophylla*) that pro-

duces mammoth-sized leaves to three feet long and truly spectacular flowers centered among leaf clusters high in the trees. The sweetbay magnolia (*M. virginiana*) is a semi-evergreen tree with silver color on the back sides of the leaves. Its white flowers are about two inches across. Other great natives include Ashe magnolia (*M. ashei*), Fraser magnolia (*M. fraseri*), pyramidal magnolia (*M. pyramidata*), and umbrella magnolia (*M. tripetala*). Each of these has beautiful flowers and interesting seed pods. These natives are normally associated with sandy streams and forest bluffs.

Use caution when handling magnolia blossoms. They bruise easily and turn brown at the slightest touch. Moisten fingers with cool water before touching flowers. This prevents damage from the natural oils in the skin. Wear soft cotton gloves that have been moistened often, if your hands must come into contact with the flower petals.

Malus spp.
(MAY-lus)
CRABAPPLES
Family: Rosaceae
Zone: 5–8. Size: 10–20 feet by 15 feet

The crabapples offer extraordinary features, both in flowers and in fruit, so they are also included in

The big leaf or cowcumber magnolia is a native tree noted for its beautiful foliage and flowers. NGO

Japanese crabapple is one of hundreds of flowering crabapples that produces beautiful flowers and handsome fruit in the upper South. NGO

'Foggii', a lesser-known banana shrub, produces large, creamy-white flowers. T. E. POPE

the section of the book on fruit. Flower colors include white, pink, and red. The Southern crabapple (*M. angustifolia*) grows over most of the South and is tolerant of a wide range of soils from dry to relatively wet, clay soils. This crabapple produces an abundance of rosy-pink buds that open into beautiful pink, fragrant, five-petalled flowers. The northern part of the region has many more options for spectacularly-flowering crabapples. Most trees need several hundred hours of chilling below fifty degrees to satisfy their dormancy requirements. In the Deep South, where this condition is not regularly satisfied, trees bloom sporadically and are relatively short-lived. Although there are

several hundred cultivars of the *M. floribunda* group listed in the trade, here are a few names that you might consider for an early spring display of gorgeous color in the upper South: 'Adam' (red), 'Callaway' (pink), 'Centurion' (red), 'Katherine' (double pink), 'Sargent' (white), 'Selkirk' (pink), 'White Angel' (white), and 'Zumi' (red). Many of these have wonderful fruiting qualities in addition to the spring flowers, and the group is also covered in the fruiting section of the book.

Branches of crabapples make excellent cuttings for arrangements. Slightly crush the basal ends of the stems and condition cuttings in warm water that contains a floral preservative for a

couple of hours before placing cuttings in an arrangement. Petals begin to fall after a couple of days, but their spring beauty is worth every effort, if only for a short duration.

Michelia spp.
(ma-KEL-li-a)
BANANA SHRUBS
Family: Magnoliaceae
Zone: 8–9. Size: 10–20 feet by 10 feet

The banana shrubs are among the South's most beloved large shrubs or small evergreen trees. Although native to China, they have been growing in Southern gardens for many years. The most common of the group is the banana shrub, *M. figo*, sometimes referred to as "magnolia fuscata." The upright growing shrubs are dense, with the tips of the branches turned slightly upward. In recent years, several others have found their way to prominent positions in Southern gardens because of the delightful fragrance from the thick, fleshy-petalled flowers these banana shrubs produce. Cut flowers last only a couple of days, but the foliage is much longer lasting, provided the water has been treated with a floral preservative.

Philadelphus coronarius
(fil-a-DEL-fus kor-o-NA-ri-us)
MOCK ORANGE, PHILADELPHUS
Family: Saxifragaceae
Zone: 5–9. Size: 8–12 feet by 6 feet

Mock orange is one our most enduring Southern garden shrubs. As the South's exuberant display of spring-flowering trees and shrubs begin to fade, the mock oranges of the region surprise us as they come into their full glory. Having a flower somewhat like the floral parts of the dogwood, and in fact sometimes called "English dogwood," this upright-growing deciduous shrub with arching branches never fails us. It tolerates a wide range of soil types and performs well in full sunlight to par-

Mock orange is a favorite heirloom, and a pest-free, spring-flowering shrub. NGO

tial shade. Mock orange is pest-free. One caution: this shrub tends to "walk" in a shrub border by means of *stolons* (underground stems/suckers), and a large specimen can spread and virtually take over a section of a bed. Dig and share these volunteers with friends. Long, ascending stems of the white, fragrant mock orange flowers with yellow centers are glorious indoors, especially at night under artificial light. Flowers begin dropping petals in a couple of days after cutting, but cuttings in the bud stage continue to open. For making arrangements where they are only needed for a day, like in churches and for weddings, there is no more versatile white-flowering shrub than the mock orange.

Prunus americana
(PROO-nus a-mer-i-KA-na)
AMERICAN PLUM, WILD PLUM
Family: Rosaceae
Zone: 4–9. Size: 15–20 feet by 10–15 feet

Plums are among our earliest spring-flowering trees. In addition to the American plum, the Chickasaw plum (*P. angustifolia*) is also quite common in the region. Both species form thickets of root suckers that develop around the base and in close proximity to a mature specimen. Although in full bloom, and hence usually assertive for only a relatively short period during the year, plums are in fact common around old homesites, along highway and railroad rights-of-way, fence rows, and other tracts of fallow land. Their clusters of white flowers are arranged along slender branches. Plums grow best in well-drained soil and need full sunlight to pro-

Multiple stems of American plum provide spectacular cuttings. NGO

American plum in bloom. NGO

The Taiwan flowering cherry blooms in mid-winter. NGO

an extended period. The rosy-pink, bell-shaped flowers occur in clusters, and a mature tree can make a dramatic display of blooms at a time when most other plants are in their deep winter dormancy. Volunteer seedlings are common in the vicinity of a large specimen, because birds pick every seed that this cherry produces and deposit them over a wide area. Cut branches last several days in water, but indoors under artificial light the flowers take on a more purple color and are quite recessive, not making the same show indoors that they do outdoors. Consequently, provide as much natural light as possible.

Prunus glandulosa
(PROO-nus glan-dew-LO-sa)
FLOWERING ALMOND
Family: Rosaceae
Zone: 5–8. Size: 3–5 feet by 4 feet

The flowering almond forms a mass of straight stems covered with closely-arranged double pink or white flowers, depending on the cultivar, in very early spring. After bloom, the multiple-stemmed plant is rather nondescript for the remainder of the year. Periodic grooming and pruning make plants much more thrifty; consequently plants bloom better, although a plant or a small grove of this ornamental almond can live on a site for many years in a cultivated or uncultivated state. Unusual for members of the rose family, this old garden favorite is relatively pest-free. Provide a well-

duce flowers and fruit. Flowers have a rather unpleasant odor up close. Cut branches are delightful indoors, but last only a couple of days in arrangements.

Prunus campanulata
(PROO-nus cam-pan-u-LAY-ta)
TAIWAN FLOWERING CHERRY
Family: Rosaceae
Zone: 8–9. Size: 12–20 feet by 10 feet

The Taiwan flowering cherry has received a great deal of attention in recent years because it is one of a relatively few flowering cherries that perform well in the Gulf South. It has a very low chilling requirement; consequently it is well adapted to the region. Flowering can occur in early January, and because temperatures are rather low, flowers persist for

The white form of the flowering almond is the lesser-known of the flowering species. NGO

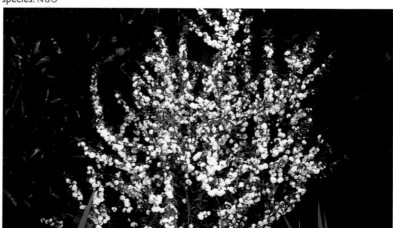

The Okame flowering cherry is an early and highly reliable flowering tree in the upper South. NGO

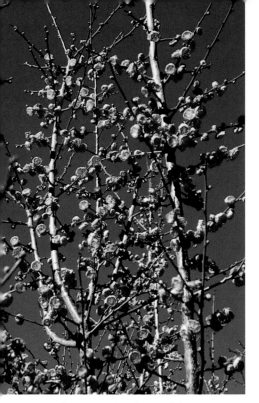

Japanese apricot is one of the most celebrated early spring-flowering trees in Japan. NGO

drained soil and full sunlight for best growth. Cultivar 'Alba Plena' is a beautiful white selection being used frequently in gardens. The long, stiff stems with lovely flowers are ideal for spring arrangements.

Prunus mume
(PROO-nus MU-me)
FLOWERING APRICOT
Family: Rosaceae
Zone: 6–9. Size: 20 feet by 12 feet

The flowering apricot, a somewhat lesser known member of this genus of the Southern flowering trees, is highly prized in its native Japan, where it has been in cultivation for 1,500 years. Over 250 cultivars are currently being offered in the trade in Japan. A few warm, sunny days in January or early February will force this tree into full bloom, thus giving it the distinction of being the earliest of our flowering trees, even coming into flower before the Oriental magnolias and cherry trees. Prominent pink buds and beautiful, delicate clear-pink open

The Yoshino, or Japanese flowering cherry, in full bloom at Afton Villa Gardens, St. Francisville, Louisiana. NGO

flowers with pale yellow centers are breathtaking on a mature specimen which has set a bountiful crop of flowers. Provide full sunlight and a well-drained soil for this small deciduous tree, as is the case for all members of the rose family. 'Peggy Clark', one of several fine cultivars in this country, has a deep, rose-colored flower. White-flowering cultivars are also available. To condition members of this group, slightly crush the basal ends of cut specimens before placing them in warm water containing a flower preservative.

Prunus spp.
(PROO-nus)
FLOWERING CHERRIES
Family: Rosaceae
Zone: 4–8. Size: 15–25 feet by 15 feet

Flowering cherries are among our most beautiful spring-flowering trees. The many ornamental types have somewhat narrow climatic and environmental niches where each performs well, and trees should be selected with these requirements in mind. The earliest of all to bloom is the Taiwan flowering cherry (*P. campanulata*). Most are in full flower in late January, but they are restricted to

The double-flowering peach is the preferred selection for ornamental landscape uses. T. E. POPE

the very warm coastal area, because they require only a few hours of cold temperatures below 50° F to satisfy their dormancy. Flowers are rosy-red; when cut and brought inside, they appear quite dark and recessive, unless they are in a well-lighted room— preferably good natural light. Okame cherry (*P. × incam* 'Okame') is a sensational flowering tree throughout the region. This upright tree produces a mass of rich, rosy-pink flowers in early spring. The cherry of Tidal Basin, Washington, D.C., fame is the Yoshino cherry (*P. × yedoensis*). Trees produce a cloud of white to cottony-pink, almond-scented flowers in early spring. This species is often used as a neighborhood street tree. The Japanese flowering cherry (*P. serrulata*) is a highly popular small tree that is noted also for its white- and pink-flowering cultivars. The cultivar 'Kwansan' produces large, pink, carnationlike flowers, and 'Mt. Fuji' is a delightful white-flowering form. The weeping Higan cherry (*P. subhirtella* 'Pendula') is famous for its specimen appeal as a grand accent tree.

Prunus persica
(PROO-nus PER-si-ka)
FLOWERING PEACH
Family: Rosaceae
Zone: 5–9. Size: 12–15 feet by 10 feet

The standard flowering peach tree grown for fruit production needs little defense as an ornamental flowering tree in its own right.

Flowers are generally small, however, and so must be seen en masse to really make an impact. There are several selections that have been introduced specifically for their outstanding ornamental features. Peaches for the most part are short-lived trees, and have several plant pests, so they are relatively high-maintenance choices. For trees grown for their edible fruit, spraying is required frequently while the fruit develops. All peaches require full sunlight and a well-drained soil. Ornamental flowering peach trees produce spectacular flowers in early spring. Several outstanding

cultivars include 'Alba Plena', a double-flowering white; 'Double Peppermint Stick', with its mottled red and white striped flowers; and 'Double Pink', with its fluffy double, bright-pink flowers.

Punica granatum
(PEW-ni-ka gra-NA-tum)
POMEGRANATE
Family: Punicaceae
Zone: 7–9. Size: 10–15 feet by 10 feet

The pomegranate is among our oldest fruiting plants in cultivation, and many have found their way into Southern gardens, possibly because of the common legend that the pomegranate is a symbol of fertility. There is no orange color quite like the intense orange of pomegranate flowers. The double-flowering forms are especially good for ornamental purposes. Because of their clear, intense color, pomegranate flower buds and open flowers make a strong presence under artificial light, both indoors and outdoors. This slender, upright-growing tree needs full sunlight and well-drained soil. Pomegranates are rel-

Pomegranate thrives in hot coastal areas. This large-flowering, pest-free shrub is especially attractive at night under artificial lights. NGO

Ornamental flowering pears produce beautiful branches of flowers in early spring. NGO

atively pest-free. They are subject to freezes during harsh winters, but most return from the roots following such freezes. Although not of very desirable quality because of the limited amount of juicy pulp, the cultivar 'Wonderful' is the most popular selection in the trade. 'Sweet' is reported to be much better, but is sometimes difficult to locate. The dwarf forms, 'Nana' and 'Chico', make great container specimens. Stems with several of the large, carnationlike flowers make a grand presence indoors in a container.

Pyrus spp.
(PI-rus)
PEAR
Family: Rosaceae
Zone: 4–9. Size: 20–30 feet by 20–25 feet

Pyrus is an old-world genus that is of great significance to the world of contemporary horticulture. Pears are among our most prized Southern fruiting trees. There have been hundreds of fruiting cultivars and many ornamental types introduced in the trade through the years. The fruiting types are relatively long-lived. It is rather common to see a fruiting pear that may be seventy-five or more years old struggling to survive at an old homesite. Old specimens continue to produce fruit up until the last stem dies. Make cultivar selections of the fruiting pear according to where you live, because they vary greatly in response to the amount of cold

that is required to meet their dormancy needs. The flowering ornamental pears like 'Bradford', 'Aristocrat', 'Cleveland Select', and 'Red Spire' are spectacular spring-flowering trees, but are relatively short-lived. Small, rounded, nutlike fruit is produced in abundance on a heavy-flowering specimen. They have brittle wood and narrow crotches between the trunks. Consequently members of this group tend to split due to the heavy, vertical mass typical of these ornamental trees. Popular for many years because of their beautiful white spring flowers, glossy foliage, and delightful autumn color, the flowering pears are being banned in many public plantings in cities across the country because of their splitting and high maintenance requirements. Pears need well-drained soil and

full sunlight. Flowering branches of pear make exquisite cuttings for arrangements. They have a rather disagreeable odor, but this becomes a problem only if they are approached up close.

Rhododendron spp.
(ro-do-DEN-dron)
AZALEAS
Family: Ericaceae
Zone: 7–9, Sizes: 3–15 feet by 2–12 feet

What flowering shrub better epitomizes the Southern garden than azaleas? This huge and highly complex genus comprises some our most beloved spring-flowering shrubs. It includes both azaleas, which flourish primarily in the southern United States, and the rhododendrons of the Northeast, although there are some of both in all parts of the region. In size, members of this genus range from small, dwarf forms under 2 feet in height to the giant, treelike mountain rhododendrons of the Northeast. Both evergreen and deciduous species are included. While most have been introduced into this country from Japan and China, there are important native species that enrich our forests, savannas, and other natural landscapes. Few plants offer more color options than do the azaleas. There are literally hundreds of cultivars

A close-up of the flowers of the Florida azalea, an excellent deciduous shrub for partially-shaded sites. NGO

Left: The native honeysuckle azalea has interesting branches and lovely fragrant flowers in spring. NGO

Below: 'Pride of Mobile' azalea, a very dependable cultivar, can grow to mammoth size in the South. NGO

Bottom: A planting of 'Formosa' azaleas along the Oak Avenue at Afton Villa Gardens, St. Francisville, Louisiana. NGO

Top: A mass planting of the dwarf azalea 'Snow' at the Emy-Lou Biedenharn Garden, Monroe, Louisiana. NGO

Above: A popular combination of azaleas and Reeves spirea, or bridal wreath, at Longue Vue Gardens, New Orleans. NGO

within each of the major azalea types, and scores of new ones are being released annually. A special group currently gaining considerable recognition are the repeat bloomers—those that flower in cycles over many months. Azaleas are somewhat environment- and climate-specific for optimum performance, so choosing the right type for a specific site is important.

In the South, the queen of the azalea group is the large Southern azalea (*R. indicum*), which makes a spectacular show annually and is relatively easy to grow. The smaller dwarf azalea (*R. obtusum*), often used en masse, is more difficult to grow. Several native deciduous azaleas, like the flame azalea (*R. austrinum*), native honeysuckle azalea (*R. canescens*), plumleaf azalea (*R. prunifolium*), and Alabama azalea (*R. alabamense*), perform well along woodland bluffs, on margins of sandy streams, and as understory shrubs to high-branched trees. Heavy shade reduces the flowering of these

natives. Azaleas require an acid, well-drained soil that contains a generous amount of *humus* (well-decomposed organic matter) to keep it from compacting. Roots are shallow, so mulch plants to help maintain a desirable porous soil texture for root growth.

Flowering branches of the large azaleas make spectacular exhibition pieces indoors. They can be used effectively alone and in combination with other fresh materials. Azaleas hold up for several days, if they are properly conditioned and their stems are placed in water that contains a floral preservative.

Rosa spp.
(RO-za)
ROSES
Family: Rosaceae
Zone: all, Sizes: 2 feet and greater

Roses stand alone as cut flowers, as they have no rivals for being the most popular of our home-grown flowering plants. Roses are the most aristocratic of flowers, but also rank among the most democratic, because they have been fixtures in gardens of the wealthy and mighty throughout history, while also gracing the cottage gardens of the more common people. Because of their popularity with the well-to-do, roses have been the most researched and best doc-

'Baronne Prevost', a hybrid perpetual rose growing on a Washington County, Texas, fence post. WCW

umented of all flowers. They often come with titled names for European aristocrats and came to us from nurseries in France and England. Their names appear constantly in old diaries and historic garden plans.

Roses are, for the most part, easy to propagate by cuttings. Cottage gardeners have long shared starts of their favorite types with friends and family members. As a result, modern rose collectors commonly find the finest specimens of eighteenth- and nineteenth-century roses in the humbler neighborhoods. The owners of these glorious antiques may not know the name of what they have been preserving, but they know a special beauty when they see it.

Generally, the older roses require less maintenance. They are traditionally used as shrubs in borders, as hedges, and as cover for arbors, trellises, and other garden structures, rather than being forced into the special beds where modern roses are often located, so

that their rather exacting cultural requirements may be met more easily. There is tremendous variation in the form and size of the flowers among old roses, and the perfumes are typically richer and more varied than those of modern roses. The colors of the heirloom roses tend toward pastels of pink, purple, yellow, white, and rose, and they tend to blend more easily

into garden and interior settings than the eye-catching bright reds, oranges, and yellows of the modern hybrids. But mainly, the old roses tend to be tough. Often they may be found flourishing on the grounds of abandoned homesteads and cemeteries, where they carry on without pruning, spraying, fertilization, or irrigation. These roses are not only beautiful, but they are survivors, too—survivors from an era when garden plants had to thrive without the help of modern pesticides, sprinkler systems, and other aids of modern horticulture.

More complete information on the classes and varieties, as well as culture and landscape uses, of these fascinating plants is available in *Antique Roses for the South* (Taylor Publishing Co., Dallas, 1990).

Modern roses have been developed with a strong focus on their use as cut flowers. The typical pointed buds, large flowers, and bright colors of the hybrid tea class of roses make them useful for bouquets inside the home. They have another value when compared with the older roses, as the cut flowers of many modern roses tend to last longer than their older relatives. Their stems tend to be longer and stronger as well, making them somewhat more versatile for use in large arrangements. Antique roses are particularly

'Eugene Boerner', a floribunda rose useful for the landscape and as a cut flower. WCW

during the morning hours. They will produce and live with less, but flower production suffers. However, they actually perform better when given some protection from the hot afternoon sun in Southern climates.

The ideal time for planting roses is when they are dormant in January and February. Container-grown plants may be set out at any time, but planting during the growing season requires more watering and attention.

For best flower production of everblooming roses, fertilize them every 4 to 6 weeks, beginning in the early spring and continuing until early fall. Use a complete fertilizer, such as a 6-10-4 formulation.

Prune modern hybrid tea roses severely in February to early March, depending on the part of the region where they are growing, and give them a less severe pruning in early August. Most old roses require less severe pruning. Blooming climbers and species roses should be pruned after they have completed their spring flowering cycle.

Some gardeners choose to grow old roses because they are often more resistant to insect and disease problems, but this tolerance varies considerably among varieties. Roses grown in open sunny areas with good air circulation tend to be freer of pests.

Improper cutting of flowers can injure the plant and decrease its vigor. It is best to cut few, if any, flowers during the first blooming season after planting. By removing only flowers and only a

Top: 'American Beauty' drapes a picket fence at 'Cricket Court', the former Washington County, Texas, home of William C. Welch. WCW
Above: *Rosa multiflora* 'Carnea' hangs across a tool shed at the historic Adolphus Sterne home in Nacogdoches, Texas. WCW
Below: Closeup of *Rosa multiflora* 'Carnea' at the Adolphus Sterne home in Nacogdoches, Texas. WCW

appropriate for use in historic or restored structures. It would seem equally important to use roses "of the period" as to have furniture and accessories that reflect the time of a historic structure. Since many of the older roses are available again, and they tend to be easier to grow and maintain, their popularity is likely to continue to increase in the years ahead. Today, many gardeners choose to grow a mixture of antique and modern roses to accommodate their favorites for cut flowers and landscape uses.

Roses are amazingly versatile

plants that respond favorably to a wide variety of growing conditions. They prefer a location where they receive at least a half-day of direct sunlight, preferably

A bouquet of old garden roses at the weekend home of Bill and Diane Welch in rural Washington County, Texas. WCW

small portion of stem, roses are encouraged to develop into larger, more thrifty plants by fall, at which time more flowers and longer stems may be cut. Cut flowers just above the first five-leaflet leaf, to encourage more side branching. When cutting, use sharp tools and allow at least two leaves to remain between the cut and the main stem. Roses cut just before the petals begin to unfold will open normally and remain in good condition longer. Late afternoon is the best time of day to cut roses; cut in the morning if you are conditioning roses for arranging, or to get the most fragrance for potpourri.

Place rose stems in water containing a plant preservative immediately after cutting. To hasten the opening of buds, use warm water for several hours before placing them in an arrangement. If a floral foam that absorbs water is used to anchor stems in an arrangement, be sure to soak it also in the floral preservative solution.

Spiraea spp.
(spy-RE-a)
SPIREAS
Rosaceae
Zone: 6–9. Size: 2–8 feet by 2–6 feet

Old-time gardeners in the South would seldom speak of their plantings without referring to their "azaleas and baby's breath" (or "bridal wreath") spireas. In the South, if it was white and bloomed with azaleas, it had to be spirea, although in fact such a plant could have been any number of other spring-flowering shrubs. They were often interplanted with azaleas in an alternating pattern— spirea, azalea, spirea, azalea, etc. Spireas are indeed important and deserve all the credit they have received through the years as being among our most enduring spring-flowering shrubs. Remnants of plantings that go back a hundred years are still to be found on some old homesites across the region. There have been many church floral offerings made exclusively of home-grown spireas. Spireas were among the most common plants in arrangements made for schoolteachers, hospital cheer, and memorial pieces left at the graves of loved ones. With a few cuts, an arrangement could be quickly assembled from these mainstays in the early spring gardens.

Several of the important species include Reeves spirea (*S. cantoniensis*), bridal wreath spirea (*S. prunifolia*), baby's breath spirea (*S. thunbergii*), and Vanhoutte spirea (*S. × vanhouttei*). All of these are white-flowering selections. There are other colors like the pink 'Anthony Waterer' spirea and the Japanese spirea 'Shibori', which produces pink, red, and white flowers on the same plant. Provide all spireas with a sunny location and well-drained soil. Flowers begin to shed their petals after a couple of days indoors. The long stems can provide height in arrangements, while some of the species that produce tiny flowers are good filler materials.

Syringa vulgaris
(si-RING-ga vul-GA-ris)
COMMON LILAC
Family: Oleaceae
Zone: 3–7. Size: 8–10 feet by 8 feet

Lilacs are among the most beloved flowering shrubs in the United States. Unfortunately, they grow only in a relatively small portion of the South where summer

Popcorn spirea produces long, ascending stems that are wonderful for cutting if the shrub is pruned properly. T. E. POPE

A close-up of one of America's most beloved flowers, the lilac. NGO

temperatures are moderate and winter temperatures remain low for an extended period. Gardeners who have had experiences with lilacs in the upper regions of the country long to have them when they move to the South, but are met with poor success when they try to grow them in the Deep South. The shrub is so important in the Northeast, a special day, "Lilac Sunday," an annual celebration at the Arnold Arboretum, is held in its honor. While there are hundreds of cultivars, one feature is common to all—delightful, highly fragrant, sweet-scented flowers. The dense, tubular flowers are borne in showy, terminal, conical-shaped clusters. Colors include white, pink, lilac, blue, and purple. Lilacs grow well in full sunlight to partial shade, and do best in a well-drained soil with a neutral pH. To condition, retain the leaves on stems near the flower heads. This is a unique practice for lilacs, since for most plants the removal of the lower foliage is highly recommended. Crush stems and soak deeply in water up to the flower heads.

Trachelospermum jasminoides
(tra-ke-lo-SPER-mum jas-min-OI-dez)
CONFEDERATE or STAR JASMINE
Family: Apocynaceae
Zone: 8–10. Size: 20 feet, vine

Confederate jasmine is among our most prized evergreen vines. This fast-spreading vine has long been loved for the abundance of highly fragrant, creamy-white, star-shaped flowers produced in early spring. Although this vine does not produce tendrils or other holdfasts for clinging to surfaces, it will virtually cover any object in its path with its rampant growth. Confederate jasmine is ideal for growing on garden structures like arbors, pergolas, trellises, fences, and walls. It makes an ideal covering for chain-link fencing, if the vines are trained by weaving new growth throughout the fence from the bottom to the top during its early stages of growth. Otherwise, once the vine forms a foliage mass at the top of a structure, it is difficult to train growth below the mass. This vine is not particular as to special growing conditions, but blooms best if it receives several hours of morning sunlight. Prune annually after flowering to keep growth under control. This species is much more tender than its relative, the ground cover Asian jasmine (*T. asiaticum*), and is sometimes severely damaged by hard freezes.

Clippings of the Confederate jasmine persist for about a week if placed in hot water first, to help congeal the milky sap before using the vines in arrangements or for cuttings on indoor structures. The sweet-scented flowers are ideal for use indoors. Confederate jasmine is popular for late spring weddings and other social gatherings.

Viburnum spp.
(vy-BUR-num)
VIBURNUMS
Family: Caprifoliaceae
Zone: 5–9. Size: 3–10 feet by 4–8 feet

The viburnums are a group of plants which have so many outstanding qualities that they are worthy of being included in all three sections of the book on woody ornamentals—flowering, foliage, and fruiting. This is a large and complex genus of both native and introduced species. Plant types include deciduous and evergreens, and the range of growth extends from Canada all the way to the Gulf Coast. Sizes range from the relatively low spreaders to giant, treelike shrubs. For flowering, none is more spectacular in bloom than is the snowball viburnum (*V. macrocephalum* 'Sterile'). Plants grow to 12 feet

The Confederate or star jasmine produces an abundance of star-shaped, fragrant flowers in late spring. NGO

Flowering Trees, Shrubs, Vines, and Ground Covers

Snowball viburnum, a large-flowering shrub with huge, snowballlike blooms. NGO

tall or more and produce large globular clusters of white flowers. A mature specimen of this viburnum can make its presence known a hundred yards away. Double-file viburnums, *V. plicatum* 'Mariesii' and 'Shasta', produce large, flat clusters of flowers on long, tiered stems. Flowers are followed by round clusters of bright red berries. These two are best adapted for the upper parts of the region. Arrowwood (*V. dentatum*) and rustyhaw viburnum (*V. rufidulum*) are two handsome native species that bloom well under the canopies of tall trees like pine in Southern woodlands and other naturalistic settings. Some viburnums have mildly fragrant flowers; others have a musty odor. They grow best in fertile, well-drained soils and perform well in full sunlight to partial shade.

Cut branches of flowers last several days to a week indoors if their stems are in water. Many people find the immature blooms, chartreuse in color, combine well with other flowers, and especially well with dark green foliage. Stages of development among flowers are often combined in an arrangement.

Vitex agnus-castus
(VI-teks AG-nus-CAS-tus)
VITEX, LILAC CHASTE TREE
Family: Verbenaceae
Zone: 7–9. Size: 10–15 feet by 10 feet

This large, fast-growing deciduous shrub or small tree produces a bloom somewhat similar to those of the lilac. Compound leaves, composed of five to seven 5-inch leaflets, are aromatic and resemble those of marijuana. According to legend, Roman maidens made their beds of vitex foliage during the Feast of Ceres to keep themselves chaste, hence the name "chaste tree." An abundance of showy clusters of spike-shaped flowers in colors of lavender, blue, pink, or white are produced in May and June. Provide this easy-to-grow shrub full sunlight, a well-drained soil, and lots of space. Cuttings in flower hold up for three to five days in water, but the blue color is somewhat difficult to use indoors in low light.

Weigela florida
(wy-GE-la FLOR-i-da)
WEIGELA
Family: Caprifoliaceae
Zone: 5–8. Size: 6–10 feet by 6–8 feet

Weigela blooms a bit after the grand burst of spring color from other flowering shrubs and trees. This is an old garden plant held in high esteem for its lovely 2-inch-long, funnel-shaped flowers in colors of red, rosy-pink, light pink to lavender, and white. Unlike some heirloom plants, which can persist on homesites for nearly a century, weigela is somewhat shorter-lived, but is easy to grow and has few pests. It does best in a fertile, well-drained soil and full sunlight, although it is tolerant of a wide range of conditions. Weigela is best adapted to the upper range of

Vitex is a trouble-free, drought-tolerant, summer-flowering shrub. T. E. POPE

Weigela is popular throughout the South, with flowers in shades of red, pink, and white. NGO

the region, where cold temperatures help to satisfy its dormancy needs. The cultivar 'Florida Variegata' is quite popular in garden plantings because of its green and creamy-white variegated foliage. Long, slender branches of weigela flowers make exquisite indoor floral displays, and they remain fresh for several day as cuttings. The variegated selection is attractive as cut foliage at other times during the year, when the plant is not in flower.

Wisteria sinensis
(wis-TE-ri-a si-NEN-sis)
WISTERIA
Family: Leguminosae
Zone: 5–9. Size: to 75 feet, vine

Wisteria is among our most popular deciduous flowering vines, producing showy, hanging, grapelike clusters of delicate lavender flowers in early spring. This vine can severely try our patience, as we often have to struggle to keep it in bounds in a garden setting. Pruning two or more times a year is a regular practice when plants are growing on structures. To accommodate the massive growth of wisteria, garden structures must be sturdy and very durable, because repairs are difficult to make once a vine covers a structure. One of the best ways to feature this rampant grower is to give an entire tree over to it for support and allow the branches of the vine to hang from the tree.

Unfortunately, in some parts of the South, wisteria has escaped cultivation and is growing, very much like kudzu, over acres of unmanaged landscapes. There have been many old gardens virtually destroyed by wisteria left to grow at will for years. When planted in a rich soil, a new vine can spend five or more years "colonizing" its supporting structure before it comes into flower. If you want flowers sooner, choose a plant that has already begun flowering, and do not fertilize it. Root pruning may also help to hasten flowering.

Wisteria produces grapelike clusters, one or more feet in length, of beautiful flowers just as the new foliage begins to emerge in early spring. Although lavender is the most common color, the white cultivar, 'Alba', is equally spectacular and might be slightly less aggressive. Japanese wisteria, *W. floribunda*, produces gorgeous 20-inch flowering *racemes* (hanging, grapelike clusters of pea-shaped flowers). Wisterias produce blooms on previous seasons' growth, so to ensure flowers, keep some of the previous year's growth.

Because of the exquisite line quality of wisteria branches, cuttings are most often taken in the bud stage, rather than when the flowers are full-blown. In any case, the delicate flowers last only a couple of days indoors before they begin shedding. A single branch with only young foliage is also handsome as a stand-alone piece, or used in combination with garden flowers. Slightly crush the stems of this woody vine and set the cut ends in warm water for several hours before placing stems in a bouquet.

NGO

Japanese wisteria in full bloom overhanging the Louisiana State University lake in Miss Elizabeth Williams's garden in Baton Rouge. WCW

Six

Foliage Fit for Cutting

Most of us have a bountiful source of cut foliage just a few feet away—in our gardens. Because a wide range of trees and shrubs, especially the evergreens, are used to provide dominant structure and edges to our garden spaces, they are quite accessible for cuttings. In garden design, trees and shrubs may be selected specifically for their bold, striking textures and their many and varying shades of green. The bold forms of trees and shrubs can clearly define the spatial partitions, or "rooms," in our gardens. These divisions aid in providing pleasing scale and proportion to garden settings.

The history of gardening indicates that trees and shrubs have long been used to provide strong pattern and geometry. Today, when we visit historic homes and other buildings, it is refreshing to see these traditional practices being continued in those gardens. Likewise, freshly cut greens play an important role in the ongoing life of these fine places.

Trees and shrubs are not the only sources of cut foliage. Ground cover plantings of aspidistra and some ferns, both popular for shaded sites, are good sources for cut foliage. Many evergreen vines, like English ivy and smilax, are equally important materials. And the visually assertive, variegated foliage of plants like aucuba and pittosporum add still another dimension to the list of sources for interesting cut foliage.

Many of the evergreens make a strong presence immediately as a cut material—so much so that they can often stand alone, providing that flowers are not always a necessary part of a decorative feature. Sometimes, for example, the best way to set a proper scale relationship in an interior space is by the use of one or more large cut branches. For the same size arrangement with flowers, a dozen or more stems might be necessary.

While we might readily select a large ficus (rubber) tree, philodendron, or other interior plant in a container for a specific interior space, we might be somewhat more reluctant to cut a large branch of Southern magnolia or pine and place it in a prominent place on a sideboard or other equally imposing position. Do not be timid with the use of cut foliage! Use it freely and often.

One caution: Dark green, the color of most of our popular evergreens, is a very recessive color. A branch on a tree or shrub growing in full sunlight might appear to be a perfect choice for a position indoors. But when the same branch is removed from the open sunlight and placed in a dark room, like a foyer or other interior space, this foliage often loses

A New Orleans courtyard garden dominated by foliage. NGO

much of its "life" and vitality. This is particularly true with dull, non-glossy foliage. Consequently, provide as much natural light as possible for the dark greens or place them beneath bright, directed artificial lights.

Plants having large, boldly-textured leaves or a glossy leaf surface, like the Southern magnolia, and those with variegated leaves make a relatively strong presence in darker interior spaces. When selecting foliage for dimly lighted spaces, also consider the plants that have a more yellow-green color like common boxwood and ferns and those with white and green variegated foliage like the variegated euonymus, aucuba, and one of the variegated hollies. The yellow-green shades can also be combined with the darker greens to make a strong and more visually-interesting contrast in colors than if only varying shades of green were combined.

The life of evergreen foliage is quite long when compared to the softer, herbaceous cut flowers. Flowers, when used in combination with evergreen foliage, may need replacing several times before the foliage materials begin to wane. Also, there are always periods of indeterminate length in our gardens when the sources of cut flowers can be quite limited, while the evergreens normally remain available in an unlimited supply. At such times, experiment. Allow the lighter foliage to "stand in" for flowers.

Although the general conditioning of plants is covered in a separate section of the book, for the most part, plants in this chapter have woody stems. To aid in maximum water uptake, make initial cuts at a slant when removing a portion from the parent plant. To further enhance water uptake, make a pair of longitudinal slits in the shape of a cross up the stem for about one inch. The cut edges will expose more of the conductive tissue to the water. Some peo-

The tall, spiky Artemisia 'Silver King' is a gray-foliaged perennial useful in both the fresh and dried state. NGO

ple advocate crushing the basal inch or so of woody stems, but this can cause a problem if a water-absorbing foam is used to hold the stems in their final position. Remove the lower one-third to one-half of the leaves on the woody stems. Place the cut ends and the lower one-third lengths of the stems in warm water containing a flower preservative. Allow plants to sit for several hours before arranging them. When using a water-absorbing floral foam, be sure to soak the block of foam in water containing the flower preservative. Recut stems periodically to extend the life of cut greens.

The critical eye for design will find many plants in the garden that can serve as suitable sources of cut foliage. While surely not an exhaustive listing, here are some popular evergreens that are durable, relatively easy to grow, produce a considerable amount of leafy material, and are relatively long-lived as cut foliage.

GARDEN PLANTS

Artemisia spp.
(ar-te-MIZ-i-a)
ARTEMISIA, TARRAGON, WORMWOOD, SOUTHERN-WOOD
Family: Compositae
Zone: 5–8, depending on cultivar. Size: 1–4 feet by 2 feet

Artemisias are a group of semi-woody, clump-forming perennials grown primarily for their delightful silvery-gray, aromatic foliage that makes a strong presence among the traditional greens in most gardens. Textures can range from the very fine, ferny foliage of cultivars like 'Valerie Finnis' and 'Powis Castle' to the relatively coarse-textured, velvety-lobed foliage of cultivars 'Silver King' and 'Silver Queen'. For all members of this group, provide full sunlight and fast-draining soils. They seem to fare well even in poor, dry soils. Stem and root rot are common in heavy, wet soils. *A. annua* is a reseeding annual that can be somewhat invasive. Flowers of the artemisias are relatively insignificant. Cut foliage conditioned in warm water with a floral preservative will last several days in an arrangement.

Asparagus densiflorus 'Sprengeri'
(as-PAR-a-gus den-si-FLO-rus SPRING-er-i)
ASPARAGUS FERN
Family: Liliaceae
Zone: 9–10. Size: 2–4 feet

Everyone needs a big pot of asparagus fern, even if it has to be hauled inside for protection every winter. It can provide quick cuttings to fit any occasion. Not a fern by any means, but a member of the lily family, its great virtue is its delightful, fine-textured, ferny foliage that works wonders as a cut foliage in nearly any setting. Asparagus fern can stand alone as a cut green and is also very effective in arrangements with other foliage and flowers. Through the years, it has covered many home-spun arrangement holders and other *mechanics* (all the materials used to anchor arrangements like stones, branches, and needlepoint holders).

Several seasons are required to grow a heavy mass of asparagus fern, but once established it can provide cuttings many times during the year. Generous applications of nitrogen will hasten growth. It is somewhat drought-

Asparagus fern has soft, graceful, fine-textured foliage. NGO

Aspidistra has useful, long-lasting foliage and grows particularly well in heavy shade. NGO

hardy because of the thick, underground fleshy nodules, which do not produce plants themselves, but store water for periods of drought. This is a rugged perennial that is virtually pest-free. Cuttings retain their good qualities for a couple of weeks or more.

Asparagus fern is a choice ground cover plant in parts of the region not subject to hard freezes. When the tops are injured by light freezes, cut back the brown portions in early spring, fertilize generously, and water regularly to encourage a fast recovery from cold temperatures. Garden asparagus (*A. officinalis*), a close relative, is much finer in texture and much less dense than the asparagus fern. Both ferns make good cutting material, but the asparagus fern is preferable because of the greater density of it foliage. Garden asparagus produces stiff, upright stems that can serve as an excellent "filler" material in arrangements.

Aspidistra elatior
(as-pi-DIS-tra ee-LAY-ti-or)
ASPIDISTRA, CAST-IRON PLANT
Family: Liliaceae
Zone: 8–10. Size: 18–30 inches tall

True to one of its common names, this persistent perennial is virtually indestructible. On the other hand, aspidistra has a relatively limited range of conditions where it produces the flawless foliage desired by discriminating

gardeners. Provide shade for all parts of the day, except for possibly the early morning hours. It performs well beneath canopies of evergreen and deciduous trees and in northern exposures adjacent to buildings. Clumps of the 4-inch-wide, dark green, coarse-textured leaves are particularly handsome during the winter months beneath the canopy of deciduous trees, where plants receive low-angled light and leaves shine in the winter sunlight. Initial plantings grow and spread slowly, but with time they can make a strong presence and multiply freely, especially in fertile, well-drained soils.

Grooming—cutting back the entire mass of foliage to the ground every three years—is the key to maintaining an acceptable planting of aspidistra. Otherwise, plantings will turn brown and look tattered, and old declining leaves will mar the appearance of the mass. If this cutting is timed correctly—just before new growth begins in mid-spring—the old leaves can be cut and left in place as a mulch, and the new emerging foliage will cover the old decaying foliage. Severe freezes will also injure aspidistra foliage. When this occurs, cut back the plants after the danger of freezes has passed. Cut aspidistra leaves hold their color and appear fresh for several weeks indoors. They eventually turn a pleasing brown color if left in place longer, or if the leaves are dried.

The large, coarse-textured foliage of the variegated or gold-dust aucuba. NGO

Aucuba japonica 'Variegata'
(a-KU-ba ja-PON-i-ka)
VARIEGATED AUCUBA, GOLD-DUST AUCUBA
Cornaceae
Zone: 6–9. Size: 4–6 feet by 4–5 feet

The large, coarse-textured leaves, up to 8 inches long and 3 inches wide, and the yellow blotches of the variegated foliage make the aucuba a prominent shrub in garden plantings. The strong, stiff-foliaged stems give it an equally commanding presence as cut foliage. Aucuba responds best in a fertile, well-drained soil in partial shade. Leaves scorch in hot noon-day and early afternoon sunlight during the summer months. Weak plants are quite susceptible to several leaf diseases. Aucuba is a good companion plant with English ivy, fatsia, ferns, and mahonia. Many selections are offered in the trade. Each is distinguished by varying degrees of yellow markings or blotches on the leaves. Some like 'Picturata', 'Sulphur', and 'Crotonifolia', have unusually prominent, bright yellow variegation, which can produce excellent cuttings for indoor use.

The solid green form, *A. japonica*, produces a bold, dark green foliage and also makes a very satisfactory cut foliage because of its large size, somewhat like the foliage of the Southern magnolia. 'Viridis' is a large, vigorously-growing cultivar with solid green leaves. 'Serratifolia' also has solid green foliage, but produces an added value—bright, showy red fruit in late autumn. Cuttings of aucuba foliage persist for a couple of weeks or more, and will eventually root in the container if placed in a location inside the home where they receive sunlight.

Buxus microphylla
(BUK-sus mi-kro-FIL-a)
LITTLELEAF BOXWOOD, BOX
Family: Buxaceae
Zone: 6–9. Size: 4–8 feet by 4 feet

Boxwoods have a unique place in the history of American garden design. They have been used to provide the classical geometry in gardens of the world for centuries, and in this country for over 200 years. Images of clipped box hedges and striking parterre plantings are likely to come to mind first, but there are numerous historic sites where these delightful billowy shrubs have been allowed to grow freely, and plants have reached enormous sizes. Although there are several popular species and scores of cultivars, selections of the littleleaf boxwood are the most common throughout the lower South. However, there are

Japanese boxwood in a formal planting at Afton Villa Gardens, St. Francisville, Louisiana. NGO

Top: A *parterre* planting of 'Winter Green' boxwood at Longue Vue Gardens, New Orleans. NGO

Above: An old unclipped hedge of English boxwood. NGO

able feature of this evergreen. Plantings should be mulched. Even shallow tilling can injure the roots, which grow near the soil surface. Harsh winter freezes sometime burn the leaves of boxwood. Clip away these damaged parts in late winter after the danger of freezes has passed, but before new growth begins. Varieties japonica and koreana are quite common, and are among the most cold-hardy boxwood selections. 'Green Beauty', 'Green Mountain', 'Winter Green', and 'Winter Gem' are very fine compact, relatively slow-growing cultivars.

Boxwood greens are especially popular during the end-of-the year holiday season. Seldom are large branches removed, but small terminal shoots of foliage make great backgrounds for accent pieces like wreaths, garlands, table arrangements, mantel pieces, and exhibitions of seasonal fruit. Clippings have a relatively long life after cutting, especially if they are submerged in warm water for several hours before placing them in a decorative piece. As box foliage dries, it fades and loses some of its distinctive yellow-green color.

some fine plantings of the English boxwood (*B. sempervirens*), particularly in the upper South. This species has been used in garden design for much longer than the littleleaf boxwood. Members of this genus have been on a popularity roller coaster over the past fifty years. There was a period when few people planted box—likely due to a high level of nematode infestation and root fungi problems. In recent years, it appears that boxwoods have made a remarkable comeback in popularity, not necessarily for clipped hedge plantings, but rather as free-growing specimens selected for their dense, compact forms and highly predictable evergreen character.

For best performance, pro-vide boxwood with a fertile, well-drained soil. Plantings are very sensitive to soils that hold water for an extended period. The character of box does not change significantly from growing in full sunlight to partial shade. In fact, shade tolerance is another desir-

Cephalotaxus harringtonia
(sef-a-lo-TAX-sus har-ing-TON-i-a)
HARRINGTON PLUM YEW
Family: Cephalotaxaceae
Zone: 6–9. Size: 4–6 feet by 5–6 feet

Harrington plum yew is a broad-spreading, relatively slow-growing,

The broad-spreading Harrington plum yew. NGO

'Alabama Sunset', a handsome coleus cultivar that grows quite large during the summer months. WCW

fine-textured evergreen shrub well adapted to the South. It is an excellent substitute for the true yew (*Taxus*) that is a very popular genus in the northeastern United States. The stiff, dark green, needlelike foliage closely resembles the foliage of a yew. This is an excellent choice for partially shaded to sunny sites where a low-growing, spreading juniperlike shrub is needed. Provide a well-drained soil and fertilize in late winter to encourage a more rapid growth. The dark, blue-green foliage is excellent for cutting and lasts for a week or more. It is particularly popular during the holiday season for making wreaths and for table and mantel decorations. Be patient, because it may require several years for a plant to grow large enough to be the source of foliage for cuttings.

Coleus spp.
(KO-le-us)
COLEUS
Family: Labiatae
Zone: 9–10. Size: 2 feet by 2 feet

Coleus is an annual grown primarily for its attractive, colorful foliage. In recent years there have been scores of new cultivars introduced into the trade. If handled properly, coleuses will last for several months in the garden. Prune back tall, spindly shoots that begin flowering. Cut back plants several times during the summer months to encourage plants to branch and produce even more colorful foliage. In fact, soon after acquiring a desirable cultivar, clip out the top to encourage side shoots or branches to form, so that plants will be low and bushy rather than tall and spindly. Cuttings root in a couple of weeks in water, so propagation of a favorite cultivar is easy. Fertilize plantings every month during the growing season. This is a great foliage to use in arrangements. Cuttings hold up for weeks; in fact, they will root in an arrangement, if they remain in water.

Cycas revoluta
(SI-kas rev-o-LU-ta)
SAGO PALM, CYCAD
Family: Cycadaceae
Zone: 8–10. Size: 3–6 feet by 6 feet, clumps

This primitive plant, native to Japan, is a popular accent evergreen in gardens across the lower South. It is not a true palm, but produces a relatively low-growing rosette of stiff, shiny-green, palm-like leaves. The emerald-green of the sago is a striking contrast to most other plants. Hard freezes will severely damage the foliage, and, depending on the severity, will kill unprotected plants. Sagos grow well in full sunlight to partial shade. Although slow growing, relative to the growth rate of most other ornamentals, it does best in a fertile, well-drained soil, and will become a strong specimen of considerable size in eight to ten years. Periodic grooming—the removal of old brown leaves, especially after winter freezes—is required to maintain a pleasing appearance.

The foliage of the sago palm is frequently used on Palm Sunday in many Christian churches. It holds up well with little or no conditioning. Fronds placed in water maintain good color for weeks. Dried fronds turn a pleasing brown color and make handsome structural foliage for dried arrangements.

Cyperus alternifolius
(si-PER-rus al-ter-ni-FO-li-us)
UMBRELLA PLANT, CYPERUS
Family: Cyperaceae
Zone: 8–10. Size: 3–6 feet by 3 feet

The umbrella plant is a semi-tropical that has been used in gardens for centuries to provide accent from its unique foliage. It per-

Sago or cycad palm produces stiff, long-lasting fronds useful for arrangements and popular on All Saints' Day. NGO

greens for arrangements. Cut stems last for several weeks, if they are in water. Dried leaves are useful in end-of-the-year holiday arrangements.

Elaeagnus spp.
(el-e-AG-nus)
RUSSIAN OLIVE, ELEAGNUS
Family: Elaeagnaceae
Zone: 7–9. Size: 8–15 feet by 10–12 feet

This broad-spreading to mounding, fast-growing evergreen shrub has a host of interesting features. The foliage possesses striking, silvery-gray undersides and the stems are cinnamon-brown. Long, ascending, pliable shoots, sometimes reaching 10 or more feet in length, grow from the sides and tops of mature specimens. Positioned close to other plants or small structures, Russian olive assumes a vinelike character. Russian olives grow nearly any place, since they are not too particular about soils and light conditions, although vigorous growth takes place in fertile, well-drained soils. An added feature is the very sweet-scented, buff-colored — although inconspicuous — flowers that appear in late autumn. There are numerous cultivars of eleagnus noted for their attractive golden-

Top: Two excellent cut-foliage materials are umbrella plant (left) and the splitleaf philodendron (right). NGO

Above: The Egyptian papyrus, another form of the umbrella plant, has very fine-textured foliage. WCW

injury, because eventually plants become straggly. The roots are seldom killed by freezes near the Gulf Coast. Fresh new growth will emerge in early spring.

When surveying a garden setting for cut foliage, the umbrella plant normally stands out as one of the most distinctive foliage plants among all the plants present. Regardless of whether the plant is used alone or in combination with other plants, be reassured that the foliage of the umbrella will make its presence known. The foliage of this semi-tropical has been the source of inspiration for many beginner arrangers, as well as seasoned designers who are always searching for interesting materials. It is among the most popular cut

forms equally as well growing in a container submerged in shallow water as in soil. The leaf structure is a whorl of leaves, tightly arranged at the top of a tall, green stem. Umbrella plant thrives best in full sunlight, but will also grow in partial shade. Because it is a tender perennial, some injury from freezes will occur nearly every winter, especially in the upper South, where it is often grown in containers that can be given minimal protection. Cut back old, brown, freeze-injured foliage in late winter, just before new growth begins. Occasionally cut back all foliage to the ground, even if plants do not sustain freeze

Elaeagnus, or Russian olive, is a popular foliage for arrangements and wreaths with its long, soft, pliable shoots. WCW

yellow and green-variegated foliage. Several of these include 'Aurea', 'Maculata', 'Variegata', and 'Sunset'. *E. angustifolia*, another species that also goes by the common name "Russian olive," is a small tree form with striking, silvery-colored foliage. *E. multiflora*, the cherry elaeagnus, is a broad, spreading shrub that produces a bountiful crop of beautiful, cherry-red, edible fruit in mid-summer. Birds relish the fruit.

Stems and branches of Russian olive make a strong showing as cut foliage because of their handsome line quality. They hold up well if cuttings are properly conditioned in water that contains a floral preservative. The long shoots are often used as a substitute for grapevines to form wreaths and other decorative pieces. The silvery undersides of the foliage are especially attractive under artificial light, as they reflect the light.

Loquat, or Japanese plum, has large, bold leaves and produces edible fruit in spring near the Gulf. NGO

Equisetum hyemale
(ek-kew-SE-tum hi-e-MA-le)
HORSETAIL, EQUISETUM
Family: Equisetaceae
Zone: 7–10. Size: 3–4 feet tall

A plant of prehistoric origin, this rather obscure, upright growing, green-stemmed perennial is reputed to have once covered large portions of the earth as huge forest trees, but today it is little more than an element of visual enrichment in our gardens. It is often a source of serious concern in farming operations, especially to rice and sugar cane farmers, because of the aggressive spread of the plant in fertile, moist soils. Barriers set several inches deep can keep horsetail from escaping its designated positions in planting beds. A small patch of horsetail growing either in water or in soil can be the source of fine cuttings for use when line materials are needed in arrangements.

Eriobotrya japonica
(e-ri-o-BOT-ri-a ja-PON-i-ka)
LOQUAT, JAPANESE PLUM
Family: Rosaceae
Zone: 8–10. Size: 20 feet by 15 feet

Loquat, a small evergreen tree, is especially well-suited for relatively small garden spaces. It produces large, stiff, coarse-textured leaves to 8 inches long and 3 inches wide. The upper surface of each leaf is smooth, dark green, and somewhat shiny, while the underside has a feltlike texture. As is the

case for most members of the rose family, loquats must have well-drained soil and full sunlight for most of the day. Branching is especially handsome because of the curvature of the small branches, each possessing a unique line quality. Fragrant, creamy-white flowers are produced in clusters in autumn. Following mild winters in its upper range, and nearly every year in the southern zone, clusters of yellow, sweet-tasting, edible fruit resembling apricots are produced in spring. Like other members of the rose family, loquat is susceptible to fire blight and other leaf diseases. It is a relatively short-lived evergreen tree.

Loquat can be the source of beautiful cuttings. Pieces may be selected for particular settings and for precise positioning within an arrangement form. Added features can include clusters of tiny, cream-colored, sweet-scented flowers that appear each autumn followed by spring fruit, if temperatures do not dip much below the freezing point.

Eucalyptus cinerea
(you-ka-LIP-tus sy-NEER-ee-a)
EUCALYPTUS, SILVER DOLLAR TREE
Family: Myrtaceae
Zone: 8–10. Size: 40–50 feet by 20 feet

Few plants produce a more aromatic fragrance when cut than does the eucalyptus. The aroma can fill a room, and remains strong for weeks. Somewhat tem-

Horsetail, or equisetum, is noted for its green, segmented, leafless stems, but can be invasive if not contained. NGO

Silver-dollar eucalyptus is useful for both dried and fresh arrangements. NGO

peramental as to soil types, trees grow rapidly in sandy, well-drained soils but fare poorly in heavy, water-logged soils. Trees are also subject to winter kill. Although trees can be quite untidy in appearance after freezes, periodic freezing of the upper canopy causes plants to resprout and form multiple-stemmed masses. These new trunks produce long, well-proportioned branches of round-shaped leaves highly desirable for cuttings. Leaves on old, mature trees are more lance-shaped. In fact, some people intentionally prune back their trees so they will continue to produce an abundant source of immature foliage suitable for cuttings. The resulting form is hardly the accent specimen to feature on the front lawn, however! As trees age, the size of the leaves decreases considerably, and trees lose some of their more desirable qualities.

The silvery-gray, coin-shaped leaves of the eucalyptus are among our most popular evergreen cut foliage. The light color of the foliage makes them stand out in positions indoors with low light. Leaves remain soft and pliable for weeks, and if left in place for extended periods, they dry without discoloring and may be used over and over.

Fatsia japonica
(FAT-si-a ja-PON-i-ka)
FATSIA
Family: Araliaceae
Zone: 7–10. Size: 4–8 feet by 5 feet

A mainstay in the shade garden, fatsia is noted primarily for its bold, multi-lobed, coarse-textured leaves, although in the warm parts of the region stems of striking off-white flowers produced in winter and clusters of black fruit in spring are additional features. Mature specimens form multiple-stemmed masses of large, fan-shaped, leathery leaves to 8 inches across. The periodic removal of old stalks will force parent plants to produce basal shoots of new growth. Old plants become thin and treelike, with relatively few leaves atop thick trunks. This shrub performs

best beneath the canopies of tall trees like pines and adjacent to buildings that shield it from direct sunlight during the hot parts of the day. Companion plants include aucuba, English ivy, azaleas, and camellias.

Sometimes tufts of terminal growth are cut from fatsia for indoor uses, but more frequently single leaves are combined with flowers and other foliage. The thick leaves persist for a lengthy period.

Hedera helix
(HED-er-a HE-lix)
ENGLISH IVY
Family: Araliaceae
Zone: 5-9. Size: twining vine

English ivy is among the most celebrated evergreen vining plants in the South. Its versatile qualities include being an outstanding low-growing ground cover and a climbing, self-clinging vine that can adhere to almost any structure by its aerial rootlets. However, do not allow this vine to grow on wood surfaces. It is also widely used in container plantings where trailing plant growth is desirable. The classic, dark blue-green, lobed or heart-shaped leaves are easily recognized by most people. In the upper South, English ivy grows well in both full sunlight and in shade, but in the lower South plants fare much better in partial shade. Select a site with porous, well-drained soils. English ivy is an ideal ground cover for areas too

Fatsia, with its bold, leathery foliage, thrives in partially shaded locations. T. E. POPE

English ivy, in its multitude of forms, is likely the most widely used garden-grown cut foliage. NGO

Hosta spp.
(HOS-ta)
HOSTA, PLANTAIN LILY
Family: Liliaceae
Zone: 4–9. Size: 1–2 feet by 1–3 feet

Hostas are among our most admired garden perennials grown for both their distinctive foliage and flowers. The large, bold, coarse-textured species can be used as stand-alone accent plants, while the smaller-foliaged types make handsome ground covers, pocket plantings, and borders in shaded positions in the garden. Hostas need a fertile, moist, well-drained soil and protection from direct sunlight during mid-morning through mid-afternoon in summer months. Hostas die back to the ground in early winter, but return in early spring. Depending on the species and cultivars, these dense-mounding perennials give rise to tall, stalked terminal clusters of white, blue, or lilac hyacinthlike flowers from early summer through early autumn.

H. sieboldiana is a particularly handsome species with large, blue-green leaves. Cultivars 'Honeybells' and 'Royal Standard' are two very dependable choices

shaded for turf. Be patient—the first year plants sleep, the second year they creep, and the third year they leap. Unfortunately, in some sections of the lower South, this ground cover is highly susceptible to a root fungus that takes a big toll on large mass plantings during the hot, humid months, mostly in July and August. When used as a ground cover, it is often accented with plantings of bulbs, especially the spring-flowering types. There are many fine cultivars available in the trade noted for their petite leaves that are more tightly arranged along the flexible stems than the regular English ivy.

English ivy is likely the most popular of all the vines for cut foliage purposes. Cut only fully mature growth, because new growth wilts badly. It is widely used for weddings and other special occasions where plants are needed to soften structures that are a part of staging. Cuttings remain turgid out of water for up to a day without wilting, if only mature plant parts are taken and these are submerged in water for

up to a half day prior to using them in interior settings. Cuttings in water root in a couple of weeks. After they are used indoors, the vines can be planted in the garden.

Hosta leaves (and flowers of some species) are excellent for cutting. NGO

Top: Ornamental sweet potato 'Marguerite' covers an arch in Van Chaplin's garden in Birmingham. WCW

Above: A close-up of the highly popular ornamental sweet potato 'Marguerite' in Patti McGee's Charleston garden. WCW

foliage. They are perennials, but are often used as annuals in parts of the South that experience freezing temperatures. The vines grow rapidly and can cover a garden structure very quickly in the spring. These tropical vines are also handsome in hanging containers. Fertilize vines regularly to promote accelerated foliage growth. Cut back foliage to the ground in late autumn and protect the underground "potatoes" with a heavy mulch, or if there is a danger of hard freezes, dig and store the fleshy roots in a frost-free storage unit. Cuttings root readily in water, so propagation is easy. They make handsome additions to arrangements; the foliage is so colorful, it is very decorative standing alone in a container of water.

Juniperus virginiana
(jo-NIP-er-us ver-jin-i-A-na)
EASTERN RED CEDAR
Family: Cupressaceae
Zone: 4–9. Size: 30–50 feet by 25–30 feet

The Eastern red cedar, not really a cedar but a juniper, is one of our tallest-growing junipers, and is indigenous to parts of the region with alkaline soils. In fact, it is a good indicator plant of soils with outcrops of limestone. Under these conditions the species can be quite dominant, but in other parts of the region only a single specimen can be seen growing here and there, especially around old farmsteads, on cemetery grounds, and along fence rows where birds have deposited seeds. The crushed foliage has a rather unpleasant odor. In the western part of the region the cedar or Ashe juniper (*J. ashei*) is prevalent.

Cedar wood has been used for many years to line closets, chests, and other winter clothing storage units to give protection from moths. In the early days before western trees were shipped to the region, cedar trees were frequently cut for Christmas trees. Most were cut from the native

for the lower South because they are profuse bloomers in late summer and produce an abundance of foliage. The bold, rounded to heart-shaped leaves are excellent for use in arrangements, but should be conditioned a couple of hours in warm water before they are placed in arrangements. The leaf stems are soft and are difficult to push into water-absorbing floral foams, so they are best placed directly into the water in containers.

Ipomoea spp.
(ip-po-MEE-a)
ORNAMENTAL SWEET POTATOES
Family: Convolvulaceae
Zone: 9–10. Size: 6–10 feet, vine

The ornamental sweet potatoes have become quite popular in recent years. Several cultivars of *I. batatas* have unusually attractive foliage. 'Blackie' produces a black-purple foliage; 'Marguerita' a beautiful lime-green foliage; and 'Pink Frost' pink, cream, and green

A close-up of the Texas Ashe cedar berries. SIMPSON

The Florida leucothoe provides beautiful branches of foliage and flowers in spring. T. E. POPE

Greek laurel, or bay, is an excellent container plant for cut greens and for culinary uses. NGO

landscapes. Through the years, cuttings from this popular evergreen have been used for the foundations of wreaths and other decorative holiday pieces. Several cultivars of the Eastern red cedar having different-colored foliage are available in the trade. 'Canaertii' has stiff, dark green foliage, and 'Glauca' produces a bluish-gray foliage. All of these are relatively dense, upright-growing forms. As with all members of the juniper family, select a site with a porous, well-drained soil where plants can receive full sunlight.

Related species like the horizontally-growing 'Pfitzer', 'Blue Vase', and 'Tamarix' junipers produce similar foliage useful for cuttings. The foliage of cedars is highly flammable because of the resins, so keep foliage a safe distance from flames. Cedar and juniper foliage holds up well outdoors, but dries relatively quickly if stems are not in water.

Laurus nobilis
(LAW-rus NO-bil-is)
LAUREL, BAY
Family: Lauraceae
Zone: 7–9. Size: 10–25 feet by 15 feet

The laurel or bay has had an interesting history going back to ancient Greece and Rome, when sprigs of this evergreen tree were used to make crowns and wreaths for conquering heroes. In addition to being one of our popular culinary herbs, it is a lovely, upright-growing large shrub to small tree. Bays grow slowly, especially as young plants. Every household that includes a serious cook needs at least one of these delightful, dense-foliaged trees in the garden, to provide fresh bay leaves for Italian and other special cuisine. The leathery, stiff, wonderfully aromatic foliage that gives off a spicy fragrance is popular for holiday decorations. The foliage persists for an extended period in water, and dries very nicely as well. In a dry state, leaves hold their aromatic quality for a long time. People use bay to keep insects like roaches out of their cabinets.

Leucothoe populifolia (Agarista populifolia)
(lew-KOTH-o-ie pop-u-li-FOL-i-a)
FLORIDA LEUCOTHOE, PIPE-STEM WOOD
Family: Ericaceae
Zone: 8–9. Size: 8–12 feet by 6–8 feet

This upright-growing, multiple-stemmed evergreen shrub with an umbrellalike canopy is a relatively new introduction to our gardens. It has handsome, leathery leaves closely arranged on long ascending branches. Funnel-shaped, creamy-white flowers resembling lily-of-the-valley flowers are tightly arranged in profusion along the stemmy canes in early spring. This leucothoe grows well beneath the canopy of high-branched trees such as pines. In full sunlight the foliage tends to become bleached during the hot months of the year. It performs well in most well-drained soils. This introduced species blends well with natives in natural settings.

The long sweeping, slightly curving branches, with or without flowers, make beautiful cuttings for arrangements and hold up well in water. Florida leucothoe is always a hit when used because of its graceful line qualities. It is relatively new to Southern gardens and few people know much about it. The flowers last only a day or so, but the foliage alone is long-lasting.

Magnolia grandiflora
(mag-NO-li-a gran-di-FLO-ra)
SOUTHERN MAGNOLIA
Family: Magnoliaceae
Zone: 7–9. Size: 40–75 feet by 40 feet

The genus *Magnolia* includes many deciduous species and cultivar selections that produce very large, handsome flowers. This particular grand, stately Southern native produces beautiful evergreen foliage with reddish down on the underside, showy creamy-white flowers in late spring and summer, and red-fruited cones in early autumn. A specimen magnolia is a strong accent in any landscape setting, and in mass these trees provide strong spatial structure, screening, and other forms of privacy control. This native species produces lustrous, dark green, stiff, leathery leaves to nearly 10 inches long and 4 inches wide. The foliage of the Southern magnolia is among the most popular cut greens in the region, yet there are numerous cultivars in the trade today that have been

Dramatic foliage of the variegated-foliaged "blood" banana. NGO

introduced because of their even more striking foliage. These include 'Samuel Sommer', 'Russet', and 'Majestic Beauty'. 'Little Gem' is a selection with a petite leaf and a tight, upright growth form.

Magnolias grow in a relatively wide range of soil conditions, but perform best in fertile, well-drained soils. Provide full sunlight for most of the day to produce a dense tree canopy. Unfortunately, the foliage is sometimes marred by leaf fungi and leaf-eating insects. These problems appear to be quite regional in nature and vary in degree of severity from year to year. Magnolias are relatively high-maintenance trees because they shed leaves over most of the year. If the lower tree limbs are left intact, many of the shedding leaves will drop under the canopy and be concealed by the low, spreading branches. Cuttings of the Southern magnolia retain their fine qualities for weeks. They are appropriate for all kinds of occasions where a strong presence of foliage is desirable.

Musa spp.
(MU-za)
BANANA
Family: Musaceae
Zone: 8–10. Size: 10 feet by 6 feet, clumps

In the tropical regions of the world, there is not a more versatile cut foliage than the banana. The huge, thin, arching, and gracefully folded membranous

Dwarf banana produces attractive flowers during the summer months and fruit in late autumn. NGO

Dwarf myrtle produces lovely, fine-textured cut foliage that is frequently used in wedding bouquets. WCW

flowers with prominent stamens somewhat hidden among the plant's small leaves. It is well adapted to planting in pots and other containers. The dwarf forms, 'Compacta' and 'Microphylla', are relatively small, compact shrubs that grow to only 2 feet tall and produce tiny leaves.

Myrtles make great cut foliage. Their small, aromatic leaves have a clean, elegant quality that complements larger, more assertive, coarse-textured foliage and flowers.

Phormium tenax
(FOR-mi-um TE-naks)
NEW ZEALAND FLAX
Family: Agavaceae
Zone: 8–10. Size: 4 feet by 4 feet, clump

This striking grasslike perennial adds a unique foliage quality to a garden setting when used in combination with other plants. The

leaves are used for everything from cooking utensils or food wraps to building structures that shield people from the harsh elements of the tropics. The bold, dramatic qualities of the foliage make a strong presence in any garden setting. Plants grow rapidly in a fertile, moist soil. They will perform best in full sunlight, but do reasonably well in partial shade. Moderate freezes kill banana foliage, and harsh winds riddle the foliage of plants in unprotected places. All banana plants need periodic grooming. The removal of dead and dying foliage, caused either by freezes, old age, or wind, greatly improves the appearance of this tropical.

One problem with banana leaves used as cut foliage is their tendency to curl after being cut, even when recommended conditioning practices are followed. In this condition they still make a strong impact as cut foliage, because of the dramatic size of each leaf. Brown leaves taken from plants late in the season are also quite striking in autumn arrangements.

Myrtus communis
(MER-tus kom-MEW-nis)
MYRTLE
Family: Myrtaceae
Zone: 8–9. Size: 12–20 feet by 8 feet

A native of the Mediterranean region, this evergreen shrub's crown-shaped foliage is reported to have been a more-prized pos-

session than gold in ancient Greece. Myrtle foliage was used as crowns for military victors, and represented peace and joy in the Holy Land. This delightful, old-garden evergreen can be used in the southern part of the region, especially near the coast, on sites with fast-drained, alkaline soils. Myrtle cannot tolerate cold, wet soils. Plants produce an abundance of petite, white, fragrant

Variegated New Zealand flax in a Southern garden. NGO

clumps with long, arching, sword-shaped leaves are easy to manage, even as they expand to rather large, imposing sizes in the garden. Select a protected position in the garden that receives full sunlight and provide a well-drained soil; otherwise, root rot will occur in a heavy, clay, water-logged soil. New Zealand flax is an ideal plant to feature in garden containers like planters and large pots. There are several selections in the trade that have very attractively colored foliage other than green. These include the bronze or purple flax, 'Atropurpureum'; the variegated green and creamy-yellow foliaged 'Variegatum' and 'Tricolor' cultivars; and the red cultivar, 'Rubrum'. Although the leaves are somewhat soft and limber, they are popular cut foliage in arrangements because of their length and color. They hold up well in water for an extended period.

Pinus spp.
(PI-nus)
PINES
Family: Pinaceae
Zone: 5–9. Size: 100 feet by 30 feet

Nearly every part of the South has its unique soil or other special environmental niches where at least one and sometimes many species of pine are native and grow well. In some areas like South Louisiana and Coastal Mississippi only small "islands" of isolated pines grow here and there along slight ridges of well-drained soils. In other parts of the region, pine forests cover much of the countryside and even shade whole neighborhoods in communities across the region. To the casual observer, all pines are basically alike, but upon closer observation the species vary greatly in plant form, foliage color, density, and needle length. Pines are normally associated with upland soils, but landscape planting sites can be amended to accommodate a few of these tall-growing evergreens. They grow fast, but require well-

A branch of slash pine, one of the numerous species of pines that grow in the South.
CHARLES F. FRYLING JR.

drained soil and full sunlight for acceptable growth.

Slash pine (*P. elliottii*) and loblolly pine (*P. taeda*) are the most common species in the South. They are quite similar in plant form and have clusters of needles to 10 inches long. These two are quite tolerant of a broad range of soil types. Longleaf pine (*P. palustris*), on the other hand, is a taller, more open-growing species that produces clusters of needles up to 15 inches in length. This pine is quite particular about where it will grow well, and must have very well-drained soil with a high sand content. Two species with relatively short needles include the shortleaf pine (*P. echinata*) and the spruce pine (*P. glabra*). Their canopies tend to be more dense than some of the others that allow filtered light through their branches. Other pines of the region include the Scotch pine (*P. sylvestris*), Virginia pine (*P. virginiana*), and to a lesser degree, the white pine (*P. strobus*).

No discussion on foliage would be complete without references to the pines, because this foliage is normally readily available to any household, and a single tree can be the source of a considerable amount of cut foliage for

holiday decorations. Even a carefully selected single branch can be quite dramatic in form and presence when placed in a large container indoors.

Pittosporum tobira
(pit-o-SPO-rum *or* pi-TOS-po-rum toe-BIR-a)
PITTOSPORUM
Family: Pittosporaceae
Zone: 8–10. Size: 10 feet by 15 feet

Pittosporum is a broad-spreading evergreen shrub that produces whorls of small, leathery, olive-green, slightly convex leaves at the tips of the somewhat horizontally-growing branches. They require a well-drained soil and preferably full sunlight, although this shrub grows quite well beneath a high canopy of trees like the pines. Companion plants that grow in the same conditions include azaleas, many of the hollies, nandina, and several of the viburnums. The paler, cream-colored leaves of the variegated pittosporum (*P. t.* 'Variegata') are very popular cut foliage because they combine well with the solid greens of other plants. It is not uncommon to see both solid green and variegated foliage on the same plant. This is due to the variegated form reverting back to the parent, solid green

Pittosporum with green and variegated forms on the same plant. WCW

type. If the solid green portions are not removed, the solid green foliage will eventually take over the entire plant. Both green and variegated selections produce dense foliage when grown in full sunlight, and somewhat thinner, more open-branching patterns in partial shade. Pittosporums also produce sweetly-scented, creamy-white flowers that yellow after several days.

Both long branches and the smaller tip clusters may be cut from pittosporums. Cuttings hold up a couple of weeks before drying and shriveling on the stems. Cuttings of 'Variegata' are highly effective in darker indoor spaces because of their light, creamy-white coloration.

Podocarpus macrophyllus
(pod-o-KAR-pus mak-ro-FIL-us)
PODOCARPUS, JAPANESE YEW
Family: Podocarpaceae
Zone: 8–10. Size: 10–20 feet by 8–12 feet

This popular, slow-growing evergreen is often planted as a hedge for privacy control either in a clipped or natural state, because of its slender, upright form. Individual specimens can become sizable evergreen trees in the lower coastal part of the region. It is incorrectly called a "yew" because the foliage and the plant form are somewhat similar to members of the *Taxus* genus, a group of evergreens that performs much better in the upper Southern and northeastern parts of the country. The dark green, narrow leaves, up to 4 inches long, are somewhat glossy. Podocarpus grows well in full sunlight to partial shade and must have a well-drained soil for satisfactory performance. The variety Maki is more shrublike in character, but produces similar foliage. A lesser-known relative that also grows in the South is the coarser-textured *P. nagi*, the broadleaf podocarpus.

Podocarpus foliage holds up quite well as cuttings and is very useful as "filler." The narrow leaves combine well with other foliage, especially the broader, more coarse-textured materials.

Rosmarinus officinalis
(ros-ma-RY-nus o-fis-i-NA-lis)
ROSEMARY
Family: Labiatae
Zone: 7–9. Size: 2–4 feet by 3–4 feet

Rosemary is a hardy, aromatic culinary perennial or half-shrub native to the Mediterranean region. This old garden plant is receiving considerable attention today as culinary and medicinal herbs regain popularity in contemporary gardens. One or more rosemary plants can be easily integrated into any garden setting, if plants receive full sunlight and are planted in a fast-drained soil, even if the soil is relatively infertile. For this reason these plants are well adapted to container culture. What this perennial cannot tolerate is shade and cold, wet soils. As plants age, they form large mounds of delightfully fragrant foliage on twisted stems. During the late spring and summer months, small purple flowers are

Podocarpus, or Japanese yew, in fruit, a good Southern substitute for the true yew (*Taxus*). NGO

Rosemary is useful for both ornamental and culinary purposes. NGO

produced among the narrow leaves. Plant rosemary adjacent to paths and other passageways, so that casual contact with the plant will release into the atmosphere the aromatic fragrance (oils) of the foliage. Every sunny garden needs this herb for a readily-available source of fresh rosemary for cooking. There are many different cultivars in the trade. They vary in plant size, flowering quality, color of foliage, and winter-hardiness. Cuttings retain their fresh quality for an extended period, if stems are in water.

Setcreasea pallida
(set-CREAS-ea PAL-id-a)
**PURPLE HEART,
SETCREASEA**
Family: Commelinaceae
Zone: 9–10. Size: 10–12 inches tall and spreading

The violet-purple foliage of purple heart makes a strong presence in landscape plantings, and plants are also popular for container gardening. In raised plantings, the relatively fast growing shoots with long, pointed leaves hang gracefully over the edges. Depending on the cultivar, white, pink, or purplish flowers are an added feature. In warm, protected positions in the lower South, purple heart makes an excellent permanent ground cover. It combines nicely with many other plants and is a

strong contrasting color to most other foliage. This is a very easy perennial to grow. Provide morning sunlight and a fertile, moist soil. Cuttings root easily and are excellent for use in arrangements.

Smilax smallii
(SMI-laks)
SOUTHERN SMILAX
Family: Liliaceae
Zone: 7–9. Size: 20–30 feet, vine

"Garlands of Southern smilax draped over candelabras and lattice work, clustered at the ends of the church pews, and hung throughout the reception hall." These often repeated phrases have been associated with many Southern weddings over the years. There is in fact a "romantic" character to smilax that makes it right at home in weddings, but it has been equally as popular at other celebrations. Need a beautiful evergreen vine to make a holiday wreath, mantle piece, or table arrangement? Smilax is a great cutting green. With its shiny, dark green leaves, the natural form of smilax as a clipped specimen is

Purple heart combines well with many grasses and other perennials. T. E. POPE

Smilax is a graceful vine, traditionally used for decorations in Southern weddings and special holidays. NGO

unparalleled in plant growth. A single stem can stand alone in rare elegance or long strands can soften trellis work, arbors, and other structures associated with various celebrations. It is common in Southern woodlands, but is sometimes difficult to capture and bring down from its perch atop trees and other tall vegetation.

After cutting, submerge the entire vine in a big vat of water and allow it to stay for a half day or more before using the material in an arrangement. Smilax retains its beautiful quality for a couple of days out of water, and for a week or more if cut stems are placed in water containing a preservative.

Vinca major
(VING-ka MA-jor)
VINCA, BIGLEAF PERIWINKLE
Family: Apocynaceae
Zone: 7–9. Size: to 10–12 feet

Vinca is an evergreen, viny ground cover ideally suited for naturalistic areas because it always appears very casual and a bit untidy, but is quite persistent. Vinca should be planted in shaded places, because direct sunlight burns the foliage and causes a planting to be unthrifty. Coverage is rather rapid for plantings placed on 12–18-inch settings. For best results add a considerable amount of organic matter to planting beds and fertil-

ize a couple of times annually to encourage more rapid and denser coverage. The variegated form, with its creamy-white and green leaves, is particularly popular in containers, as the runners cascade nicely over the sides of raised plantings. Cuttings placed in water with a floral preservative will last for several weeks.

FERNS

Because of the intense heat in the Deep South during summer months, we normally strive to plant an abundance of trees to produce much-needed shade.

When the light is reduced by fifty to sixty percent, the number of plants that can grow beneath the canopy of large trees is correspondingly reduced. For example, do not attempt to grow turf—turf grasses will not grow in positions where sunlight has been reduced by this amount, regardless of the horticulture practices used to encourage them. Ferns do extremely well in these shaded places in our gardens. These flowerless perennials reproduce from spores borne on the lower sides of their fronds. There are over ten thousand species of ferns, and many of them make excellent ornamentals for deeply-shaded locations where many other plants will not grow. They can provide delightful fresh foliage each spring and bold textures during the growing season in some parts of the garden that might otherwise have been abandoned.

Ferns grow best in positions that receive early morning sunlight for several hours, but become shielded from hot noonday and afternoon sunlight during summer months. They do best in moist soils heavily fortified with humus such as compost and leaf mold. To maintain a high level of humus, add 3–6 inches of fresh leaf mulch each year during late

This large-leaf variegated vinca, a popular ground cover, produces long, graceful stems of foliage useful for containers. T. E. POPE

winter. Ferns also respond well to heavy feeding in the early spring, just as new growth begins. Use a general, all-purpose, complete fertilizer following the recommendations given by the manufacturer. Ferns normally perform poorly in heavy, wet, compacted soils. Cut back deciduous types to near the ground in mid- to late December after the foliage has been killed by winter freezes and its clear, brown color begins to fade. At this time apply a new layer of mulch.

A partial listing of some of the most popular ferns for shade gardens include the following: **maidenhair fern** (*Adiantum capillus-veneris*) is a clump-forming fern with delicate, fine-textured, fan-shaped leaves. The leaves have a delightful yellow-green color that contrast nicely with their dark purple to black stems. This fern does well planted directly into a surface layer of rotted plant growth formed from years of accumulation of leaves and other organic matter. It will even grow on moss-covered brick and in decaying wood. Fertilize in early spring. The **Northern maidenhair fern** (*A. pedatum*), a deciduous fern, does well in the upper South, growing under similar conditions. **The holly leaf fern** (*Cyrtomium falcatum*) is a highly popular evergreen that forms mounding clumps of arching leaves to nearly 30 inches long. This one should be protected from harsh freezes below about 25° F. Good grooming practices will keep this species from becoming untidy. Remove all browning fronds just as the new growth emerges in early spring. Very large clumps can be lifted, divided into several parts, and replanted in late winter. **Boston fern** (*Nephrolepis exaltata* 'Bostoniensis') is a species most often seen growing in large pots and hanging baskets, but in the mild sections of the South it forms a wonderful ground cover, when planted in a humus-rich soil. The stiff, upright, sword-shaped fronds add a unique texture to the

Top: The delicate-foliaged maidenhair fern growing on a brick retaining wall in Natchez. NGO

Middle: Holly fern, a popular evergreen for shade gardens. JO KELLUM, ASLA

Above: The sword or Boston fern is an excellent ground cover in the lower South, and is a good choice for hanging baskets and other containers. NGO

great accent specimen for planting among other perennials, in low-growing ground covers, and other places in a naturalistic garden. The **leatherleaf fern** (*Rumohra adiantiformis*) produces firm, plastic-like triangular fronds and is among the most popular for use in bouquets. It is a great fern to use in clumps, eventually forming small colonies of rich, dark-green leaves, although spread is relatively slow when compared to most other species. Early frosts will damage the fronds, but if plantings are cut back and mulched heavily with leaves, new growth will reappear in late spring.

Marsh or **wood fern** (*Thelypteris palustris*) is a delightful native fern that can be seen growing in moist places over the entire region. It makes an ideal ground cover beneath the canopy of trees, where few other plants will grow. The light yellow-green leaves and bold texture can really lighten up otherwise dark, moody positions in the garden. Cut back the fronds in winter and mulch heavily with leaf mold. Fertilize in early spring. A second crop of this fern can be produced if the old, maturing fronds are cut in mid-summer and plants are fertilized and watered thoroughly. This is one of the easiest of all ground covers to grow. There will be slightly over three months during the winter when there is no foliage, but a clean mulch of pine-straw or leaves will usually be acceptable, even for gardeners who require a well-groomed appearance.

Top: A clump of royal fern makes a strong presence as a single specimen. NGO
Above: Leatherleaf fern, a popular commercially produced fern for the florist industry, is easy to grow in the home garden. T. E. POPE
Below: Marsh or wood fern is common throughout the South, and makes an excellent summer ground cover. NGO

group of traditional ground covers, which are predominantly flat. Cut back all of the top growth in mid-winter and mulch the basal crowns with a heavy layer of leaf mold. Fertilize the emerging new foliage in early spring.

Royal fern (*Osmunda regalis*) is a delightful clump type that produces tall, arching fronds to nearly 30 inches high, and a center cluster of tall brown fronds extend out of the center of mature plants in summer. This can be a

A demonstration planting of ornamental grasses showing the many diverse sizes and forms. NGO

ORNAMENTAL GRASSES

Ornamental grasses have received much attention in recent years. Only a relatively short time ago, about all that was offered in the trade were the turf grasses, possibly pampas grass, and a couple of other ornamental selections. Today, however, the story is quite different. Ease of cultivation, freedom from most plant pests, low water requirements, adaptation to a wide range of soil conditions, good heat and cold tolerances, diversity of form, and, most of all, their unique foliage and flower characteristics—these are but a few of the advantages giving rise to entire sections of many nurseries being devoted to this very special group of plants. Grasses comprise a very large and complex family (*gramineae*) of plants that, worldwide, are among our most important plants. Members of this group include the major commercial agricultural cereal crops like wheat, corn, rye, oats, and rice, and a big specialty crop in Louisiana and Florida, sugar cane. The ever-increasing number of grasses being introduced for ornamental uses are mostly clump grasses. They vary in height over a range of from less than 1 foot to 12- or even 15-foot tall species.

Most of the grasses share common requirements for growth—full sunlight, well-drained soil, and most should be cut back in mid- to late winter, even in parts of the region where the foliage is not killed by freezes, so as to encourage fresh foliage growth in the spring. Most are tolerant of a wide range of soil types, and although they do not require much care otherwise, an annual application of fertilizer is beneficial.

Cuttings of both flowers and foliage of the grasses are popular materials in arrangements, both in the fresh and the dried state. Dried flower heads of grasses shed rather badly indoors after they become fully mature. If possible, cut them before they reach this stage. For those species that produce heavy plumes like ravenna grass and pampas grass, spray the heads with hair spray to reduce the amount of shedding.

Arundo donax
(a-RUN-doe doe-NAKS)
GIANT REED
Zone: 7–10. Size: 10–15 feet

Giant reed is one of our most dramatic grasses because its towering canes reach a height of 15 feet or more in a mature planting. This is a large, clump-forming grass, and consequently should be reserved for large garden spaces that can

A colony of giant reed in early spring showing the heavy green and white variegation. NGO

Top: A forest of giant timber bamboo. NGO
Above: Clumps of hedge bamboo. NGO

accommodate its mammoth height and spread. The form 'Variegata' is especially attractive with its distinctive white- and green-striped leaves. As warm weather arrives, much of the variegation fades into a dull green that persists for the remainder of the growing season. Keep the spread of giant reed in check by cutting back old growth to the ground every year. Both the foliage and the prominent silky, buff-colored flower heads, produced in late summer, are popular materials for arrangements.

Bambusa, Phyllostachys, and *Sasa* spp.
(bamb-OO-sa, fillo-STACH-ees, SASS-ah)
BAMBOO
Zone: 7–10. Sizes: 2–20 feet

Bamboos can be either friend or foe, depending on where they are planted and the uses intended. For some gardeners the very thought of bamboos brings on alarming images of aggressive growth and spread by underground runners that are nearly impossible to control. Others, however, deem them both an essential plant form and the theme plant for certain Oriental garden settings. Bamboo clumps form very tight, competi-

tive root systems and heavy canopies that essentially limit the growth of other ornamentals close by. However, for centuries these grasses have been used in gardens for privacy control (the hedge types, *B. glaucescens* or *multiplex*); as fencing, from the cut poles of the timber types (*Phyllostachys* spp.); as an integral part of Oriental garden water features; and for their dramatic towering forestlike quality when the timber types are planted in groves. Bamboos have a delightful foliage texture, and the hedge types are quite elegant planted in contained clumps to provide graceful movement from the tall, slender canes. These grasses are worth having, if for no other purpose than for introducing some movement in a garden setting. Every garden needs at least one small clump of bamboo to be the source of handy garden stakes for vegetable and ornamental plants.

Bamboo foliage is relatively difficult to condition. Immediately after cutting, submerge stems and foliage in hot water. Condition the material in water for several hours before using the cuttings in arrangements.

The giant bamboos are often crafted into containers for floral arrangements. Leora Moore of North Charleston. South Carolina, and Mrs. D. S. Asbill of Columbia. South Carolina, have shared their instructions for conditioning and preserving pieces of giant bamboo: Cut the bamboo into lengths that you desire for containers. Use two large containers—in one container add white vinegar, and in the other add water and salt at the ratio of one tablespoon of salt to one quart of water. Use enough of the liquids to cover only one to three pieces of bamboo. Boil the pieces in the vinegar for five minutes, turning them with a wooden spoon. Remove the bamboo and wipe off the sticky film with paper towels. After cleaning, drop the cleaned pieces into the boiling salt solution. Turn off heat under each container and allow the bamboo to soak for one hour in the salt solution. Remove bamboo and allow to dry overnight. If desirable the inside of the containers can be sprayed with lacquer.

Chasmanthium latifolium
(chas-MAN-thium lat-i-FOL-i-um)
INLAND SEA OATS
Zone: 7–10. Size: 3 feet by 2 feet

This popular ornamental grass native to Texas produces drooping, one-sided heads of flattened oats and loosely tufted, rich green, arching foliage. For an ideal situation provide a rich, fertile soil with a generous amount of organic matter. However, this grass will grow in dry, sandy, infertile soils. The seed heads, or *oats*, are nice for cutting and using in arrangements as filler materials.

Cymbopogon citratus
(sim-bo-PO-gon sit-TRAY-tus)
LEMONGRASS
Zone: 8–10. Size: 3 feet by 3 feet

This is a clump-forming grass grown for its graceful, lemon-scented foliage and as the commercial source of lemon oil. The light yellow-green, upright-arching foliage and mounding form in mature specimens are special features, but this ornamental grass is subject to winter-kill if there are hard freezes.

Erianthus ravennae
(er-i-AN-thus ra-VEN-nae)
RAVENNA GRASS
Zone: 6–9. Size: 10–12 feet

Ravenna grass is a stiff, upright-growing grass that stays in a relatively tight clump and produces a showy mass of silvery-colored, 2-foot-tall flowering heads above the 3-foot-high foliage in mid- to late autumn. Spray fully mature flower heads with hair spray to reduce the shedding of flowers indoors.

Soft foliage and interesting seed heads on sea oats. WCW

The soft, graceful foliage of lemongrass is ideal for container growing. NGO

The stiff, columnar form of ravenna grass in a planting at the Brooklyn Botanic Garden. NGO

Is there is any doubt about which grass is the Japanese blood grass in a planting of other grasses in late autumn? NGO

Autumn sunlight on a flowering clump of the very popular maiden grass, at the Missouri Botanic Garden in St. Louis. NGO

Imperata cylindrica
(im-per-A-ta si-LIN-dri-ca)
JAPANESE BLOOD GRASS
Zone: 5–9. Size: 18–24 inches

No grass produces a more striking foliage than does Japanese blood grass. The bright red color stands out in a planting as far as the eye can detect the plant is indeed a grass. This species can do a bit more spreading than most of the ornamental grasses, other than bamboo, but it is not overly aggressive. When used in a planting, it usually becomes the accent in any composition, especially in late summer and autumn. The leaves are somewhat shorter than

those of many other ornamental grasses, and clusters of the leaves are normally used in arrangements.

Miscanthus sinensis 'Gracillimus'
(mis-KAN-thus si-NEN-sis)
MAIDEN GRASS
Zone: 4–9. Size: 3–4 feet by 5 feet

Maiden grass is among the most popular of the ornamental grasses. The long, thin, fine-textured, gracefully-arching foliage and open, airy flowers arise from very manageable clumps that are miniature forms of its much coarser relative, pampas grass. Two highly rated cultivars are the variegated selections 'Siberfeder' and 'Zebrinus'. These two cultivars provide nice contrasts to coarser-textured woody and herbaceous plants. *M. s.* 'Variegata', variegated Japanese silver grass, always makes a strong presence in a landscape setting because of its variegated white and green foliage. Members of this genus produce branched flower heads. They can be very handsome when used to provide a light, airy quality to an arrangement.

Muhlenbergia dumosa
(muh-len-BER-gia du-MO-sa)
BAMBOO MUHLY
Zone: 6–9. Size: 6 feet by 6 feet

This ornamental grass has extra fine-textured foliage, although clumps grow to nearly 6 feet in a

A clump of zebra grass in a bed of yellow marigolds and red zinnias at Biltmore Estate, in Asheville, North Carolina. USED WITH PERMISSION FROM BILTMORE ESTATE, ASHEVILLE, NORTH CAROLINA

The fine texture of bamboo muhly. WCW

single season. Its light, airy foliage somewhat resembles garden asparagus. Bamboo muhly has a wonderful tan color in late autumn and winter. *M. lind-heimeri*, Lindheimer's muhly, is also a rather common ornamental grass that is native to Texas. Cut back the foliage to the ground in late winter. Both of these grasses make good filler materials for arrangements.

Above: A clump of fountain grass in a herbaceous border with other perennials. NGO
Below: A mass planting of fountain grass with giant reed (Arundo donax) in the background. NGO

Pennisetum alopecuroides
(pen-i-SE-tum a-low-pee-CURE-oi-dez)
FOUNTAIN GRASS
Zone: 6–9. Size: 5 feet by 3–4 feet

Fountain grass produces relatively soft, wide-bladed leaves and fuzzy, bottlebrushlike flower heads to about six inches long. As with most of the grasses, they begin making a major impact in the landscape in mid- to late spring and reach their peak of performance in late summer, when they produce showy flower heads extending well above the foliage clumps. The purple form of this grass, 'Purpureum', has handsome reddish-purple foliage that com-

The colorful and very popular purple fountain grass makes a strong accent in a planting of annuals. NGO

bines nicely with many solid green and variegated plants. When planted in a landscape, there is usually a lot of conversation about the merits of this plant because of its handsome foliage.

Selections from this genus are the source of flowers often used to give an airy quality to arrangements. Cut specimens persist for several days in a fresh state and also dry quite nicely. Spray flowers with a hair spray if they begin shedding.

Stipa gigantea
(STI-pa ji-gan-TE-a)
GOLDEN OATS
Zone: 7–9. Size: 4–5 feet by 6 feet

Golden oats is a tufted perennial ornamental grass that produces extremely fine-textured foliage from which silvery to purplish, very airy flower heads arise in summer. This grass makes a delightful specimen planted among other perennials. It has an interesting winter character as well. Tall, slender stems of flowers and seed pods extend well beyond the overall height of the clumped foliage.

PALMS

Palms offer some of our most dramatic foliage for cuttings. For interiors large enough to accommodate their grand leaves, they offer great potential for making a bold presence at a relatively small cost. Palms are well adapted to a relatively wide range of soil types and other growing conditions commonly found in the South, provided they receive full sunlight for most of the day. Growth is much faster, however, in a fertile, well-drained soil that has been fortified with a lot of humus, and when they are fertilized at least on an annual basis. Because palms continue to grow throughout the warm periods of the year, an application of fertilizer two or three times a year is both possible and

beneficial in our region. To condition palm fronds, cut the leaf stems and place cut ends in warm water.

Ironically, the **cycas** or **sago palm** (*Cycas revoluta*), which is really not a palm but is often included in groupings of palms, is likely the most popular palmlike plant for cuttings; it is covered in a separate entry in this section. Among the true palms, perhaps the leading candidate for the title of "most decorative" is the **dwarf palmetto** (*Sabal minor*), a native palm that grows over the entire region. Although it is very difficult to transplant from the wild, due to a horizontally growing tuberlike root that is normally cut during transplanting, it is otherwise not particular about where it grows, and in fact is often a pest in farming operations. This very non-treelike palm, which normally reaches no more than 6 feet in height, grows well in heavy, clay soils that remain wet for most of the year, and performs equally well in sandy, well-drained soils, although the fronds are normally much smaller on plants growing in dry soils. Its large, fan-shaped leaves are ideal for use indoors in arrangements, provided containers are sufficiently heavy to support the size and weight. A close relative, the **cabbage palm** (*Sabal palmetto*), grows in the warm parts of the region, usually near the Gulf Coast and along the Atlantic Coast in the southeastern United States. It produces very large leaves on long stems. The

The bright yellow-green color and soft tips of the Chinese fan palm fronds. NGO

Palmetto at Peckerwood Gardens, Hemstead, Texas. WCW

A young specimen of the windmill palm.
CHARLES F. FRYLING JR.

Chinese fan palm (*Livistona chinensis*) produces handsome yellow-green fronds with drooping tips. In locations which do not experience severe freezes, this is a great one to add for a distinctive, tropical touch in a planting that needs a bold foliage. Although there are spines along the leaf stems, this is a very manageable palm that remains as a rather tight cluster of fronds for several years before it begins producing a trunk. In areas that can accommodate large leaves, the leaves of this palm are excellent for big arrangements.

The **lady palm** (*Rhapis excelsa*) is another palm with a fan-shaped leaf, but the leaves are much smaller and more manageable in arrangements than some of the large leaves of most other species. It is quite cold-tender and must be given some protection from freezing temperatures. Consequently, it is frequently grown in large tubs as an accent specimen on patios and terraces during the warm months of the year. Especially useful are its multiple stems covered with a burlap-like fiber and dense foliage. An old multi-stemmed specimen can supply both cut foliage, and sometimes entire stems are used for large indoor arrangements. Cuttings last for an extended period in water. At the other end of the leaf size scale from the lady palm is the **windmill palm** (*Trachycarpus fortunei*), widely adapted to most of the region and likely the most frequently planted palm of all. The large, stiff, fan-

A grove of cabbage palms in Sea Island, Georgia. NGO

shaped leaves are divided into narrow, pleated segments and are borne on long stems. Trunks are covered with a shaggy, burlaplike fiber. It transplants easily in large sizes, and makes a strong presence with its dark green, leathery, fan-shaped leaves up to 3 feet across.

OTHER PLANTS

There are a host of other plants that on occasion might be selected for their distinctive foliage, although this foliage is normally shorter-lived in a cut state than others covered in this chapter. When a particular effect is desirable, however, the following plants offer many possibilities:

Two wonderful native huckleberries of the region, **winter huckleberry**, *Gaylussacia dumosa*, and **sparkleberry**, *Vaccinium arboreum*, have delightful small, leathery leaves that remain a deep red late into the winter. These two shrubs also have interesting lines in their branching. **Wax myrtle**, *Myrica cerifera*, another native evergreen shrub, is noted for its aromatic foliage and its silvery-blue berries from which bay candle fragrances are made. It makes a good filler foliage for a relatively short period. The **Leyland cypress**, × *cupressocyparis leylandii*, is a relatively new conifer for the South. It is receiving considerable attention because of its rapid growth rate and dense upright form. The soft, yellow-green, cedarlike foliage is frequently cut during the holiday season for a variety of decorative uses. Similar to the foliage of most conifers, the leaves dry rather quickly after being cut, especially when used indoors.

Among shrubs, **nandina**, *Nandina domestica*, offers a delightful, fine-textured foliage, but does not hold up well as a cut foliage. After a day or so in water, leaves begin to shed. Its clusters of bright red berries are longer-lasting in a cut state. **Red-leaf photinia**, *Photinia glabra*, has soft, pliable foliage in the mature state. New foliage is a striking red color, but leaves in this early stage must "harden" on the plant before being cut and conditioned for arrangements. Several of the introduced viburnums have evergreen foliage that is versatile as cut foliage. These include **Japanese viburnum**, *Viburnum japonicum*; **Laurustinus viburnum**, *V. tinus*; **Sandankwa viburnum**, *V. suspensum*; and **sweet viburnum**, *V. odoratissimum*. All of these grow well in the South and are reasonably cold-hardy. Each has a strong, bold foliage that holds up well.

Finally, several of the yuccas are used as cut foliage because of their strong line qualities. Since they are quite spiny, this foliage is somewhat dangerous if used in close proximity to people. The **soft leaf yucca**, *Yucca filamentosa*, has a distinctive silvery-green foliage. This gray color is a nice contrast to some of the more traditional greens. The **Spanish dagger yucca**, *Y. aloifolia*, has stiff-pointed, emerald-green leaves. A stalk of yucca flowers makes a dramatic presence in an arrangement, although a single plant will produce only one flower stalk. Flower stalks on the native species are tall, thin, and somewhat airy, while those that produce heavy foliage are normally short and dense. If cut in the bud stage, yucca flowers will last several days in water.

NGO

Seven

Fruiting Plants of Distinction

Autumn is a very special time of the year for fruiting plants in the South, for this is the season when our gardens and natural areas become dotted with their colorful fruit. While some plants produce fruit at other times, around harvest time each year berries and other forms of fruit become quite showy on many of our ornamental plants. They offer numerous possibilities for indoor decorating. This year, on a fine day in September (or October, if you are in the Deep South), take a stroll through your garden and note how many plants display attractive fruit; many of these can be worthy specimens for indoor use. An entire fruiting branch of pyracantha, for example, can make a splendid display standing alone or in combination with other materials.

By technical definition, a fruit is the seed-bearing organ of a plant. There are several types, including (along with an example of each) the following: berry (holly), nut (pecan), drupe (cherry), pome (apple), capsule (daylily), legume (wisteria), and several others. Fruiting follows flowering. A fruit can be a simple, single-seeded nut (like a pecan), or a complex, aggregate fruit (such as the cone of a pine or Southern magnolia, and the even more complex seed-bearing capsule of the pomegranate). Each of these structures has its unique sculptural form. In order to enjoy these forms to the fullest, we normally delay gathering ornamental fruit until it matures, although for some plants fruit in the immature state can have highly decorative qualities as cut specimens. Foliage, flower, and fruit are sometimes combined to express the entire life cycle of a plant.

The earliest records of man's relationship with nature in paintings and other art forms indicate the widespread use of fruit such as apple, pear, fig, and grape in prominent positions in the home. Early Egyptian paintings depict bowls and baskets of carefully arranged fruit on the grand banquet tables of the nobility. Celebration garlands and wreaths of fruit were common in Renaissance art.

What can be more gratifying than going into our private gardens and picking edible fruit from trees that we have grown, then exhibiting the bounty of our harvest in a bowl on a table in a prominent position? Few of us have the luxury of an orchard of fruit trees, but nearly every landscape can accommodate a tree or two and possibly a vine providing edible fruit. In the more temperate areas of the region, consider apple, crabapple, pear, and plum trees. Along the Gulf Coast, citrus can be grown with considerable success for varying lengths of time before a hard freeze interrupts the growth. Other fruiting trees for the lower South include fig, mayhaw, pear, pomegranate, persimmon, and jujube. Whatever its kind, there is always something special about picking fruit from trees in our care.

Fruit, like flowers and foliage, has unique textures, geometric forms, and colors, and is equally as interesting and challenging to work with as flowers and foliage. Some kinds of fruit are usually exhibited with their associated foliage, as is the case with many of the evergreen hollies. For plants like the persimmons and deciduous hollies, the foliage is often plucked off, or gathering is delayed until natural leafdrop has occurred. Fruit can be displayed on its own branches or removed and placed in a container alone or with other items in an artistic arrangement.

The life expectancy of fruit varies considerably. For many berry-producing plants, such as pyracantha and Burford holly, cuttings can remain attractive for a couple of weeks before the berries begin to shrivel, fade, and eventually fall. For a cut specimen of nandina, the period of decline is much more rapid, only a few days in a fresh state. When conditioning cuttings with berries, be sure

An abundance of red berries clustered among the glossy foliage of the aptly-named "Christmas Berry." T. E. POPE

to start the conditioning process with warm water. To the water add the recommended amount of a floral preservative and allow plants to condition for several hours before placing them in an arrangement. Recutting the stems periodically will extend the life of cuttings.

FRUITING PLANTS

Ardisia crenata
(ar-DIZ-i-a kre-NA-ta)
CHRISTMAS BERRY
Family: Myrsinaceae
Zone: 8–10. Size: 2–3 feet by 1 foot

Christmas berry, sometimes called coralberry, is an outstanding fruiting plant in shade. In fact, plants perform poorly in full sunlight, except in early morning sun. Clusters of bright red berries are produced just below the dark, shiny green leaves. Cultivar 'Alba' produces white berries, and there is a less common coral pink cultivar. This is one of the few plants that fruits heavily in shade. Christmas berry is somewhat tender to low, freezing temperatures.

When the tops are killed by freezes of around 20° F, plants usually return the following spring from the roots, if they are mulched with leaves. It takes two years before berries return. Self-seeding is common where plants drop their berries into leaf mold that has accumulated for several years. Excellent companion plants include aspidistra, ferns, hostas, camellias, and English ivy, all shade-loving species. In areas subject to hard freezes, the Christmas berry can be grown as a very attractive tub specimen and moved to protected areas in winter. The rich, dark green serrated leaves and tight clusters of bright red berries make handsome holiday decorations. Cut stems of Christmas berry stay attractive for weeks indoors.

Callicarpa americana
(kal-li-KAR-pa a-mer-i-KA-na)
FRENCH MULBERRY
Family: Verenaceae
Zone: 6–9. Size: 6–8 feet by 6 feet

French mulberry is a prolific self-seeding species native to our Southern fields and woodlands. It grows best where plants receive sunlight for several hours each day. Plants grow relatively well beneath the canopies of large trees, but berrying is somewhat sporadic. This deciduous shrub is not very temperamental as to soil and fares quite well in poor, dry soils. French mulberry foliage drops in early autumn, well before the first frost, and what remains are numerous tight clusters of purple beadlike berries, arranged at close intervals along flexible stems that are ideal for cutting. 'Lactea' is a white-fruiting selection, and Japanese mulberry, *C. japonica*, produces violet-colored berries. Farther north, Bodinier beautyberry (*C. bodinieri*) and purple beautyberry (*C. dichotoma*) are excellent choices for their bountiful production of berries. Long stems of mulberry are effective in arrangements, but the dark purple berries are quite recessive and do not show up well in dark indoor spaces, so provide as much light as possible. Cut specimens persist for up to two weeks, provided the berries show color and most are fully developed. Foliage is normally removed. Place stems in hot water at the time of cutting. A floral preservative helps to lengthen the life of French mulberry.

A long stem of the French mulberry. T. E. POPE

Bittersweet berries just before foliage drop. T. E. POPE

Celastrus scandens
(se-LAS-trus SKAN-denz)
BITTERSWEET
Family: Celastraceae
Zone: 4–8. Size: 25 feet, vine

This is a vine grown in the upper South that can be considered either a friend or a foe, depending on where it is growing.
Bittersweet is a highly-prized vine in the upper region of the South because of its bright, orange-red berries. Stems of bittersweet with their string of tightly arranged berries sell for high prices in plant shops, beginning around the middle of October and going through the Thanksgiving season. Berries persist for a long period in a dried state. The vine, which can be obnoxious at times because of its fast, entangling growth, goes virtually unnoticed until the leaves fall after the first frost and the seedpods split to expose the orange-red berries. This is a good vine to use in a location isolated from other plantings, but close enough to permit convenient harvesting of its stems with handsome autumn fruit. Berries persist for an indefinite period in a dried state.

Cocculus carolinus
(KOK-u-lus ka-ro-LY-nus)
CAROLINA SNAILSEED
Family: Menispermaceae
Zone: 7–9. Size: 20–30 feet, vine

Carolina snailseed is a twining, wiry, evergreen vine native to the southern region. This vine with its heart-shaped leaves goes virtually unnoticed until the bright red berries appear in late autumn. Although Carolina snailseed is seldom grown in a cultivated state, it is surely worthy of more consideration because it is much more manageable than many of the more highly promoted ornamental vines. Volunteer plants can be quite pesky in the garden where they are not wanted. The Carolina snailseed is not particular about where it grows, but produces an abundance of fruit, as is shown in the photograph, only if grown in full sunlight. Cuttings hold their berries for several days in water, but cuttings of the vine alone will persist for several weeks indoors.

Crataegus spp.
(kra-TE-gus)
HAWTHORNS
Family: Rosaceae
Zone: 5–9. Size: 15–20 feet by 15–18 feet

Hawthorns ("haws") grow over most of the United States. This is a very large and complex genus, comprising both ornamental flowering trees and trees that are planted for their edible fruit. Members of this genus adapt to a wide range of soils—from the relatively wet bogs where mayhaws grow to the high, well-drained upland soils best suited to the Washington and green hawthorns. All hawthorns are relatively small flowering trees, and are ideal for plantings in small gardens, although most have thorns, especially when young. A Southern favorite is the mayhaw, *C. opaca*, the source of fruit for prized mayhaw jelly and preserves. It produces a bountiful mass of five-petalled, white, clustered flowers

Carolina snailseed in heavy fruit. T. E. POPE

Parsley hawthorn fruit and foliage. T. E. POPE

Mayhaw fruit is ready for harvest in May. WCW

Diospyros kaki
(di-OS-pi-ros KAH-kee)
JAPANESE PERSIMMON
Family: Ebenaceae
Zone: 7–9. Size: 15–20 feet by 15 feet

Japanese persimmon is among our most spectacular fruiting trees in late autumn. This relatively small, deciduous tree is easy to grow, taking only a small amount of space with full sunlight and a reasonably good soil to meet the requirements for this delightful fruiting tree. The tree's picturesque branching pattern is only enhanced when the huge, bright orange fruit come into full view following early autumn leafdrop. Fruit can be removed just prior to becoming soft and stored in a warm room for several days before it is eaten, or kept in a bowl as a beautiful display until the fruit softens. Since persimmons are *dioecious* (male and female floral parts on different plants), a male plant is needed to provide pollen to the female, fruiting plant. There are many good cultivars of Japanese persimmon. Some of these include 'Eureka', 'Fuyugaki', 'Tanenashi', 'Hachiya', and 'Saijo'. The native persimmon (*D. virginiana*) produces a bountiful crop of relatively small orange-colored fruit that turn a purplish color after the first frost—about the time they fully ripen. This native can be found over the entire region. The Texas or black persimmon (*D. texana*) grows in colonies of small trees in the dry soils of Texas and produces black

with purple *anthers* (pollen-bearing parts of the flowers) in very early spring, and showy red, applelike fruit in May. One cultivar, 'Super Spur', is known for its outstanding fruiting qualities. Parsley hawthorn, *C. marshallii*, is a delightful small-flowering tree with clusters of white flowers and parsleylike leaves. Two species noted for their beautiful autumn fruit are the Washington hawthorn, *C. phaenopyrum*, and the green hawthorn, *C. viridis*. Both of these produce clusters of white flowers followed in the autumn with bright red berries somewhat similar to pyracantha berries.

As cuttings, hawthorn flowers

persist for a relatively short period of a few days before beginning to shed, but cuttings with fruit are much longer lasting, especially if stems are conditioned in water containing a floral preservative.

Japanese persimmon fruit silhouetted against a late autumn sky. WCW

Strawberry bush at the "hearts a-bustin'" stage. I. E. POPE

Ilex decidua
(I-leks de-SID-you-a)
DECIDUOUS HOLLY
Family: Aquifoliaceae
Zone: 5–9. Size: 12–15 feet by 10 feet

This small, deciduous, berrying tree goes virtually unnoticed in the native landscape until late autumn, when its leaves begin to fall sooner than most deciduous trees and the berries turn a brilliant red color. There is also a less-common orange-berried variety. Single specimens of the deciduous holly are particularly prominent along fence rows, highway rights-of-way, woodland edges, open fields, and other disturbed landscapes where birds have deposited seeds. As with most hollies, both a male and a female plant are necessary for pollination and heavy berry production. In the wild

fruit. Cut entire branches of persimmon to include in arrangements, or pick the fruit to use it in a variety of ways indoors.

Euonymus americana
(you-ON-i-mus a-mer-i-KA-nus)
STRAWBERRY BUSH, WAHOO, HEARTS-A-BUSTIN', BURSTING-HEARTS
Family: Celastraceae
Zone: 6–9. Size: 5 feet by 4 feet

Strawberry bush is an interesting native, deciduous shrub that grows along sandy streams and on the edges of upland forests as an understory species to large trees. The strawberry bush goes virtually unnoticed until autumn, when its red, strawberrylike fruit become quite showy. If the strawberry bush is planted in a soil with a high humus content, or if a generous amount of leaf mold is placed around a healthy specimen, it will spread and form a small colony of plants. The tall, wiry, green stems with small, sparse leaves make great cuttings for arranging indoors. Condition cut stems for a couple of hours in warm water before placing them in an arrangement. Other relatives of the strawberry bush, like the variegated euonymuses, *E. fortunei* 'Silver

Queen' and *E. fortunei* 'Emerald 'N' Gold', also make excellent cuttings for arrangements.

A heavily-fruiting branch of Burford holly. NGO

A bountiful crop of deciduous holly berries in winter. T. E. POPE

there can be as many as seven male plants for every one seed-producing female plant, but only the female plants make a strong impact in the landscape because they are the ones producing the colorful berries. Throughout most of the South, fortunately, there is sufficient holly pollen present in the environment that a single female tree can be selected for a planting scheme with reasonable confidence that it will bear fruit. The berries persist throughout the winter, until birds clean the trees in early spring, generally favoring the red-berrying variety over plants bearing orange berries. An outstanding selection of the decid-uous holly is 'Warren's Red'. *I. verticillata*, winterberry or black alder, is another deciduous holly that produces a heavy fruit set. It tends to be more shrublike in character, and its berries are larger than those of deciduous holly. Handsome cultivars of deciduous winterberry holly are 'Winter Red' and 'Red Sprite'. Harvest the branches of this holly in late autumn after the fruit is fully mature. Most people delay cutting until the foliage has fallen.

Hollies grow best in fertile, moist soil and open sunlight, although members of this genus are quite tolerant of extremes in soils from wet to dry and varying amounts of sunlight exposure. They grow well over the entire

South and are a part of nearly every garden setting. In addition to being widely used to establish garden boundaries, many of these strong, usually dark green foliaged plants are selected specifically for their striking red fruit. Most of the fine berry-producing types are not native, but have been intro-duced into the region. The native species tend to have a yellow-green leaf color and are not among the favorites for cutting greens and berry production. Our American holly, *I. opaca*, is an example of a native holly that has attractive berries, but its foliage is sometimes an anemic yellow color. Some of its cultivars like 'Bounti-ful', 'Miss Helen', and 'Jersey Princess' are superior to the indi-genous species, but are not always readily available. There are yellow-fruiting selections also, but they have not gained the recognition that the red-fruiting hollies enjoy.

Another native is yaupon, *I. vomitoria*, is an excellent berry producer, but the dark blue-green leaves are very small; cuttings of this holly do not have the visual impact as that of the more positive introduced hollies. The berries of the yaupon do not persist for an extended period as fresh cuttings.

Burford holly, *I. cornuta* 'Burfordii', a Chinese introduc-tion, produces dark, glossy-green, modestly-spined leaves and an abundance of large berries. It is

among our most durable species, although considerable space must be provided for its massive height and spread. A forerunner of the Burford holly, the Chinese holly, *I. cornuta*, has handsome, lustrous foliage, but its spines are trouble-some.

Several hybrid hollies have been introduced into the trade because of their fine fruiting quali-ties and good foliage characteris-tics. Some of these include selec-tions of the *I.* × *attenuata* group such as 'Savannah', 'East Palatka', 'Hume #2', and 'Fosters.'

In the northern part of the region where temperatures are colder, several of the "Meserve" (*I.* x *meserveae*) hybrids grow quite well and produce fine foliage and berries. Exceptional berry-producing female possibilities include 'China Girl', 'Blue Girl', and 'Blue Princess'. 'Blue Boy' is reported to be an excellent male selection. The English hollies (*I. aquifolium*) are especially good hollies for cut foliage and many have excellent fruiting qualities. Several cultivars have attractive variegated yellow and green foliage. Although the English group contains some of the best species for cutting because of their lustrous, glossy-green foliage, members of this group are best adapted to the cooler regions of the country, especially to the northeastern United States.

Cut foliage and berries have a relatively long life, especially if stems are conditioned prior to use in decorations. The hollies most frequently used as cuttings are the dark green, imported ones with their bright red fruit. The color combination has traditionally been found perfect for the holiday sea-son. Two of these are 'Burford' holly and 'Nellie Stevens' holly. Native, yellow-green foliaged species like the American holly have been less favored as have, of course, the really prickly types like the Chinese holly. The lighter-foliaged species offer a field for experimentation, especially those

Seedpods of the golden rain tree. NGO

Malus spp.
(MAY-lus)
FLOWERING CRABAPPLE
Family: Rosaceae
Zone: 4–8. Size: 14–25 feet by 20 feet

Crabapples may be best described as trees for all seasons. It is difficult to judge which season for the crabapple is the most spectacular—the spring, when the trees provide a glorious array of color, or the autumn, when certain cultivars exhibit a dazzling display of beautiful fruit. A fine native Southern crabapple, *M. angustifolia*, produces handsome dark-pink buds that open into delightfully fragrant pink flowers, but its fruit is not that sensational. Those that have unusually striking fruit are best adapted to the northern part of the region where cold temperatures satisfy their dormancy needs. Here the colors both in bloom and in fruit can be quite striking. Somewhat short-lived, crabapples need full sunlight and well-drained soils. There are literally hundreds of crabapples offered in the trade. Flower colors include white, pink, red, and rosy-red. Fruit can be small—well under an inch in diameter, to quite large—nearly 2 inches across. Colors include red, orange, and yellow. The edible apple, *M. sylvestris*, is a member of this select group that produces large fruit.

with yellow fruit. Supply a generous amount of water for cut branches, because they can take up a considerable amount in a short period.

Koelreuteria bipinnata
(kol-roo-TEER-ri-a by-PIN-na-ta)
GOLDEN RAIN TREE
Family: Sapindaceae
Zone: 8–10. Size: 30 feet by 25 feet

Golden rain trees bloom at an unusual time of year. While most trees bloom in spring and the summer, this Southern tree blooms in late September and October. The flowers are borne in large, showy, yellow, branched flower heads and occur on the outer canopy of the tree, but last for only about a week. Flowers are followed by seeds contained in prominent papery sacs that first appear pink, then turn a beautiful salmon color, and finally a warm, clear tan. The large clusters of fruit are prized materials for dried arrangements because they are so attractive and hold up indefinitely as a cut material. Unfortunately a golden rain tree has to be about five to seven years old before it comes into its flowering stage, and trees are subject to periodic freeze injury over most of the South. The northern golden rain tree, *P. paniculata*, blooms in mid-summer, and its fruiting bodies are not as handsome as those of the Southern species. The northern species is very cold-hardy and really needs low temperatures to perform well. Both species grow fast and in a wide range of soil types. Provide full sunlight because trees will not bloom in shade. Cut the seedpods as they turn a pinkish-tan. They can be used in a relatively fresh state or placed in a warm storage room to complete the drying process before using them in a permanent, dried arrangement.

One of the many crabapple varieties in heavy autumn fruit. NGO

Cluster of berries among the fine-textured nandina foliage. NGO

region. Although it may not be a plant to feature at the front door because of the dangerous thorns, this open-branched, large deciduous shrub to small tree produces handsome green stems, highly fragrant, typically sweet-scented orange tree blossoms, and hard, lemonlike, non-edible fruit in late autumn. The wild orange will grow in virtually any soil in full sunlight to partial shade, but plants flower and fruit best in full sunlight. Fruit picked in the fall and placed in a bowl in a warm, humid room will emit a pleasing citrus fragrance, and the scent lasts for several weeks.

Pyracantha spp.
(pi-ra-KAN-tha)
PYRACANTHA, SCARLET FIRE THORN
Family: Rosaceae
Zone: 6–9. Size: 8–12 feet by 6–8 feet

Among the most prolific fruiting shrubs for landscape plantings are the pyracanthas. Although not easily trained into manageable shrubs, few ornamentals offer a more striking display of berries. Pyracantha shrubs are heavily armed with sharp thorns that will cause terrible skin inflammation if they stick into the skin, so be very careful when handling branches. As with all members of the rose family, provide well-drained soils and full sunlight. They grow

Nandina domestica
(nan-DI-na do-MES-ti-ka)
NANDINA
Family: Berberidaceae
Zone: 6–9. Size: 3–6 feet by 3 feet

Nandina is one of the all-time favorite shrubs of the South. Its ease of growth, tolerance to a wide range of growing conditions, and freedom from most plant pests are but a few of the reasons why this evergreen shrub has been with us for such a long time. The delicate-textured foliage and clusters of red berries hanging atop the tall slender canes make it a tempting specimen for cut foliage and fruiting canes. Nandina fruiting is much more prolific in full sunlight, but the plants perform quite well in shade. It does best in a fertile, well-drained soil but is not a very temperamental plant at all. Cut foliage is reasonably good for short-term use and the red berries separated from the foliage are somewhat longer lasting.

Poncirus trifoliata
(pon-SY-rus tri-FO-li-ata)
WILD ORANGE, TRIFOLIATE ORANGE
Family: Rutaceae
Zone: 7–10. Size: 8–10 feet by 10 feet

The wild orange, hardiest of the citrus, has escaped cultivation and is prevalent over much of the

Wild orange fruit in late autumn. WCW

Pyracantha in heavy fruit. T. E. POPE

rapidly and become gangly if not pruned on an annual basis. Plants bear berries on the previous season's growth. Consequently, when pruning in late winter, be sure to retain some of the former year's growth to insure a bountiful fruit-set. There is not much emphasis given to the flowers of pyracantha, but the blooming of a fully-mature specimen can be quite spectacular with its mass of small white flowers for a short period in early spring. Two popular species in the trade include *P. coccinea*, with bright, orange-red, rounded fruit, and *P. koidzumii*, also a red-fruiting selection, that produces slightly flattened berries.

Viburnum spp.
(vy-BUR-num)
VIBURNUMS
Family: Caprifoliaceae
Zone: variable according to the species
Size: 6–12 feet by 8 feet

Although this is a genus that contains a huge number of species, each viburnum species has its climatic and environmental niche where that selection performs beautifully while others struggle because of soil, temperature, moisture, or other factors that affect their acceptance in landscape plantings. Viburnums flourish across the entire Southern region. There are both evergreen and deciduous types, and a range of sizes from low-growing shrubs to those attaining treelike stature. The viburnums do not have the reputation for spectacular fruiting enjoyed by some of the other plants like the fruiting hollies, but several make impressive displays with their autumn fruit. Among the most proven selections are Linden viburnum (*V. dilatatum*), which produces a huge quantity of red fruit borne in flat clusters. A particularly good cultivar is 'Erie'. The European cranberry viburnum (*V. opulus*) has clusters of translucent berries in September and October. Some people consider the double-file viburnum (*V. plicatum*) to have some of the most spectacular fruit of all. Bright-red berries are borne prominently on the upper side of strong-tiered branches in early autumn. There are some equally fine native species that produce black berries such as the rustyhaw and arrowwood viburnums, and

A tier of 'Shasta' viburnum in autumn at the Arnold Arboretum. NGO

Top: Mature cluster of black Spanish grapes ready to be picked. wcw
Above: Mature muscadines and foliage. T. E. POPE

all of these have a showy flowering stage in early spring.

Viburnum berries do not normally last for an extended period after they are cut, but they can still be used very effectively in short-term decorations.

Vitis spp.
(VY-tis)
GRAPE, MUSCADINE
Family: Vitaceae
Zone: 5–9. Size: 20–40 feet, vine

There are two major species of grapes that produce delicious fruit in the South. Commercial grapes, *V. vinifera*, and the Southern muscadine, *V. rotundifolia*, produce a bounty of fruit and are also excellent vines for growing on garden structures. Special care should be taken to select the recommended cultivars for particular parts of the region because they vary greatly in productivity, fruit quality, and disease susceptibility. Also the fruiting habits and pruning requirements vary greatly among grapes and muscadines. Provide full sunlight and a well-drained soil. To produce good fruit, the soil need not be fertile since the objective is normally to produce fruit rather than a mass of foliage, especially after the first year following establishment. In addition to the fruit that should be available in the autumn, vines from both grapes and muscadines are quite pliable and thus are ideal for making wreaths, garlands, and forming into other shapes for holiday decorations.

NGO

Eight

Conditioning

Extending the Life of Cut Flowers and Other Plants

When a plant part is removed from its source of water and nutrition, it begins a declining process that continues until the cutting dies. Sometimes this decline is quite rapid, but at other times the process may be delayed, depending on the condition of the cutting and the treatment given at the time the cutting is made. The objective is to reduce the rate of decline and extend the vase life of cut material as long as possible.

Fortunately, there has been considerable experimentation over the years by a huge plant industry whose survival depends on how well they can condition plants to hold up after they are cut. This industry is growing rapidly. The per capita purchases of cut flowers in the United States is estimated to be slightly over twenty dollars per year, and increasing. In other countries this figure is much larger—in several countries in Europe per capita purchases are double that in the United States. A considerable amount of research conducted by this worldwide industry can be drawn upon to learn how best to condition materials from our gardens for indoor use.

Conditioning is the process whereby cut plant material is subjected to a variety of treatments to prolong its life and viability. This can involve rather complicated procedures for some plants that are marketed commercially, since they are often handled by several people before reaching their final destination in a container.

Wholesalers, retailers, and other commercial handlers of live plants must practice rather extensive procedures for prolonging the life of their highly perishable products if they are to be successful. For a more complete and comprehensive reference on this subject refer to *Specialty Cut Flowers* by Allan M. Armitage (Varsity Press, Timber Press, 1993 and subsequent editions).

The length of time that plants are subjected to the stress factors that shorten their lives can be greatly reduced at home and in the garden, because they can be placed in more favorable environmental conditions almost immediately. This section will focus on basic steps that can be taken to condition materials cut from our gardens, although the guidelines are applicable to plants found in other situations as well.

Plants are quite variable in their requirements for post-harvest care. Recommendations unique to specific plants are covered in the sections on the various plant categories. Here are some basic guidelines, applicable to most plants, that will help prolong the life of garden plants.

Plant Condition and Stage of Development

Healthy plants provide the best source of material expected to last a satisfactory period after cutting. While one advantage of making cuttings from the garden is the many choices available, try not to cut from weak, stunted plants, as these seldom produce long-lasting flowers, fruit, and foliage. Vigorously-growing plants, with their built-up food reserves, can be expected to have longer post-harvest lives. Yet, never discount the value of uniquely-shaped stems, branches, flowers, fruit, or foliage from plants that are less than "perfect" horticulture specimens. Home cuttings need not measure up to the clearly-defined classes or grades plants must adhere to in the floral industry.

When to Cut

A general rule of thumb is to cut flowers when they begin to show color. For spike-shaped flower structures this is normally at the stage when the first two or three florets begin to show color. For the round-shaped flowers, buds half to three-quarters open usually give the best post-harvest longevity. Flowers in tight bud seldom open satisfactorily, while those fully open begin fading quickly. There are commercial bud-forcing solutions available from florists that will aid in the opening of flowers in the bud stage. One such material is Quick Dip.

Time of Day

There are varying opinions as to what part of the day is best to make cuttings for indoor use. Some authorities advocate early morning harvest because at this time plants are holding the greatest amount of water they contain all day. This is particularly important for plants that wilt quickly, because such plants are prone not to take up supplementary water as readily as others. This category includes plants like the hydrangeas, viburnums, poinsettias, and other woody species, which will be covered more completely in the plant sections. Yet, during the morning hours, especially very early, plant foliage is normally wet with dew, and it is more susceptible to leaf diseases in this condition. For many plants, however, this is not a factor, because most of their foliage is normally removed after cutting.

Other authorities prefer late afternoon cutting, arguing that at this time of the day plants have had a full day to manufacture their foods (carbohydrates), and the high levels of these reserves help extend their lives following harvest. Those of us who are not "morning people" may choose to become adherents of this latter position.

Luckily for those of us who seek unambiguous guidance, nearly all plantsmen agree on one point—mid-day, especially in hot weather when temperatures are above 80° F, is the least desirable time of all for cutting flowers and other materials. Plants are usually at their highest point of stress during the mid-day hours. High temperatures cause rapid water loss and a fast rate of respiration and resulting food loss; consequently the rate of food consumption is greater than the amount being manufactured during this stressful period.

Cutting Stems and Removing Foliage

Use a sharp knife or hand shears to cut fresh materials. Make stem or branch cuts on a slant so as to expose as much of the interior, conductive tissue to the water as possible. Studies indicate that most of the uptake of water is through the basal cut end and not through stem walls. Many plants respond favorably to having their stems recut (at the ends) under water, following their initial removal from the main plant. The underwater cut pulls water up into the stem and reduces air blockage. This is particularly important for some of the woody plants, like roses, that tend to have air bubbles form at the basal cut, thus impeding the rapid uptake of water through their stems. This condition is evident when flower heads droop soon after being cut, although stems are in water. Other plants besides roses, such as viburnum, hydrangea, forsythia, and jasmine, are reported to benefit from this procedure and can be expected to have a longer post-harvest life as a result of it. One product that is reported to help prevent a sudden wilt or bent-neck stems in cut flowers is Vita Flora Pre-Treatment by Floralife. Another formulation, Hydraflor Quick Dip, is a treatment that aids in the accelerated passage of water through the stems.

If possible, place cut flowers and other plants in a container of water containing a flower preservative for a minimum of two hours before placing them in an arrangement. Even if a preservative is not used, placing cuttings in water immediately after they are made is very important. This step is the key to longer vase life, particularly where a preservative is not used.

Remove as much foliage as possible from the lower stems of cut materials before placing it in water. This is particularly important for portions of the stem that will come in contact with the water. When foliage is set in water it deteriorates quickly, thus setting the stage for the development of bacteria/fungi-infected water that will reduce the vase life of all plants placed in it.

The Weight of Water

Water is likely the single most important factor that influences the life of cut plant materials. Many studies on the post-harvest physiology of plants show the life and condition of cut plants are influenced by such factors as water quality, mineral content (pH), temperature, and the addition of floral preservative supplements.

Place cut plant material in water immediately. Even short delays result in valuable water loss from the plant parts, the formation of air bubbles in the base of the stems, clogging of the conductive tissue, and the possible inception of bacterial action at the basal cut area. From personal experience, and talking with people in the industry, I've concluded that plants take up warm water more rapidly than cold tap water. Warm water with a temperature of around 105 degrees F. is effective for woody plants. It may also help other plants that have become limp due to water loss, and limp foliage on plants without fully developed foliage and flowers. For heavy, woody plant stems much warmer water (around 175 degrees F) is beneficial to bring back turgidity to plant stems, flowers, and foliage. Some flowers, like poppies and poinsettias, exude a milky substance when they are cut. This material hardens relatively quickly, forming a barrier to the flow of water through the stems. For plants that produce this milky sap, place the cut ends in hot water immediately to keep the sap from hardening and plugging the conductive tissues.

Studies indicate that there is little benefit in submerging stems into deep water, since little water is absorbed through stem walls. A few inches deep is sufficient, especially if foliage is retained on the stems. If possible, allow plants to stand in water a minimum of two hours before arranging them. Some authorities recommend a conditioning period of twelve hours. Home-grown flowers do well if they stand in water overnight.

Plant life is reported to be longer if the pH of the conditioning water is acidic (a range of 3.0 to 5.5) rather than alkaline (above 7.0). Water uptake is more rapid from an acidic water. Most floral preservatives work best if the water is more acid. However, there are commercial preservatives for alkaline water supplies. Microorganism activity is slower in acidic water. Studies also indicate that air bubbles seem less prevalent in water more acidic than basic pH. Some city sources of water high in fluorides are quite detrimental to certain flowers like Gerbera daisies and freesias.

Floral Preservatives

Among the most researched strategies for prolonging the life of cut plant material has been the addition of specially formulated compounds to water to help prolong plant life. Several products that go by various trade names are available on the market for this purpose. Using one or more of these products can increase the vase life of plants significantly. While some people advocate the virtues of one commercial preparation over another, they all improve the post-harvest life of cut flowers more than plain water.

Floral preservatives normally contain a source of plant energy food (sucrose) and a hydration ingredient that lowers the pH to improve water uptake. Some also contain an inhibitor to stem-plugging, which helps reduce the development of bacteria and fungi. For homeowners and other small consumers, manufacturers of floral preservatives have prepared small five- or ten-gram packaged units, with a single package of the powders or crystals being sufficient to treat about one quart of water. The compounds dissolve quickly in warm water. These small packaged products are often provided at the purchase of fresh flowers and other materials.

One of the most popular plant preservatives is Floralife. The company, Floralife Inc., in Burr Ridge, Illinois, offers several other products to help extend the life of flowers. Robert Koch Industries of Bennett, Colorado, has a preservative, Prolong. The Gard Environmental Group in Algonquin, Illinois, produces several products for both commercial and consumer users. One of their popular preservative formulations is Rogard RS. Pokon & Chrysal USA of Miami, Florida, produces the floral preservatives Chrysal Universal and Chrysal Select. Experimentation with these and other preservatives will help determine which performs best with the water supply and for any given plant. If using a water-absorbing floral foam to hold plants in arrangements, be sure to soak the foam in the preservative prior to placing flowers in the foam. One experiment increased the life of roses from seven days in plain water to eleven days, as a result of soaking the foam in one of the preservatives.

A very important caution: Follow the manufacturer's directions very closely when using any of these products, because miscalculation of the amount of the product to use will result in poor performance by flowers and other plants. Keep these products in airtight containers, safely stored away from children and pets. Because they are manufactured compounds, they have a certain "shelf-life." Consequently, the materials should not be kept for extended periods. Purchase only what can be used for the stated life of the chemical. To maintain the freshness and clearness of vase water, second and third treatments of these products can be beneficial, if made at several-day intervals. The frequency depends on the amount of *plant mass* (number of stems), the volume of water, and the conditions in the location where the plants are being maintained.

Some people make their own home-brew preservative by adding a teaspoon of household bleach (to kill disease organisms) and one teaspoon of sugar (for plant nutrition) to a quart of water. They recommend allowing plants to condition in this mixture for several hours before arranging.

Ethylene Gas

Many plants are highly sensitive to ethylene gas after they are cut. Ethylene acts as an important hormone in early flower formation and development, but after plants are cut ethylene is no longer beneficial and when present will hasten the decline of flowers and other plant materials. This gas is also a by-product of old, declining flowers and ripening fruit. It is routinely produced in refrigerators that contain ripening fruit, especially items like apples and pears. Certain flowers, if stored in a refrigerator that contains such fruit, will become quite droopy, and many will drop their florets prematurely even though they are in water. Bulbs, such as tulips and hyacinths, that require six weeks of chilling in the South are often adversely affected by this gas.

Keep cut flowers and cold-stored bulbs away from fruit, and discard old flowers in the same storage area. Ethylene inhibitor products that reduce the impact of this gas on flowers are available, but they are primarily used in commercial markets where large volumes of flowers are stored. Some plants that are especially sensitive to ethylene gas are: agapanthus, alstroemeria, snapdragon, delphinium, larkspur, gladiolus, stock, carnations, freesia, Queen Anne's lace, and some of the lilies.

Temperature and Other Environmental Conditions

Protect cut flowers, fruit, and foliage from direct sunlight, drafts, and heat sources such as the tops of television sets and other units that give off even small amounts of heat. Warm air temperatures increase the amount of water loss in plants. The cooler the interior spaces in which they are held, the longer the flowers and other cut materials will last.

Temperatures that make for comfortable conditions for people will hold cut flowers and other materials for a reasonable amount of time. To hold for extended periods and reduce the aging process before they are arranged, flowers and cut greenery should be stored at much lower temperatures of between 34 and 38 degrees F, and in a high humidity of at least eighty percent to reduce water loss—the general conditions in refrigerator store units used by florists.

Always begin the conditioning process with clean containers, since old plant residue is often the source of rapid bacterial and fungal activity once new plants are placed in water. Most containers are used over and over. Consequently over time they become highly contaminated. Floralife produces a product, D.C.D., used to clean containers and other materials in the flower arranging area. It contains a disinfectant, cleaner, fungicide, sanitizer, and deodorant. A small amount of household bleach will aid in destroying the organisms in flower containers.

PRESERVING PLANT MATERIAL

There is a huge and growing demand today for dried flowers and other plant materials. Processing dried materials has become a major part of the wholesale and retail markets across the country, and fortunately naturally dried plants are becoming available to homeowners and others who choose to go with natural materials over artificial plants.

There are several methods of preserving plants in a natural state. Success depends to a large degree on the stage of development and the degree of freshness at the time fresh cuttings are made. Two relatively easy methods of preserving plants include the following:

Glycerin and Water

Some foliage plants like eucalyptus, aspidistra, eleagnus, palm fronds, artemisia, myrtle, magnolia, and other evergreens can be preserved and kept in a very natural, soft, pliable state if their stems are placed in a solution of glycerin and water. Flowers that can also be preserved by this method include hydrangea, lavender, money plant, strawflower, and celosia (cockscomb). A solution can be easily prepared by mixing two parts glycerin (by volume) with one part warm water. A small amount of a surfactant, like a mild detergent, placed in the solution aids in the mixing process. Recut and crush the stem ends of woody branches that are not more than 18 inches long and recut the stems of flowers and other materials. Place cut ends into a solution about 2 inches deep. Plants being treated should remain in the solution for 2–3 weeks in a well-venti-

A floral arrangement of aspidistra, hydrangea, and eucalyptus dried at home by the dehydration method, designed by Lou Riddle, Columbia, South Carolina. NGO

lated area at a temperature of about 80 degrees F. Following the treatment, wash the solution from the stems and hang plants to dry or place them directly in an arrangement.

Dehydration

Some plants preserve well if they are placed in a dry, warm place like an attic, furnace room, or garage to dry from the loss of water or dehydration. The storage unit must have a low relative humidity for drying plants. In places with a high humidity, a very serious problem but a more normal condition in most of the Gulf South, mold and other fungi growth will form on the materials and make them virtually useless.

To dry plants—first, strip the leaves from stems of flowers to be dried. Next, hang plants in bunches from a ceiling or beams in one of the places as noted previously. Some people advocate placing flowers upside down hanging in brown paper bags. In a hanging position, the stems and flower heads dry in their more natural forms. Thin, airy material may be bunched, but thick-stemmed materials do best if they are hung as separate stems, to permit good air circulation among the plant parts. Hang materials for three to four weeks.

Some plants that preserve well by dehydration and retain a nice natural color include many of the wildflowers, nearly all of the

PROLONGING THE LIFE OF CUT FLOWERS

Conditioning Tips
- Cut plant material in the late afternoon or early morning
- Remove the foliage on the lower one-half of the stems
- Place floral preservative in clean water
- Three to four inches of water in the container is sufficient
- Slightly crush stems of shrubs and trees (woody plants) and use warm water to begin the conditioning treatment
- Provide supplementary water to fresh materials in arrangements as needed

ornamental and cereal crop grasses as well as wild grasses, hydrangeas, statice, celosia (cockscomb), strawflower, lavender, artemisia, globe thistle, feverfew, and Queen Anne's lace, just to name a few. Plants that have a high water content like the irises, most of the exotic tropicals, and thick-petalled flowers like carnations, peonies, callas, some roses, and lilies do not normally dry well by this method.

In 1590 Honso Komoku, a famous herbalist, recommended this formula for prolonging the usefulness of cut flowers:

Gather the young shoots of "sweet" cooking chrysanthemums in March, the leaves in June, the flowers in September, and the stems and roots in December—each on a certain day of the sexagenary cycle. Dry all these parts of the plant in the shade for 100 days. Powder and mix an even quantity of each on a dog day of the sexagenary cycle. Take a small spoonful of the mixture three times a day.

If the dosage is continued for 100 days, one becomes nimble and generous, and one's white hairs turn black within a year. If the dosage is continued for two years, new teeth will grow where the old ones fell out. In the fifth year, an old man of 80 will become like a boy again.

Komoku was probably wrong about the power of dried flowers to prolong life, however carefully selected or timely picked. Few would dispute, however, that the enjoyment of flowers, whether growing in our gardens or cut and lending their beauty to our homes, has the power to make life better.

NGO

Nine

Marketing the Bounty

A growing interest in developing small, owner-operated cut-flower production businesses has emerged in recent years. Making the transition from hobby gardener to commercial production is a step many people are considering. The Texas A&M University Agricultural Extension Service has conducted workshops in Houston and other places designed to help emerging producers with management and production. The information in this chapter is designed to help those interested to evaluate their dream and examine it objectively.

Gardening is one of America's favorite leisure-time activities, because it is rewarding on many levels. There's the enjoyment of growing beautiful flowers, tasting vegetables fresh off the vine, and improving the aesthetics of the outdoors. However, a few gardeners also find enjoyment in *selling* bounty from their gardens. These *market gardeners*, as they are called, usually get started because their interest in gardening has gradually expanded until they can no longer "consume" all they have produced. While many of these market gardeners reach this point and realize that this type of business was not cut out for them, others go on to build rather profitable businesses.

Ask any market gardener which crop usually sells and pays off the best and chances are the answer will be "fresh-cut flowers." There are people that grow up disliking vegetables (in spite of their mothers), yet almost everyone likes fresh flowers and knows they are a very special item—and costly. A huge gift basket of fresh fruits and vegetables can be sent for $40, but a really nice bouquet is hardly available for that amount. Thus, given their relative profitability, cut flowers have gained popularity in recent years as an alternative crop for market gardeners. However, before entering the cut-flower business, a gardener should have a firm grasp of the following information:

- A thorough knowledge of the physical and cultural characteristics of the plant;
- A sense of the market potential for the floral crop(s) being considered;
- A crop budget, including production and marketing costs, and expected returns;
- An estimate of the amount of capital and space that will be devoted to production;
- What retooling or upgrading might be necessary to properly grow and handle the floral crop(s);
- The details of the production and handling systems to be used; and
- An idea about services that may be provided with the product.

A commercial field of lilies in South Louisiana, photographed in 1943. NGO

Growing flowers is one thing, but the real question is—*after you grow the flowers, how do you profitably market them?* Potential market outlets available to market gardeners include floral wholesalers, supermarket distribution centers, direct sales to supermarkets, retail florists, direct retail, and pick-your-own retail. The type of market outlet utilized depends on the "personality" of the individual gardener's cut-flower business.

Sales to floral wholesalers and supermarket distribution centers are generally at lower prices and require a relatively high volume, making this goal well out of reach for smaller "mom & pop" market gardeners. Some operators try delivery to retailers, and while this generally brings a higher per-unit price, it can also be extremely time-consuming. Also, it is unlikely that a flower producer can sell directly to both retailers and wholesalers in a given trade area.

Some roadside stands and pick-your-own operations (PYO) have strategically added cut flowers to their product line. Research shows that many of these businesses are increasing the proportion of flowers they sell, and in turn, reducing vegetable-growing space every year. Many wedding participants and caterers will travel to roadside stands or PYO farms to build their own outstanding bouquets for what they *perceive* to be relatively little money. Even retail florists from nearby towns drive out to "save" money by picking their own flowers. Tourists visit pick-your-own farms to enjoy selecting their own flowers and admiring the beauty of the vast fields (benches) in full bloom.

Many flower growers living on busy roads construct roadside stands with bouquets placed in water buckets under shade. Some market gardeners merely leave a bolted-down cash box out on the stand, relying on the honor system, and find their bouquets bought and paid for without a hitch.

Betsy Arriola creates beautiful bouquets from her Country Petals at New Ulm, Texas. This arrangement features larkspur, roses, bells of Ireland, stock, mock orange, and clarkia. "The flower business has so many opportunities. It is not competitive in production, but in the style that one has to offer. I love the design part and to get my hands dirty in the garden."—Betsy Arriola, April 3, 1999. WCW

Saturday flea and farmers' markets are becoming very popular places to buy and sell great bouquets of fresh flowers: cottage flowers, old-fashioned flowers, Victorian flowers, English garden flowers—call them what you will. They are very *fresh* and will last all week, so for about the cost of taking the family to the movies, people can decorate their homes with lovely bouquets.

What about local business offices, restaurants, or bed & breakfast operators? They each use and are interested in purchasing bouquets. Local florists will also probably be delighted to buy fresh garden flowers, as will the wholesale florist supply house in the nearest city.

Marketing specialty cut flowers can be very difficult, however. A market gardener may be

Flower stand at Country Petals. Customers can "self serve" on weekends, leaving money in a box by the flowers. Plastic bags, ties, and water are available inside. WCW

attempting to introduce a relatively unknown product in a market where demand is often dictated by holidays or special occasions such as weddings or funerals. In this market, demand shifts rapidly and selling prices fluctuate accordingly. In addition, the product is extremely perishable and there is a limited secondary market (that is, drying of the flowers). Also, it is difficult to guarantee buyers that sufficient quantity and quality can be supplied.

Even when a new crop is successfully developed by a producer, there is often a short opportunity time for the crop because local markets are easily saturated by other growers also introducing the crop. Sometimes the supply of major crops such as carnations, roses, or mums floods the market at low prices. These products instead of specialty crops are easily picked up by wholesalers.

Despite all of the cautions, opportunities seem to exist. The potential of the cut-flower market

is enormous, as the average United States consumer currently purchases approximately half as many flowers as their European counterparts. As Americans continue to become more frequent purchasers of cut flowers, specialty cut-flower crop sales are likely to expand.

INFORMATION GROWERS SHOULD ACQUIRE

Profitable cut-flower growers must have critical information at their disposal, much of which is constantly changing. By collecting and evaluating the following information, floral market gardeners will make informed and more profitable decisions:

Production Costs

The cost of producing flowers must be known. Without this knowledge it is nearly impossible to determine if the sales price will be profitable until it is too late. A basic but convenient method to

figure out production costs is to estimate the cost to plant and maintain an area (bench or bed) and divide it by the yield or output (dozens or sprays) obtained from that same area.

For example, first get an idea of the number of square feet of benches or beds that are being used for growing flowers. Then keep track of the costs of planting and maintaining this space (labor, seed, water, fertilizer, pest control, and so forth) and the typical yield (number of marketable flowers per year) produced from this space. Dividing costs by the number of flowers will give the cost per flower, which must be covered in order to break even. A grower armed with this type of knowledge can better evaluate price offers or different pricing schemes to make sales.

Market Prices

Unlike the fresh fruit and vegetable market, there is little timely information about market prices for cut flowers. However, cut-flower prices do not typically vary as much as prices for fresh fruits and vegetables.

When negotiating with retail buyers, recognize that most price their product on a "cost plus margin" basis. For example, a flower retailer may need to cover a thirty-five percent margin on all flowers in order to cover labor, management, rent, and spoilage to maintain profitability. The retailer will attach the appropriate margin to the price paid for the product. Of course, depending on market conditions and store promotions, the retailer may change the margin to achieve certain sales goals. Gaining experience in dealing with retail buyers helps to better estimate the price that can be received.

Credit Risk

Unfortunately, wholesale and retail flower businesses have a high turnover rate. A grower should check into the credit rating of a particular buyer before approaching them, as growers often must wait a few weeks for payment. Some good indicators of credit worthiness are years in business or bank references. Ask them for references or call the Better Business Bureau.

Seasonality in Production and Demand

Both flower production and demand vary over the course of the year. Growers should be knowledgeable about the "peaks and valleys" associated with their flower production. A grower shouldn't over-commit to a buyer during times when production is typically low. On the other hand, during times of peak production a grower may need to market the product more aggressively, and perhaps (as a last resort) accept a lower price.

Growers also need to know about the rise and fall in customer demand. Generally, demand is down during the summer months

Bells of Ireland provide hundreds of spikes for fresh and dried use at Country Petals. WCW

(when production is often at its highest) and increases around holiday times or special occasions, such as Christmas, Mother's Day, and Valentine's Day. Demand for flowers may vary by variety as well. For example, poinsettias are popular at Christmas, while lilies are popular at Easter. The grower should adjust to these situations.

Grades

Almost all flower buyers have certain quality standards for the flowers they purchase. Growers should routinely familiarize themselves with these standards. Not only is this knowledge valuable during price negotiations, but many buyers prefer the grower to do the grading.

Competition

Direct competitors in the floral industry might be other wholesale greenhouses, retail greenhouses, retail nurseries, garden centers, florist shops, and supermarkets. Direct competitors appear to sell the same products as the new market gardener, although the addition of services, store image,

and merchandising techniques may make their products marginally different. *Indirect competitors* are those who compete for the consumer's discretionary income, but who do not sell floral products.

Identify direct and indirect competitors and make some assessment of their market share and power. Estimate the sales potential for the market in question and determine what might happen if another competitor enters the market or makes an aggressive attempt to change market share.

While competition is very likely to increase for cut-flower producers, there are currently market niches a small producer can fill locally which allow reasonable profitability. However, entry into the market is relatively easy for any vegetable producer in the market area by simply diversifying. If a small five-acre producer sells 8,000 bunches of a particular cut-flower species per acre per year in a market area of 250,000 people, what would happen to his market if the next year another

Rows of larkspur were direct-seeded in October and bloom in April and May at Country Petals. WCW.

producer in the area produced ten acres of the same species? Also, as cut-flower operations grow, they are forced to seek markets outside their local area. As their market expands, they encroach on local growers. Eventually production favors those areas with distinct seasonal advantages, and filling market windows becomes more critical.

Even when a successful new crop is established by a market gardener, domination (first mover advantages) of that market may be brief because others will begin to grow the same crop. Try to answer the following questions about possible competitors by visiting their operations, reviewing their advertising, and talking with their customers:

- Who grows and sells plants and flowers in the target market area?
- How many "competitors" are there? (Be sure to include supermarkets and other non-traditional outlets.)
- Where are competitors located? How large are they and how "healthy" economically? What is the "atmosphere" of each outlet?
- What do competing firms sell? What is their product mix in terms of specific floral products? What sizes and colors are grown and in what proportions? How are the plant products packaged?
- What is the price structure (wholesale and retail) for plant products in the market area(s) under consideration?
- When are the various floral products sold and are the sales seasonal or year-round? Where do the floral products come from? How is the quality of what is produced and sold? What is not available that might be a promising floral product in the market? How fast do the products move and what is "left over" as the season progresses? What floral products would the buyers in each type of market outlet like to have, if they could get them?
- What services do growers need to provide retailers or other customers to enhance image, etc.? Rate the general knowledge and experience level of consumers in the market area related to the use of plants and flowers.

WHY DO SOME MARKET GARDEN BUSINESSES FAIL AND OTHERS SUCCEED?

Most individuals hoping to begin a market garden flower business think of themselves as hard working, enthusiastic, responsible, energetic, and resourceful. The difference between entrepreneurs who succeed and those who are less successful seems to be how those traits are used. Many see themselves as responsible, but then fail to make sound plans. Others see themselves as creative, but fail to draw together the resources to make their idea a reality. In either case, success will be difficult to achieve.

Why do market garden businesses often fail within the first year of operation? Here are some key reasons:

- Limited resources available because of the business's small size.
- Inexperience of the business owner.
- Inadequate planning.
- Poor decision making.
- Difficulties in getting enough capital (money).
- Lack of careful financial management.
- Inability to manage growth and expansion.
- Extensive local and regional competition.
- Failure to recognize the value of a team approach in business start-up.
- Too many risks taken.

The first important task of rookie entrepreneurs is to decide if they have what it takes to be successful in business. Few people have all the necessary characteristics and skills needed in the beginning. Most people work with at least one partner who will offset their weaknesses, or use resource people to perform tasks they do not like or do not have the skill to do.

HOW TO GET STARTED

Starting a business is like planting a tree. The landscape surrounding a tree may look right, but the real test comes in knowing (and planning) when and how to till, plant, water, fertilize, and weed properly. A well-thought-out, written plan is as important to the market garden business as the roots are to a tree. Such a plan will help ensure the finances, resources, products, services, and tools when you need

them, so business runs smoothly.

Planning and managing a business requires anticipating both good times and bad, just as a tree will have periods of drought and abundant rain. The bad times may require hard work and creativity to keep the business healthy and strong. Successful conditions can also be challenging when they bring opportunities for rapid growth and expansion of the business.

One proven way to minimize the high risk of business failure and manage for success is to develop a complete, written business plan. A business plan will bring together all the necessary information to guide in planning and managing the business. A business plan should include a description of the business, goals and objectives, legal structure, and plans for marketing, finances, record keeping, and management.

Begin by writing down all of the goals and objectives for the business. These goals then become the outline for the business plan. It is important to keep in mind that business plans change over

time. Plans should be updated periodically when business conditions change.

The business owner must be keenly aware of all that goes on around the business to keep it heading in the right direction. Making informed, and often quick, decisions requires skill, experience, and persistence. Some information will be readily available, while other data will require considerable searching. Most of the information will be generated by the owner, who must analyze opportunities, learn about the marketplace, assess financial positions, and determine what is needed to get the business up and running.

CHARACTERISTICS OF A SUCCESSFUL AND PROFITABLE FLOWER GROWER

There are many books and references detailing the attributes needed to be successful in business. But probably the most important characteristics a cut-flower grower must have to be profitable would include:

Customers at Wildseed Farms, Fredericksburg, Texas, are provided clippers and containers to harvest their own flowers for a modest cost. In addition to bluebonnets, larkspur, cosmos, daisies, and many other flowers are grown and offered for "pick your own" bouquets. WCW

A bouquet of hybrid musk roses arranged by Henry Flowers at the Antique Rose Emporium in Independence, Texas. Varieties include 'Penelope', 'Ballerina', 'Prosperity', and 'Andenken an Alma de L'Aigle'. G. MICHAEL SHOUP, ANTIQUE ROSE EMPORIUM

Quality Flowers

Across the board, flower buyers require high-quality flowers that: (a) last a long time (have a good shelf life), (b) are available when their customers demand them, and (c) reduce costs through less spoilage (shrink). Remember, there are literally thousands of flower growers worldwide. For this reason, retail florists and other flower buyers usually have no problem getting quality flowers throughout the year. In order to remain in the market and stay competitive, flower growers today need to consistently provide top-quality flowers.

Dependable Service

Retail buyers need to have flowers always on hand. If a grower fails to deliver flowers on time or in the correct quantity, the retailer can lose potential sales. In the retail business, many sales are repeat. The loss of even one customer can affect future sales of the store, so retailers tend to work with the most dependable suppliers.

Frequent Deliveries

Most retail buyers lack the equipment and space to keep a large number of fresh flowers; therefore, they prefer growers who can make regular deliveries several times a week.

Product Variety

In general, buyers prefer to deal with growers who can provide a number of flower varieties, to reduce business transactions. However, providing a significant amount of one or two varieties may establish a strong niche.

Competitive Prices

A retailer will have several possible sources of supply, so growers must price their flowers competitively. To do this effectively, growers need to have thoroughly researched the questions and information presented earlier in this chapter.

IS THE MARKET GARDEN FLOWER BUSINESS THE RIGHT CHOICE?

Ultimately, the time comes when every potential entrepreneur must make a firm commitment to the business. Few enterprises are as intrinsically and aesthetically rewarding as a cut-flower business, but the rewards are accompanied with a certain degree of risk. No one is guaranteed a market for their flowers. In some years Mother Nature is not always cooperative. However, market gardeners tend to treat their business as a passion, and sometimes that dedication and tireless energy are exactly what it takes to make a business like this successful!

Dr. Charles R. Hall

Dr. Hall is an Associate Professor and Extension Economist with the Texas A&M University Agricultural Extension Service. In addition to growing up on a family-owned nursery, Dr. Hall is trained as an agricultural economist as well as a horticulturist. He also conducts applied research regarding the economics of producing and marketing nursery/floral products.

Sources for Plants and Seeds

Antique Rose Emporium
Rt. 5, Box 143
Brenham, Texas 77833
800-441-0002
Beautiful, informative catalog
$5.00
Hundreds of varieties of antique roses for the South. Both mail order and retail. Retail facilities in San Antonio, Texas; Independence, Texas; and Dahlonega, Georgia, are beautiful and inspirational for garden ideas.

Brent and Becky's Bulbs
7463 Heath Trail
Gloucester, Virginia 23061
804-693-3966
Free catalog

Camellia Forest Nursery
125 Carolina Forest Road
Chapel Hill, North Carolina 27516
919-967-5529
Informative catalog
Incredible mail-order source of camellia species and cultivars, Asian plants, and other hard-to-find items, including magnolias, sweet olives, banana shrubs, Chinese quince, and citrus.

Canyon Creek Nursery
3527 Dry Creek Road
Oroville, California 95967
530-533-2166
Informative catalog $2.00
Mail-order source of uncommon perennials, including nine cultivars of rosemary and thirty-five different violets and violas.

Carroll Gardens
444 East Main Street
Westminster, Maryland 21157
800-638-6334, 410-848-5422, fax 410-857-4112
Catalog $3.00 deductible with first order
Good mail-order source of perennials and uncommon plants, including blackberry lilies, iris, roses, bay laurel, wisterias, honeysuckles, azaleas, boxwoods, flowering quinces, deutzias, pearlbushes, hydrangeas, crape myrtles, magnolias, mock oranges, spireas, vitex, and weigela.

Daisy Fields
12635 SW Brighton Lane
Hillsboro, Oregon 97123-9051
503-628-0315
Nice catalog $1.00
Mail-order source for "old-fashioned perennials and cottage garden plants."

Ferry-Morse Seeds
P.O. Box 488
Fulton, Kentucky 42041-0488
800-283-6400
Free catalog, Seeds, bulbs, gifts, and garden ideas.

The Flower and Herb Exchange
3076 North Winn Road
Decorah, Iowa 52101
Annual membership and listing $7.00
A unique "seed savers" exchange group with over 250 members offering more than 2,000 rare flowers and herbs that are seldom found in modern catalogues.

Flowerplace Plant Farm
P.O. Box 2865
Meridian, Mississippi 30304
800-482-5686
Informative catalog $3.00
Good mail-order and retail source of Southeastern perennials and natives, including crinums, honeysuckles, *Gladiolus byzantinus,* bigleaf magnolia, mock oranges, etc.

Forest Farm
990 Tetherow Road
Williams, Oregon 97554-9599
541-846-7269
Excellent catalog $3.00
Large mail-order selection of hard-to-find trees and shrubs, including boxwoods, deutzias, pearlbushes, hydrangeas, flowering quinces, spireas, crape myrtles, magnolias, mock oranges, flowering almond, common quince, Chinese quince, roses, weigelas, and irises.

Fox Hollow Herb and Heirloom Seed Company
P.O. Box 148
McGrann, Pennsylvania 16236
Informative catalog $1.00
Good source of heirloom vegetable, herb, and flower seed, including rosemary and cockscombs.

Fragrant Path
P.O. Box 328
Fort Calhoun, Nebraska 68023
Informative catalog $2.00

Excellent mail-order source for fragrant and heirloom flower seed, including petunias, four-o'-clocks, cockscombs, bachelor's buttons, zinnias, blackberry lilies, rosemary, irises, boxwoods, roses, vitex, sweet bay, myrtles, pomegranates, and Chinese wisterias.

Glasshouse Works
Church Street
P.O. Box 97
Stewart, Ohio 45778-0097
740-662-2142
Extensive catalog $2.00

Long list of rare and hard-to-find mail-order plants, mostly tropical and/or Victorian, including crinums, amaryllis, jasmines, pomegranates, boxwoods, hydrangeas, variegated privets, and nandinas.

Green Hill Nursery, Inc.
5027 Highway 147
Waverly, Alabama 36879
334-864-7500, fax 205-864-9400
Free catalog (wholesale only)

Excellent wholesale source of old-fashioned shrubs, including deutzias, pearlbushes, althaeas, hydrangeas, crape myrtles, mock oranges, honeysuckles, pomegranates, flowering almond, roses, spiraeas, vitex, and weigelas.

Heirloom Old Garden Roses
24062 NE Riverside Drive
St. Paul, Oregon 97137
503-538-1576
Extensive catalog with color pictures $5.00.

Very interesting source for all kinds of hard-to-find own-root roses, including many old-fashioned varieties.

Heritage Rose Gardens
16831 Mitchell Creek Drive
Fort Bragg, California 95437
707-964-3748
Catalog with dates of introduction $1.50

An excellent mail-order source for old garden roses.

Heronswood Nursery
7530 288th Street NE
Kingston, Washington 98346
360-297-4172
Extensive catalog $3.00

Excellent mail-order source for rare and hard-to-find plants, including hydrangeas, honeysuckles, mock oranges, rhododendrons, roses, irises, and violets.

Kelly's Plant World
10266 East Princeton
Sanger, California 93657
559-292-3503
Descriptive list $1.00

Fabulous mail-order selection of rare and unusual plants for the connoisseur, including crinums, amaryllis, hymenocallis, tuberose, and lycoris (twenty-plus cultivars available).

Landis Valley Museum
Heirloom Seed Project
2451 Kissel Hill Road
Lancaster, Pennsylvania 17601
717-569-0401
Informative catalog with approximate dates of introduction $2.50.

Excellent source of limited quantities of Pennsylvania German heirloom vegetable, herb, and flower seed, including cockscombs.

Logee's Greenhouses
141 North Street
Danielson, Connecticut 06239
860-774-8038, fax 203-774-9932
Extensive catalog $3.00

Excellent mail-order source for mostly showy tropical and semi-tropical plants, including camellias, gardenias, Carolina jessamine, roses, citrus, boxwoods, bay laurel, myrtles, rosemary, violets, oleanders, jasmines, and pomegranates.

Louisiana Nursery
Route 7, Box 43
Opelousas, Louisiana 70570
318-948-3696, fax 318-942-6404
Extensive selection and catalogs: Magnolia and Other Garden Aristocrats catalog $6.00, Daylilies and Louisiana Iris catalog $4.00, Fruiting Trees, Shrubs and Vines catalog $3.00, Crinum and Rare bulb catalog $3.00, Bamboo and Ornamental Grass catalog $3.00; catalog price deducted from first order

Mail order and retail. Unequaled source for hard-to-find Southern plants, including amaryllis, boxwoods, bay laurel, camellias, flowering quinces, fruiting quinces, citrus, crinums, lycoris, tuberose, hymenocallis, persimmons, figs, grapes, jujubes, gardenias, Carolina jessamine, hydrangeas, irises, jasmines, crape myrtles, azaleas, roses, pomegranates, wisterias, and spiraeas.

Lowe's Own-Root Roses
6 Sheffield Road
Nashua, New Hampshire 03062
603-888-2214
Catalog with dates of introduction $2.00

Good mail-order source.

McClure and Zimmerman
108 West Winnebago
P.O. Box 368
Friesland, Wisconsin 53935
920-326-4220
Free extensive catalog

Extensive mail-order listing of rare and hard-to-find bulbs, including daffodils, jonquils, narcissus, spider lilies, snowflakes, Byzantine gladiolus, Roman hyacinth, and amaryllis.

Mellinger's
2310 West South Range Road
North Lima, Ohio 44452-9731
330-549-9861, fax 330-549-
3716, orders 800-321-7444
Free extensive catalog
  Extensive mail-order listing of
hard-to-find trees and shrubs,
including flowering quinces, honeysuckles, trumpet vines,
hydrangeas, rosemary, magnolias,
flowering almond, and mock
oranges.

Old House Gardens
536 Third Street
Ann Arbor, Michigan 48103
734-995-1486
Informative catalog with dates of
introduction $1.00
  Excellent mail-order source of
heirloom bulbs for the North and
South, including jonquils, daffodils, narcissus, authentic Roman
hyacinth, and authentic Byzantine
gladiolus. Many bulbs offered are
actually produced in the South
instead of Holland!

Old Sturbridge Village
One Old Sturbridge Village Road
Sturbridge, Massachusetts 01566
508-347-3362 Ext. 270, fax 508-
347-5375
Catalog $1.00
  Good mail-order source of
antique flower, herb, and vegetable seed, including bachelor's
buttons, cockscombs, four-o-
clocks, Johnny-jump-ups, and zinnias. Also offers period garden
supplies and books.

Park Seed
Cokesbury Road
Greenwood, South Carolina
29647-0001
803-941-4480
Free catalog
  Dependable mail-order source
of vegetable and flower seed,
including cockscombs, bachelor's
buttons, zinnias, Johnny-jump-
ups, and many more.

Petals from the Past
16034 County Rd. 29
Jemison, Alabama 35085
205-646-0069
  An emerging mail-order source
for antique roses, perennials, and
shrubs. Retail garden center with
idea gardens featuring heirloom
plants and garden objects.

Pickering Nurseries
670 Kingston Road
Pickering, Ontario L1V 1A6,
Canada
416-839-2111, fax 905-839-4807
Extensive catalog with dates of
introductions $3.00
  Excellent mail-order source of
antique and hard-to-find roses.

Plantation Bulb Co.
Box 159
Ty Ty, Georgia 31795
Extensive catalog $1.00
  Fabulous mail-order selection
for Southern bulbs and plants,
including amaryllis, sprekelias,
hymenocallis, narcissus, lycoris,
leucojums, irises, hibiscus, and a
large selection of crinums.

Plant Delights Nursery
9241 Sauls Road
Raleigh, North Carolina 27603
919-772-4794
Interesting catalog available for
just 10 postage stamps or a box of
chocolates

Roses of Yesterday and Today
802 Brown's Valley Road
Watsonville, California 95076
831-724-3537
Informative catalog $2.00
  Long established source for old
garden roses.

The Roseraie at Bayfields
P.O. Box R
Waldboro, Maine 04572-1919
Informative catalog
  Good mail-order source of pri-
marily Old European roses.

Seeds Blum
Idaho City Stage
Boise, Idaho 83706
208-324-0858
Informative catalog $3.00
  Good mail-order source of heir-
loom vegetable and flower seed.

Select Seeds
180 Stickney Road
Union, Connecticut 06076-4617
860-684-9310
Informative catalog with reference
dates $3.00
  Good mail order source of
antique flower seed.

Shepherd Garden Seeds
30 Irene St.
Torrington, Connecticut 06790
860-492-3638
Catalog $1.00
  Vegetable, herb, and flower
seed.

**Southern Exposure Seed
Exchange**
P.O. Box 170
Earlysville, Virginia 22936
804-973-4703
Free catalog
  Heirloom vegetables, flowers.

Sunlight Gardens
174 Golden Lane
Andersonville, Tennessee 37705
865-494-8237, orders 800-272-
7396
Informative free catalog
  Good mail-order source of
natives and perennials of the eastern United States, including
asters, coneflowers, yarrows, Joe-
Pye weed, etc.

**Thomas Jefferson Center for
Historic Plants**
Monticello
P.O. Box 316
Charlottesville, Virginia 22902
Very informative newsletter and
seed list $1.00
  Great mail-order source of
Jefferson–grown flower and veg-
etable seed.

Thompson & Morgan
P.O. Box 1308
Jackson, New Jersey 08527
732-363-2225, 800-274-7333
Free catalog.
Many unusual seeds.

Vintage Gardens
2227 Gravenstein Highway South
Sebastopol, California 95472
707-829-2035
Beautiful, informative catalog with extensive listings and dates of introductions $4.00
Excellent mail-order and retail source of many interesting antique roses.

Wayside Gardens
1 Garden Lane
Hodges, South Carolina 29695-0001
800-845-1124
Beautiful color catalog $1.00
Good mail-order source of perennials and hard-to-find trees and shrubs, including roses, azaleas, honeysuckles, hydrangeas, flowering quinces, gardenias, mock oranges, etc.

White Flower Farm Southern Edition
P.O. Box 50
Litchfield, Connecticut 06759
800-503-9624
Color catalog $4.00
Annuals, perennials, shrubs, and bulbs collected from around the world.

William R. P. Welch
Grower of Narcissus Tazettas
P.O. Box 1736
Carmel Valley, California 93924-1736
408-659-3830, pager 408-645-0816
Free informative price list
World's most diverse selection of old polyanthos (cluster-flowered) narcissus. No orders accepted or sent out after October 1, as these like to be planted in late summer. Be sure to order 'Grand Primo', 'Erlicheer', and 'Golden Dawn'. Will also identify, at no charge, old narcissus samples sent to him.

Woodlanders
1128 Colleton Avenue
Aiken, South Carolina 29801
803-648-7522
Extensive catalog $3.00
Outstanding mail-order listing of hard-to-find trees and shrubs for the South.

Yucca Do Nursery
Peckerwood Gardens
P.O. Box 655
Waller, Texas 77484
409-826-6363
Detailed catalog $3.00
Excellent mail-order source of rare and hard-to-find plants, many from Mexico, including native magnolias, a number of mock oranges, Chinese quince, honeysuckles, desert willow, and prickly pears.

Bibliography

Armitage, Allan M. *Specialty Cut Flowers*. Portland, Oregon: Timber Press, 1993.

Bailey, Liberty Hyde. *The Standard Cyclopedia of Horticulture*. New York: Macmillan, 1917.

Bourne, H. *The Florist's Manual*. New York: Munroe and Francis, 1833.

Bowles, E. A. *The Narcissus*. London: Waterstone & Cook Ltd., 1985.

Buist, Robert. *American Flower Garden Directory*. New York: C. M. Saxton, Barker and Co., 1860.

De Zavala, Adina. "In Grandmother's Old Garden Where the Rose Reigned as Queen." *San Antonio Express* (September 2, 1934).

Dirr, Michael A. *Dirr's Hardy Trees and Shrubs*. Portland, Oregon: Timber Press, 1997.

Downing, Andrew Jackson, ed. *The Horticultural and Journal of Rural Art and Rural Taste*, Vol. 4.

Earle, Alice Morse. *Old Time Gardens*. New York: Macmillan, 1902.

Fell, Derek, and Carolyn Fell. *Impressionist Bouquets*. New York: Friedman/Fairfax Publishers, 1998.

Gainey, Ryan. *The Well-Placed Weed*. Dallas: Taylor Publishing Co., 1993.

Griswold, Mac, and Eleanor Weller. *The Golden Age of American Gardens*. New York: Harry N. Abrams, Inc., 1991.

Henderson, Peter. *Henderson's Handbook of Plants and General Horticulture*. New York: Peter Henderson & Co., 1890.

Hill, Madalene, and Gwen Barclay, with Jean Hardy. *Southern Herb Growing*. Fredericksburg, Texas: Shearer Publishing Co., 1987.

Hobhouse, Penelope. *Color in Your Garden*. Boston: Little, Brown and Co., 1985.

———. *Flower Gardens*. Boston: Little, Brown and Co., 1991.

Hume, H. Harold. *Camellias in America*. Revised Edition. Harrisburg, Pennsylvania: J. Horace McFarland Co., 1978.

Jekyll, Gertrude. *Wood and Garden*. London: Langmans Green & Co., 1899. Reprint. Salem: The Ayer Co., 1983.

Jones, David L. *Encyclopedia of Ferns*. Melbourne: Lothian Publishing Co. PTY LTC, 1987.

Lawrence, Elizabeth. *Gardening For Love*. Durham, NC: Duke University Press, 1987.

———. *A Southern Garden*. Chapel Hill: University of North Carolina Press, 1984.

———. *Through the Garden Gate*. Chapel Hill: University of North Carolina Press, 1990.

Liberty Hyde Bailey Hortorium. *Hortus Third*. Revised and expanded from materials compiled by Liberty Hyde Bailey and Ethel Zoe Bailey. New York: Macmillan, 1976.

Martin, Laura C. *Southern Gardens*. New York: Abbeville Press Publishers, 1993.

M'Mahon, Bernard. *The American Gardener's Calendar*. Philadelphia: M'Mahon, 1806.

———. *The American Gardener's Calendar*. Ninth Edition, Greatly Improved. Philadelphia: A. M'Mahon. 1839.

Newcomb, Peggy Cornett. *Popular Annuals of Eastern North America 1865–1914.* Washington, D.C.: Dumbarton Oaks, 1985.

Odenwald, Neil, Charles F. Fryling Jr., and Thomas E. Pope. *Plants for American Landscapes.* Baton Rouge: Louisiana State University Press, 1996.

Odenwald, Neil, and James Turner. *Identification, Selection and Use of Southern Plants for Landscape Design.* Third Edition. Baton Rouge: Claitor's Publishing Division, 1996.

Pregill, Philip and Nancy Volkman. *Landscapes in History, Design and Planning in the Western Tradition.* New York: Van Nostrand Reinhold, 1993.

Robinson, William. *The English Flower Garden.* Fifteenth Edition. London: The Amaryllis Press, 1984.

Ryan, Julie. *Perennial Gardens for Texas.* Austin: University of Texas Press, 1998.

Scourse, Nicolette. *The Victorians and Their Flowers.* London: Croom Helm, Portland: Timber Press, 1983.

Sunset Books and Sunset Magazine. *Sunset Western Garden Book.* Menlo Park, CA: Lane Publishing Co., 1988.

Verey, Rosemary. *The Flower Arranger's Garden.* Boston: Little, Brown and Co., 1989.

Welch, William C. *Antique Roses for the South.* Dallas: Taylor Publishing Co., 1991.

———. *Perennial Garden Color.* Dallas: Taylor Publishing Co., 1989.

Welch, William C., and D. Greg Grant. *The Southern Heirloom Garden.* Dallas: Taylor Publishing Co., 1995.

Index

About the Authors

WILLIAM C. WELCH

William C. Welch is an Extension Landscape Specialist in the Department of Horticulture at Texas A & M University. A critically acclaimed speaker on the use of flowers in the South, Welch has also authored two other gardening titles, *Perennial Garden Color* and *Antique Roses for the South*, and co-authored *The Southern Heirloom Garden* for Taylor Publishing Company. He has also written numerous magazine articles. For the past 28 years, Welch has served on the Board of Texas Garden Clubs, Inc., and is a Member-at-Large in the Garden Club of America.

A graduate of Louisiana State University with masters and doctoral degrees in Extension Education and Horticulture, Welch also completed a two-year term on the Board of Directors of the Southern Garden History Society.

Welch and his wife, Diane, live in College Station, Texas. He is creating eclectic gardens at his farms near Winedale, Texas, and Mangham, Louisiana.

NEIL G. ODENWALD

Neil G. Odenwald, Ph.D., ASLA, is a professor of Landscape Architecture at Louisiana State University. He is a highly regarded speaker, as well as an honored member of the National Council of State Garden Clubs. The author of the award-winning *Southern Plants* and *Live Oak Splendor: Gardens Along the Mississippi, from Natchez to New Orleans*, he has served as a consultant for Time-Life's series of gardening books. *Attracting Birds to Southern Gardens* is Odenwald's most recent book with Taylor Publishing Company.

Odenwald lives in Baton Rouge, Louisiana.